John - Franz
Jean - Louis

THE POLITICAL ECONOMY
OF DEVELOPMENT

SUNY SERIES IN RADICAL SOCIAL AND POLITICAL THEORY
ROGER S. GOTTLIEB, EDITOR

THE POLITICAL ECONOMY OF DEVELOPMENT

Development Theory and the Prospects for Change in the Third World

BERCH BERBEROGLU

STATE UNIVERSITY OF NEW YORK PRESS

Published by
State University of New York Press, Albany

© 1992 State University of New York

Printed in the United States of America

For information, address State University of New York
Press, State University Plaza, Albany, N.Y., 12246

Production by E. Moore
Marketing by Dana E. Yanulavich

Library of Congress Cataloging-in-Publication Data

Berberoglu, Berch.
     The political economy of development : development theory and the
prospects for change in the Third World / Berch Berberoglu.
         p.   cm. — (SUNY series in radical social and political
theory)
     Includes bibliographical references and index.
     ISBN 0-7914-0909-0 (CH : acid-free). — ISBN 0-7914-0910-4 (PB :
acid-free)
     1. Developing countries—Economic policy. 2. Capitalism.
3. Dependency. 4. Economic development. I. Title. II. Series.
HC59.7.B38855   1992
338.9′009172′4—dc20
                                                                            91-2498
                                                                                CIP

10 9 8 7 6 5 4 3 2 1

*Dedicated to
the memory of my mother, Silva,
and to
my father, Suren*

CONTENTS

PART III:
CASE STUDIES OF THE STATE AND DEVELOPMENT
IN THE THIRD WORLD

TABLES

PREFACE

Many of the issues discussed in this book are the cumulative product of three decades of analysis and debate over the nature and prospects of development in the Third World. The questions raised and the approaches developed to tackle the problems of development have shifted in three different directions during this period—each becoming the dominant mode of analysis extending over a decade. Thus we have seen a shift from developmentalism in the 1960s to dependency theory in the 1970s to class analysis in the 1980s. This paradigmatic shift from mainstream modernization theories of the early 1960s to Marxist modes of theorizing and analysis in the 1980s parallels changes in the structure of development in the Third World: away from policies linked with the so-called Alliance for Progress and the "green revolution" and their attendant contradictions, toward class-based movements for change arising from the contradictions of the new international division of labor that ushered in during the 1970s a restructuring of the world economy through the expansion of capitalism and capitalist relations of production in the Third World.

Hailed as a cure for centuries of backwardness and underdevelopment, export-oriented industrialization became the primary mode of capitalist accumulation in a growing number of states in the Third World during the 1980s. It is partly in response to the resulting contradictions of this path of development in the Third World that new class forces emerged in a number of countries and began to assert themselves against the structures of exploitation still operative under a new set of conditions. And, finally, it is in this context of changes in the nature and dynamics of class contradictions that an increasing number of intellectuals and development analysts have come to adopt a class analysis approach informed by Marxist theory.

Applying the basic concepts, method, and approach provided by class analysis to the study of the political economy of development in the Third World, a growing number of critical social scientists around the world have taken up the major task of examining the process of development and change through a concrete analysis of capitalist development as it has been taking place in the Third World in recent decades. It is in this spirit of advancing our knowledge of the real sources of development and social transformation that this book was originally conceived. Written over a period of sixteen years, the essays contained in this book represent the culmination of my thinking and research as they have evolved to their present state. Building upon the works and analyses of previous generations of critical scholars in the field, this volume provides a macrosociological view of the development process based on a class analysis approach that is rooted in the principles and precepts of historical materialism.

Given the unfolding contradictions of capitalist development in the Third World, in a period when the internationalization of capital has fostered increasing rivalry and conflict on a world scale, it is inescapable that development theory and its ability to explain developments in the Third World are, and will continue to be, tied to and reflective of the great changes now taking place throughout the Third World—changes whose prospects for revolutionary social transformation on a societal scale are becoming more and more real in this final decade of the twentieth century.

ACKNOWLEDGMENTS

A project of this nature, extending over a period of nearly two decades, involves the contributions of many people. Those who have played a key role in the development of many of the positions arrived at in this book include Larry Reynolds, Blain Stevenson, James Petras, Paul Sweezy, and Albert Szymanski.

I would like to thank David Elliott, Marty Hart-Landsberg, Fikret Ceyhun, David Dickens, Peter Limqueco, Paresh Chattopadhyay, Sohrab Behdad, and Cyrus Bina for valuable discussions on issues related to development in the Third World. I would also like to thank students and colleagues in a number of graduate seminars on the political economy of development conducted at the University of Oregon in the late 1970s, and students who took part in my seminars on development at the University of Nevada, Reno, during the 1980s.

Finally, I would like to thank Roger Gottlieb and Clay Morgan, my editors at SUNY Press, for their encouragement, dedication, and professionalism, and for making the publication process a pleasant one. My thanks go also to Denise Schaar and Cinda Christie for typing various chapters of the manuscript, and to the government publications librarians of the University of Nevada, Reno, and the University of California, Berkeley, for their assistance in locating much-needed sources and data included in this book.

My wife, Suzan, and my sons, Michael and Stephen, have, as always, provided much support and encouragement to complete this project; for this, as well as for their understanding and appreciation of my work, I thank them.

INTRODUCTION

In this final decade of the twentieth century, when major changes of unprecedented proportions are rapidly taking place throughout the world, it is becoming increasingly clear that problems of development in the Third World are of such magnitude that they require urgent attention of world-historic proportions. These problems, at root economic and global in nature, affect all aspects of social life in the Third World, including long-entrenched political, institutional, and regional, as well as global, structures.

Confronting these and other obstacles to development in the Third World, which have plagued the less-developed countries of Asia, Africa, Latin America, and the Middle East for many decades, development theory has provided a number of approaches to explain the predicament of many states in the Third World.

Developmentalism, dependency/world-system theories, and Marxism have provided three distinct approaches to the study of the nature and contradictions of the development process in the Third World over the past four decades. Each of these major theoretical approaches, with its own conceptual framework and domain assumptions, has developed a comprehensive theoretical perspective on the problems of development in the Third World in a world-historical context. We examine and critique each of these approaches in Part I.

It is argued in this book that major paradigmatic shifts have occurred in development theory during the period from the 1950s to the

1990s, from developmentalism (which dominated the field of development studies in the 1950s and 1960s), to dependency and world-system
theories (which became influential in the 1970s), to Marxist class analysis (which reemerged as a viable alternative in the 1980s). These shifts in
development theory have not occurred in a vacuum and are not the
result of passing fads in development studies but are precisely the product of developments in the Third World and the world political economy over the past several decades.

Thus, just as the postwar era and the immediate postcolonial
period gave rise to the conservative and subsequently reformist theoretical perspectives and prescriptions of developmentalism of the 1950s
and 1960s, so the failure of these approaches adequately to explain (and
solve) the problems of development during this period gave rise in the
1970s to dependency theory and its variants as means of addressing the
problems confronting Third World societies. And because the dependency formulations that dominated this latter period lacked a clearly
articulated class analysis of Third World exploitation and surplus
extraction and generally could not explain the simultaneous occurrence
of dependency *and* development, where development and the exploitation of labor were both increasingly being identified as part of the process of capital accumulation on a world scale (a process based on class
exploitation, class conflict, and class struggles), Marxist theory came in
the early 1980s to fill the void and placed the development problematic
in its proper *class* context.

The shifts in development theory, from developmentalism, to
dependency and world-system approaches, to Marxism, have thus
occurred in a progressive movement toward the underlying, real causes
of the prevailing problems of development in the Third World: from ideology and apologetic pronouncements of developmentalism, to the structural and institutional description of surface manifestations of dependence and external domination provided by dependency and
world-system approaches, to an analysis of the class nature of exploitation on a world scale provided by Marxist theory, in which class relations
are examined in the context of the exploitation of labor and the appropriation of surplus value as the basis of global capital accumulation.

In Part II of this book, two alternative paths of capitalist development in the Third World—neo-colonial export-oriented industrialization and state-capitalist development—are examined in class terms. The
role of the imperial state in the context of its position in the world political economy is also examined here to highlight the dominant role of the
advanced capitalist states—especially the United States—in the Third
World development process.

Export-oriented capitalist industrialization, pursued in a number of countries in the Third World, is examined in reference to four neo-colonial capitalist states in Latin America and East Asia—Brazil, Mexico, South Korea, and Taiwan. In contrast to dependency theory, which has been hard put to explain the rapid growth of these economies within the framework of dependent relations with the imperial centers, the focus of analysis here is the impact this path of capitalist industrialization on the development of the class structure based on changes in the structure of production relations. Growth of the working class and its superexploitation by local and transnational capital are identified as the sources of the dialectical process of change that is generating attendant contradictions leading to class struggles and social transformation in these and other export-oriented neocolonial states following this path of capitalist development.

State capitalism, a second, alternative path of capitalist development in the Third World, is examined in the context of three divergent theories that purport to explain its nature and contradictions. Derived from a synthesis of the three theories, an alternative theory of state capitalism based on a class-analysis approach is provided here to help interpret the experience of a number of state capitalist regimes examined later in the book. It is argued that although independent, nationalist, state-capitalist regimes have a dynamic that is distinct from that of neocolonial states, the logic of capital accumulation under state capitalism yields essentially the same net result as that in any other capitalist society—the exploitation of wage labor. Under state capitalism this occurs through the instrumentality of the state, which plays a central role in capital accumulation on behalf of the national capitalist class—the class that currently is (or later becomes) the primary beneficiary of the policies and actions of the nationalist state.

The interrelationship of class, state, and development in different historical and comparative contexts in the Third World is the theme taken up in Part III of this book. Case studies of the role of the state in the development process, in the context of the developing class relations and class struggles in a number of Third World states—Turkey, India, Tanzania, and Peru—are provided as examples of the complex process of class politics articulated through the powers of the state in different Third World societal settings.

In examining the experience of these four states during the course of this century—Turkey from the 1920s to the present, India from the mid-1940s on, Tanzania from the mid-1960s to the late 1970s, and Peru from the late 1960s to the mid-1970s—it is shown that all have gone through a period of state-capitalist development in the early stages of their postindependence development, followed by a transition to neo-colonialism in a subsequent phase. Although there have been differ-ences in their respective historical stages of development, the processes of development and change experienced in these states reveal similar patterns of transformation, in which strong states that had earlier taken an active role in promoting capital accumulation later become instru-mental in the transformation of the state structures that set the stage for the development of neocolonialism. As the pattern of such transforma-tion is similar in all four cases, it becomes evident that the transition from state capitalism to neocolonialism is due to the logic of the contra-dictions of state capitalism developing within the context of the world capitalist economy. The class forces that assume control of the state apparatus and shift development in a neocolonial direction are shown to have emerged out of the development process unfolding under the state capitalist regimes. It is for this reason that we conclude that state capitalism, sooner or later, becomes transformed into neocolonialism.

Comprehensive in its treatment of the theories, problems, and experiences of Third World states and societies in a comparative-histor-ical context at the national and global levels, the book concludes with a chapter on the prospects for change in the Third World in the period ahead. The appendix stresses the importance of a class-analysis approach in development studies and challenges the reader to adopt such an approach so as to better understand and explain the process of development in the Third World.

While this book does not pretend to have answered all the major questions regarding the nature and prospects of development and change in the Third World, it is hoped that its focus on class, class rela-tions, class exploitation, and class struggles will help redirect attention to the real, class-based problems that lie at the roots of the contradic-tions of development in the Third World today.

PART I

Theories of Development

CHAPTER 1

THEORIES OF DEVELOPMENT AND MODERNIZATION: A CRITIQUE OF DEVELOPMENTALISM

During the postwar decades of the 1950s and 1960s, when U.S. global expansionism and domination of the world economy had reached new heights, development theory came under the grip of cold war ideologists like W. W. Rostow, who set the parameters and shaped the direction of development theory in line with U.S. foreign policy objectives. What came to be known as "developmentalism," mainstream modernization theory became the ideological arm of U.S. expansion throughout the world for the supposed purpose of diffusing "development" and "democracy" to the Third World.[1] Several theoretical variants of developmentalism thus came to complement and reinforce the establishment and later consolidation of conservative development theory that dominated the field until the late 1960s and early 1970s, when radical alternatives to developmentalist theory set the stage for a basic reorientation in studies of international development and global political economy.

This chapter provides a critical analysis of mainstream theories of development and modernization grouped under the general rubic of developmentalism.[2] It examines the main variants of this approach in a critical light and sets the stage for an analysis of alternative theories of development taken up in subsequent chapters of this book.

DEVELOPMENTALISM: A CRITICAL ANALYSIS

According to Manning Nash, a major spokesman of the developmentalist school, there are "only three modes of attacking the problem of social change and economic development."[3] These are (1) the ideal typical index approach; (2) the diffusionist approach; (3) the psychological approach. The first mode is ideal typical in that

> the general features of a developed economy are abstracted as an ideal type and then contrasted with the equally ideal typical features of a poor economy and society. In this mode, development is viewed as the transformation of one type into the other. . . .
>
> The second mode is the acculturation view of the process of development. The West (taken here as the Atlantic community of developed nations and their overseas outliers) diffuses knowledge, skills, organization, values, technology and capital to a poor nation, until over time, its society, culture and personnel become variants of that which made the Atlantic community economically successful. . . .
>
> The third mode . . . is the analysis of the process as it is now going on in the so-called underdeveloped nations. This approach leads to a smaller scale hypothesis, to a prospective rather than a retrospective view of social change, to a full accounting of the political, social, and cultural context of development.[4]

The Ideal Typical Index Approach

The index method is an attempt to deal with the problem of economic development and social change through the comparative statics of polar ideal types. This model, also referred to as the gap approach of C. P. Kindleberger,[5] has in turn two major variants: the pattern variable approach and the historical stage approach. Common to both of these variants is the assumption that underdevelopment is an original state, which may be characterized by indices of "traditionality." Further, in order to develop, underdeveloped countries must abandon these characteristics and adopt those of the developed countries—the process of "modernization."[6]

The pattern variable approach refers to the application of the Parsonian pattern variables to the study of particular underdeveloped countries or regions of the Third World. There are five pattern variables, each of which characterize the various aspects of "traditional" and "modern" societies.[7] Consisting of two polar alternatives of value orientation, these variables are (1) universalism and particularism; (2) specificity and diffuseness; (3) achievement and ascription; (4) affectivity and affective neutrality; (5) collectivity-orientation and self-orientation.[8]

The major spokesman of this approach in its application to the study of economic development is Bert F. Hoselitz.[9] Hoselitz argues that the presently developed countries exhibit the pattern variables of universalism, functional specificity, and achievement orientation—all of which are viewed as characteristics of modern society—while underdeveloped countries are characterized by their opposites—particularism, functional diffuseness, and ascription—viewed as indices of traditionality.[10]

In conceptualizing the problem in these terms, what Parsons, Hoselitz, and their functionalist followers suggest is that traditional societies (for example, underdeveloped countries) must move away from particularistic normative structures toward universalistic systems, away from role diffuseness toward role specificity, and away from ascription of one's place in society toward achievement of social position. Thus, the solution for underdevelopment requires a greater penetration of modern economic principles and institutions. And by this is meant "free markets," "free enterprise," "modern tax systems," the "rationalization of the state," and so on.[11]

In the social sphere, traditional societies, it is argued, have insufficient social mobility, due to the ascription of social position and the lack of achievement motivation among individuals. In the cultural framework, they contend that certain values associated with the developed countries, such as hard work, thrift, and achievement orientation, are absent in the underdeveloped ones. Therefore, according to these theorists, development requires programs that will instill proper values in individuals and modernize institutions; in the process, these countries will then eventually evolve from the state of traditionality to that of modern society.[12]

Another variant of the ideal typical approach that has pervaded the mainstream developmentalist literature during this period has been that of W. W. Rostow.[13] In his book *The Stages of Economic Growth: A Non-Communist Manifesto* Rostow argues that all societies pass through five stages of economic growth. The initial stage is called "the traditional society," characterized by traits supposedly typical of the rural, non-capitalist sector of underdeveloped countries. Next is the "preconditioning" stage, followed by the "take-off," the "drive to maturity," and, finally, the "age of high mass-consumption."[14]

What Rostow's theory suggests is that the underdeveloped countries are simply at a lower stage of social evolution than that character-istic of the advanced, industrial capitalist nations of the West. In fact, most of these underdeveloped countries are classified as traditional; in order to develop, they must pass through the five successive stages that Western capitalist nations passed through long ago.

There are, however, a number of major flaws in this kind of think-ing. First, as Keith Griffin points out, "it is exceedingly improbable that one can gain an adequate understanding of present obstacles and future potential for development without examining how the underdeveloped nations came to be as they are."[15] Thus, "to classify these countries as 'traditional societies' begs the issue and implies either that the underde-veloped countries have no history or that it is unimportant."[16]

Although Rostow claims to have introduced into his model histor-ical process, what we actually get from his "evolutionary" scheme is a series of snapshots that freeze the development process in five different moments of time. Hence, Rostow never clarifies how a country gets from one stage of economic growth to another. What is more, taking the developmental pattern of the Western capitalist nations as his reference point, Rostow wants to construct a universal model of development that underdeveloped societies must inevitably adopt if they wish to develop. The distortion imposed by this kind of analysis, which uses "uni-linear conceptions of historical development,"

> overlooks the degree to which the development opportunities (colonies, export markets, etc.) which existed earlier no longer exist, but have become positive advantages and weapons for maintaining dominance . . . by [the] established centers of indus-trial power. . . . The unilinear-historical dogma is both a mode of frustrating dynamic growth (as a political doctrine) and a faulty conceptual framework for examining the potentialities and neces-sities inherent in the development of the subordinate countries in the contemporary world.[17]

In neither the pattern variable approach nor the Rostovian histor-ical stage approach is there an examination of the actual structure of development in the global-historical context. "Even within its extremely narrow limits," write Baran and Hobsbawm,

> the Rostovian theory can neither explain nor predict without intro-ducing considerations that are completely irrelevant to the stage schema. It simply fails to specify any mechanism of evolution which links the different stages. There is no particular reason why

the "traditional" society should turn into a society breeding the "preconditions" of the "take-off." Rostow's account merely summarized what these preconditions must be. . . . Nor is there any reason within the Rostovian stages why the "preconditions" should lead to "take-off" to maturity, as is indeed evidenced by Rostow's own difficulty in discovering, except long *ex post facto*, whether a "take-off" has taken place or not. In fact the Rostovian "take-off" concept has no predictive value. Similarly, when it comes to analyzing the "inner structure" of the "take-off" or of any other stage, the Rostovian theory subsides into statements of the type that "things can happen in any one of a very large number of different ways," which constitute a rather limited contribution of knowledge.

Such explanations and predictions as Rostow attempts are therefore little more than verbiage which has no connection with his stages theory or indeed with any theory of economic and social evolution.[18]

"Why," Baran and Hobsbawm ask, "should a man adopt a theoretical approach so obviously defective and indeed self-defeating?" They conclude: "At least one plausible answer may be suggested. Professor Rostow, is, on his own admission, primarily concerned not with arriving at a theory of economic development, but with writing a 'noncommunist manifesto'."[19] "As to the efficacy of the policy recommended by Rostow," Frank reminds us that "no country, once underdeveloped, ever managed to develop by Rostow's stages."[20] Writing in the summer of 1967, Frank asks, "is that why Rostow is now trying to help the people of Vietnam, the Congo, the Dominican Republic and other underdeveloped countries to overcome the empirical, theoretical, and policy shortcomings of his manifestly noncommunist intellectual aid to economic development and cultural change by bombs, napalm, chemical and biological weapons, and military occupation?"[21]

The Diffusionist Approach

Closely related to both the Parsonian pattern variables scheme and Rostow's stages of economic growth is the diffusionist approach. This approach to the study of economic development is based on two major assertions: (1) that development is largely the result of the spread of certain cultural patterns and material benefits from the developed to the underdeveloped nations; and (2) that within each underdeveloped nation a similar process of diffusion takes place from the modern to the traditional sectors. The underlying assumption of both the ideal typical index approach and the diffusionist approach is the traditional/modern dichotomy. The main procedural difference between these two is that, while the former is concerned with classifying and identifying the characteristics of these societies at different stages of development, the latter examines the very same framework in terms of the penetration of certain influences from the modern to the traditional sectors. And both of these theoretical approaches are based on the notion of a "dual society."

The dualistic conception of underdevelopment centers in the common point of identifying and classifying the various characteristics of the traditional and modern sectors of the underdeveloped countries (in order to justify the transformation of the former into the institutional framework of the latter). The dual society thesis, insofar as it asserts a conceived isolation and separation of these sectors as "self-contained" entities, obscures the underlying relationships between the two sectors in the development process.

The crucial question in an analysis of the development process in actual societies is not the mere identification of two or more distinct parts; it is rather the analysis of the relationships that exist between them. Rather than advancing our knowledge on the nature of such relationships, however, the dual society thesis has served as a convenient ideological justification for not only the continuation of imperialist policies (since underdevelopment is viewed as a result of traditions that resist the international acculturation process), but for the implementation of the diffusionist approach to policy decisions, both at the inter- and intranational levels.

The acceptance of the dual society thesis, then, has led developmentalists to argue that for development to occur, capital, technology, institutions, and values must be diffused from the developed to the underdeveloped countries, and within each underdeveloped nation the same process of diffusion be repeated from the modern to the traditional sector of the economy and society.

"Modernity is not a geographical question, but a class question," James Petras reminds us. "In Latin America there exists a stratified modernity which coincides with the strata controlling the economic resources of the country."[22]

Traditionalism and modernity vary according to the levels of analysis of the socio-economic system. One can discover modernity at the level of the productive unit (techniques) and yet discover traditionalism at the level of social relations (worker-owner).
The interpenetration of modernity-traditionalism is the typ-

ical form of development of modern capitalism and command relations in the subordinate countries. It is usually expressed in the utilization of modern techniques of production and traditional social relations in order to maintain labor docile or under control. The decisive conflict hence cannot be as "dualists" would have it, between a modern sector and a traditional sector, but between those social classes having access to modern life through their socio-economic power and those subordinate classes exploited through traditional social relations.[23]

This theory, writes Johnson, "is particularly salient in providing a rationale for U.S. and international aid programs."[24] "At the very least," he adds,

> the diffusion theory represents a much more sophisticated rationalization for imperialist activities than the old doctrines of "manifest destiny" and "white man's burden." Yet in its final analysis, this theory underlies a form of cultural imperialism that accompanies economic imperialism.[25]

The wide-ranging implications of the diffusionist theory are clear.

The Psychological Approach

Perhaps the most influential exponent of the psychological approach to economic development has been David McClelland. According to McClelland, the key factor in economic development is what he calls "the need for achievement" or "n achievement motivation," which denotes "a desire to do well, not so much for the sake of social recognition or prestige, but to attain an inner feeling of personal accomplishment."[26] In McClelland's conception, economic development is a product of a high degree of individual motivation or need for achievement: "In its most general terms, the hypothesis states that society with a generally high level of n achievement will produce more energetic entrepreneurs who, in turn, produce more rapid economic development."[27] It is not the economic, political, or social structure of a society that shapes the nature and direction of its development, but rather the "values, motives, or psychological forces that determine ultimately the rate of economic and social development. . . . The Achieving Society . . . suggests that ideas are in fact more important in shaping history than purely materialistic arrangements."[28] Thus, contrary to historical materialism, this approach is rooted in the basic notion of "human nature," entangled with all of its idealist connotations.

Change, according to this view, comes from the human mind, not from the basic structures of society; nor does it come from the dynamics of the material conditions in which one finds oneself and with which one constantly interacts. No, economic growth is the result of attitudes and psychological traits.[29]

This is clearly evident, for example, in Arthur Lewis's conception of economic growth:

> Economic growth depends on attitudes to work, to wealth, to thrift, to having children, to invention, to strangers, to adventure, and so on, and all these attitudes flow from deep springs in the human mind. There have been attempts to explain why these attitudes vary from one community to another. One can look to differences in religion . . . or one can look to differences in natural environment, in climate, in race, or failing all else, in the accidents of history.[30]

For Lewis, then, one need not look at social organization or social structure to determine the presence or absence of economic growth. Of course, according to this logic, to experience economic growth the people of the underdeveloped countries must acquire, or develop, the "right" attitudes. And, short of sufficient indigenous effort on this front, the "burden of growth" in the underdeveloped areas falls, to Lewis's mind, on the knowledge, skills, and "entrepreneurial ingenuity" of the chosen capitalists of the industrial West. Lewis's concealed and subtle presentation of the problem in these diffusionist terms is an exercise in the justification of economic and cultural imperialism.

Similarly, for McClelland, the present economic, social, and political structure of underdeveloped societies does not matter at all: there is no need to change the present structural arrangements. What is needed is the diffusion of ideas: increasing n achievement; protestant conversion; education; reorganizing fantasy life. The diffusion of these values is important, according to McClelland, if the United States is to maintain a sound imperialist foreign policy toward the underdeveloped countries. Directing his message to a specific audience—the readers of the *Harvard Business Review*—he writes that, although "China was politically free under Chiang Kai-Chek . . . it lacked the dynamic of a really self-sacrificing achievement effort until it was taken over by the Communists." Thus:

> Unless we learn our lesson and find ways of stimulating that drive for achievement under freedom in poor countries, the Commu-

nists will go on providing it all around the world. We can go on building dikes to maintain freedom and impoverishing ourselves to feed and arm the people behind those dikes, but only if we develop the entrepreneurial spirit in those countries will we have a sound foreign policy.[31]

FURTHER OBSERVATIONS ON THE CRITIQUE OF DEVELOPMENTALISM

The starting point of any analysis of Third World societies should be a clear understanding of the concept of "underdevelopment. " And yet it is precisely here that a great deal of confusion seems to be centered.

Much of the writing of mainstream economists and sociologists on the question of underdevelopment assumes that underdevelopment is an "original state" characterized by "backwardness." This inherently static conceptualization of underdevelopment denies the historical process of exploitation and plunder of Third World societies by European colonialism and imperialism.

The works of a number of other developmental economists, particularly Lewis, Kindleberger, Kuznets, Nurkse, and Adelman and Morris, prompt further observations on the development process. I turn first to Lewis, since he clarifies a number of assumptions inherent in the economic analysis of development and outlines the parameters of what he calls "the theory of economic growth."

In the opening paragraphs of his widely circulated work *The Theory of Economic Growth*, Lewis states:

> First, it should be noted that our subject matter is growth, and not distribution. It is possible that output may be growing, and yet that the masses of the people may be becoming poorer. . . . But our primary interest is in analyzing not distribution but growth. Secondly, our concern is not primarily with consumption but with output. Output may be growing while consumption is declining.[32]

Lewis insists that he will carry on his study "from the angle of the growth of output, and not from the angle of the growth of consumption."[33]

Later on, we find another qualification that further narrows the scope of his study. After discussing some of the problems in defining "output," Lewis says: "We mention these problems so that pedantic reviewers shall not be able to say that we are not aware of them. We do not, however, have to solve them. For our concern is not with the measure of output, but with its growth."[34] He then explains that, for the purposes of his study, "the definition [of output] must . . . relate to goods and services—'economic' output, in the old fashioned meaning of 'economic'—and not to some such concept as welfare, satisfaction or happiness. It is possible that a person may become less happy in the process of acquiring greater command over goods and services. This frequently happens to individuals, and it may also happen to groups."[35] But for Lewis, the central question is growth. "This book," he says, "is not . . . an essay on whether people ought to have or to want more goods and services; its concern is merely with the processes by which more goods and services become available."[36] But "available" to whom? The important question here is who gets what and how, not growth toward an abstract and undefined end.

Nowhere do we see in Lewis's work a sense of concrete historical process. In a nine-page section on imperialism, he writes that it is "only marginally related to economic analysis, and we can touch it only very briefly"; and that, of all the various causes of imperialism, the one of foremost importance is that "some nations want more or better lands upon which to settle their peoples."[37] A bit later he says "migration may lead to war because other countries refuse to accept immigrants, or because they treat them badly." For Lewis, "what causes a nation to believe in militaristic glory is one of the unsolved puzzles of the universe."[38] Commenting that "class structure throws little light on the problem," he implies that Western imperialist domination is nothing more than a figment of a few radicals' imaginations, because "the richest countries tend to be peaceful, enjoying what they have, and envying none."[39]

Arthur Lewis is not alone, however, in the production of this kind of nonsense; other developmental theorists fall into a similar kind of ideological trap. "One of the great ethical issues of our time," writes Art Gallaher, Jr., the editor of *Perspectives in Developmental Change*, is "the extent to which the developed nations of the world are willing to help the less fortunate and to provide such help without binding the less fortunate to closed ideological systems."[40]

Writing at the turn of the century, the British economist John Hobson comes closer to the truth on the real motives behind such ideological statements expressed above by Lewis and Gallaher. "Industrial and financial forces of Imperialism," Hobson writes,

> operating through the party, the press, the church, the school, mould public opinion and public policy by the false idealization of

those primitive lusts of struggle, domination and acquisitiveness, which have survived throughout the eras of peaceful industrial order, and whose stimulation is needed once again for the work of imperial aggression, expansion, and the forceful exploitation of lower races. For these business politicians biology and sociology weave thin convenient theories of a race struggle for the subjugation of the inferior peoples, in order that we, the Anglo-Saxon, may take their lands and live upon their labours; while economics buttresses the argument by representing our work in conquering and ruling them as our share in the division of labour among nations, and history devises reasons why the lessons of the past empire do not apply to ours, while social ethics paints the motive of "Imperialism" as the desire to bear the "burden" of educating and elevating races of "children." Thus are the "cultured" or semi-cultured classes indoctrinated with the intellectual and moral grandeur of Imperialism.[41]

Developmentalist ideology notwithstanding, the historical record makes it abundantly clear that the history of the underdeveloped countries in the last five centuries is the history of the consequences of European expansion:

> By the end of the sixteenth century ... the agricultural economies of the Spice Islands, the domestic industries of large parts of India, the Arab trading-economy of the Indian Ocean and of the western Pacific, the native societies of West Africa and the way of life in the Caribbean islands and in the vast areas of the two vice-royalties of Spanish America [were] all deeply affected by the impact of Europeans. ... The results [of European expansion] on non-European societies were ... sometimes immediate and overwhelming.[42]

"In many cases," writes Griffin, "the societies with which Europe came into contact were sophisticated, cultured and wealthy."[43] European expansion and plunder throughout the world since the fifteenth and sixteenth centuries, while extremely beneficial for the development of the imperial centers, had disastrous effects on indigenous peoples:

> Colonialism in Latin America, as in the rest of the world, was a catastrophe for the indigenous people. In the areas of more primitive civilization the population virtually disappeared within less than thirty years. In the areas of advanced civilization the people were completely subjugated.

Spanish penetration of Latin America began in the Caribbean area. . . . The Spaniards gained control over the natives by breaking their political structure. The chiefs were liquidated and the rest of the community were allocated to individual claimants. . . . The combination of brutality, slaughter, high tribute, slavery, forced labor for gold mining, destruction of the social framework, malnutrition, disease and suicide led to the extinction of the indigenous population.[44]

And, according to the British economic historian E. E. Rich:

It has been reckoned that at the approach of the Spaniards, in 1492, total Carib population in Hispaniola was about 300,000. By 1508 it was reduced to about 60,000. A great decline had brought it to about 14,000 by 1514, as serious settlement began; and by 1548 it had reached a figure which indicated virtual extermination, about 500.[45]

Apparently, these facts have no bearing on social and economic development in the developmentalist model. The theorists of this school remain silent not only on the effects of European colonialism but also of contemporary U.S. imperialism.

Charles Kindleberger, another prominent developmentalist, writes: "Growth and development are often used synonymously in economic discussion, and this usage is entirely acceptable."[46] Further on in his essay, he gives us an ideological rationale for his interest in the underdeveloped countries, and the importance of development in these countries vis-à-vis U.S. foreign policy:

The writer is a native of the developed part of a developed country, and . . . economic and political development in the rest of the world is of concern to his country. In addition, he is persuaded that events abroad have their repercussions on the United States—not all events, to be sure, but certainly cataclysmic ones.[47]

Concerning growth and economic development in general, Kindleberger asserts that "anyone who claims to understand economic development *in toto*, or to have found the key to the secret of growth, is almost certainly wrong. . . .[48] And yet there is a positive element" to his essay, we are told. This element turns out to be that "the writer is in favor of the market":[49]

Development that ignores the market, or provides elaborate substitutes for it, is likely to fail in the grand manner. The market may not be very effective; but in the present stage of economic wisdom, when allowance is made for its evident deficiencies the result is better than any alternative.[50]

Economist Simon Kuznets puts it this way:

The populations in underdeveloped countries today are inheritors of civilizations quite distinctive from and independent of European civilization. Yet it is European civilization that through centuries of geographical, political, and intellectual expansion has provided the matrix of modern economic growth. . . .

This statement is again part of the explanation of the weaknesses in the social and political structure of underdeveloped countries today. . . . The intellectual revolution with the introduction of science, the moral revolution with the secularization of Christo-Judaic religions, the geographical revolution with the formation of national states, all occurred within the context of European civilization, not in Asia, Africa, or the Americas.[51]

Bold ideological assertions such as those above have pervaded the entire mainstream developmentalist literature, so much so that it is impossible to separate metropolitan social science from the dominant capitalist ideology.

Here is another example. Ragnar Nurkse wonders: "What is it that breaks the deadlock?"—that spurs "some parts of the world [to] economic development"? His answer: "the American economy has been abundantly supplied with the human qualities of enterprise and initiative; but we cannot take it for granted that they are present in the same degree elsewhere."[52] Later in his argument, Nurkse writes:

According to [the] Marxian or rather neo-Marxian doctrine of economic imperialism, advanced capitalist economies are under a compulsion to export capital, and in this way to dump their surplus produce abroad, in order to keep the internal economy operating at a prosperous and profitable level of activity.

My own reaction to this doctrine is that if such a compulsion existed—and it may have existed to some extent in the past—there would be nothing sinister about it. On the contrary, it would be a highly beneficent compulsion.[53]

Nurkse fails to see that, as profits from the export of capital[54] continue to pour out of the underdeveloped countries, the advanced capitalist economies experience a further accumulation of capital; this method becomes highly profitable for the metropolitan monopoly capitalists, not for the underdeveloped countries.

For Nurkse, not convinced even of his own assertion, the last resort is to go all out in defense of monopoly capital. In response to the "thesis contained in . . . the Marxian doctrine of economic imperialism [that states] the exploitation of backward areas by monopoly capitalism," Nurkse writes:

> where foreign investment has been associated with exclusive concessions in the debtor countries, there may have been some economic basis for it. . . . In order to reap an appropriate return from investment . . . [the private investor] may need an exclusive concession. This is not the whole story, but it does furnish a plausible argument in defense of the monopoly element in past foreign investment.[55]

There are, however, a number of "more sensitive" developmentalists who appear at least partially to have abandoned the ideological premises of their earlier work; among them are Irma Adelman and Cynthia Taft Morris. In their book *Economic Growth and Social Equity in Developing Countries*, Adelman and Morris seem to have arrived at a different set of conclusions on the nature and structure of recent growth patterns in the underdeveloped countries than that of their earlier study.[56] "In the 1950s," they write,

> Development economists and other specialists . . . thought that if policy actions were taken to speed up a country's economic growth, increased popular participation in the political process and a more equitable distribution of income would eventually follow. They assumed, in other words, that increases in the rate of growth of such components of economic development as industrialization, agricultural productivity, physical overhead capital, investment, and per capita GNP were closely associated with increases in the extent of political and economic participation.
>   Since about 1965, however, development specialists have begun to realize that development [i.e., neocolonial development] does not work in the expected way.[57]

Building upon their earlier work, and testing the various relationships between a long list of economic, social, and political indicators, Adelman and Morris attempt to discover "the extent to which the benefits of economic growth in underdeveloped countries during the 1950s and 1960s reached those most in need."[58] Adelman and Morris's conclusions should be instructive for those developmentalists who continue to perpetuate the old myths. "The results of our analyses came as a shock to us," they explain.

> Although we had believed economic growth to have unfavorable social, cultural, and ecological consequences, we had shared the prevailing view among economists that economic growth was economically beneficial to most nations. We had also not greatly questioned the relevance today of the historical association of successful economic growth with the spread of parliamentary democracy. Our results proved to be at variance with our preconceptions. In view of their unexpectedness, we undertook a variety of crosschecks during the two years before we sought their present publication. Case studies and other historical and contemporary evidence coming to our attention have been so overwhelmingly consistent with our findings that . . . we present them here with considerable confidence in their validity.[59]

Contrary to the "basic premise . . . that sustained economic growth leads to higher real incomes for even the poorest segments of the population" in the underdeveloped countries, "statistical analyses . . . strongly suggest that this optimistic assumption has no basis in fact."[60] Furthermore,

> inequality of income tends to be greatest where the exploitation of an abundance of natural resources coincides with a concentration of assets in the hands of expatriates. . . .
> Our analysis indicates that the relationship between level of economic development and the income share of the poorest 60 percent of the population is asymmetrically U-shaped. . . . The process of economic modernization shifts the income distribution in favor of the middle class and upper income groups and against lower income groups. . . .
> An even more disturbing implication of our findings is that development is accompanied by an absolute as well as a relative decline in the average income of the very poor. Indeed, an initial spurt of dualistic growth may cause such a decline for as much as 60 percent of the population. . . .

Our results tend to confirm Paul Baran's hypothesis that extreme inequality at the lowest levels of development occurs because the benefits of dualistic growth . . . accrue to ruling coalitions of expatriate businessmen and indigenous property owners. . . . [Thus] economic modernization has had little direct effect on the sharing of political power. . . .

We also find little warrant for the widespread belief that increased political participation leads to a more equitable distribution of income. . . . The relationship of income distribution to political power [involves] . . . those effects of the distribution of wealth on political power that provide the basis for the Marxian hypothesis that economic structure determines the structure of political power.

In short, our analysis supports the Marxian view that economic structure, not level of income or rate of economic growth, is the basic determinant of patterns of income distribution. Our conclusions . . . point strongly to the importance of social, institutional, and political transformations for the achievement of greater political and economic equality; and they underline the urgent need to discard as outmoded the view that economic growth in low-income countries typically benefits the masses.[61]

That Adelman and Morris have come a long way in formulating and asking the right kinds of questions on the structures of underdevelopment sets them apart from other developmentalists. Unfortunately, however, their deep-seated metropolitan ideology has not freed them to see the underlying realities of underdevelopment with total clarity. As apologists for capitalist industrialization, with a broad political base that includes middle-class participants, Adelman and Morris reject any kind of radical change that would disturb the power arrangements of the global political economy and weaken imperial control. To disqualify the option for revolutionary change, they offer us an ideologically-ridden statement that begs the question altogether: "Historical evidence," they write, "offers little basis for optimism on this score."[62] Puzzled with the absence of an acceptable alternative strategy for development, Adelman and Morris first tell us that "the path to social justice through greater political participation is no less thorny than the path to social justice through improving the distribution of income."[63] And in the closing lines of their book, they give us a vague and abstract statement as the ultimate paper strategy: "The only policy instruments that offer some hope for significant improvements in the standard of living of the poor . . . [are those that promote] development of the people, by the people, and for the people."[64]

The failure of modernization theory and developmentalism in general to explain the sources of the problems of development in the Third World during the past several decades has effectively discredited the mainstream theories of development economics. As one of its earlier proponents, Dudley Seers, has recently admitted in his article titled "The Birth, Life and Death of Development Economics,"

> Development economics in the conventional sense has . . . proved much less useful than was expected in the vigorous optimism of its youth. In some circumstances it may well have aggravated social problems if only by diverting attention from their real causes—indeed from the problems themselves.[65]

Similarly, a long-standing critic of developmentalism, Deepak Lal, has concluded that "the demise of development economics is likely to be conducive to the health of both the economics and the economies of developing countries."[66]

In the light of its increasing irrelevance in development studies, and in response to the rise to prominence of other modes of theorizing on the predicament of less-developed states in the global political economy, mainstream development theory has in the past decade undergone some important changes to account for its erroneous, ideologically-ridden assumptions cultivated during the cold war era. Thus, the 1980s ushered in a series of reformulated and liberalized versions of the discredited developmentalist positions of the previous three decades in a last-ditch effort to survive a paradigmatic struggle in which alternative, radical approaches—dependency theory, the world system approach, and a variety of Marxist formulations—had already taken center stage. Thus began the establishment of special panels and commissions, the publication of special reports, and declarations on the necessity of an "urgent dialogue" between "the North and the South," as well as a stream of books and studies on development issues. Proclamations by the proponents of these studies of a "new international economic order" based on "cooperation," "free trade," "debt relief," renewed "aid," and "export-oriented industrialization" schemes, within the context of a world economy controlled by the advanced capitalist states—which continue to wield economic power over the Third World through transnational corporations and banks, the IMF, the World Bank, and a host of other mechanisms of imperial control—have in reality served to institutionalize further capital accumulation in favor of the transnational monopolies and the classes that own and control them.

Remaining within such a framework, the newly refurbished main-stream development theories introduced into development studies during the past two decades (by way of systems analysis, Club of Rome reports, the Brandt Commission Report, OECD- and U.N.-sponsored studies and programs, privatization models, monetarism, world futures theory, international Keynesianism, and so on) have all failed to provide adequate answers to the problems of development in the Third World.[67]

To move on to a more penetrating level of analysis of the development process in the Third World, we explore in the next two chapters radical alternatives to mainstream development theory—the dependency and world system theories and Marxism.

CHAPTER 2

DEPENDENCY AND THE WORLD SYSTEM: TWO ALTERNATIVE THEORIES OF DEVELOPMENT

With the paradigmatic decline in legitimacy of modernization theory and developmentalism in general during the decade of the 1960s, the dependency theory filled the void in development theory and rose to prominence in the late 1960s and the early 1970s. As a radical alternative to both the conservative theorizing of the previous two decades, when U.S. global expansion was in full swing and U.S. foreign policy was tied to the fate of its imperial entanglement in Latin America and later in Vietnam, and the failure of liberal reformist initiatives in restructuring terms of trade on a world scale under the auspices of the United Nations and its various agencies,[1] the dependency theory became a popular theoretical tool of progressive scholars to critique the causes and consequences of underdevelopment in Latin America and of U.S. encroachments into the region. By the mid-1970s, dependency theory took center stage in development theory among a growing number of critical scholars in Latin America and the United States.

However, beginning in the mid-1970s and throughout the second half of the decade and beyond, the dependency theory came under strong criticism for failing to provide a complete and correct analysis of the forces at work in the development process in Latin America and elsewhere. It is in this context that a global counterpart of the dependency theory emerged in the mid-1970s that came to be known as "world system theory." Promoted by scholars previously influenced by the approach and analysis provided by the dependency theory, the globally-oriented world system approach elevated the focus of analysis onto the world level in an attempt to account for the forces at work in the global political economy.

This chapter presents an analysis of the fundamentals of the dependency theory and the world system approach, while the next chapter provides a critique of the assumptions, analyses, and implications of these theories in the context of an alternative Marxist theory of development.

THE DEPENDENCY THEORY

The dependency theory, first advanced by a group of Latin American social scientists,[2] is fundamentally different from the developmentalist theories discussed in the previous chapter. Dependence, according to Andre Gunder Frank, "is the result of the historical development and contemporary structure of world capitalism, to which Latin America is subordinated, and the economic, political, social and cultural policies generated by the resulting class structure."[3] More specifically, a clear economic conceptualization of dependence is given by Theotonio Dos Santos in his discussion of the causes of Latin American underdevelopment. According to Dos Santos, dependence is

> a situation in which the economy of certain countries is conditioned by the development and expansion of another economy to which the former is subjected. The relation of interdependence between two or more economies, and between these and world trade assumes the form of dependence when some countries (the dominant ones) can expand and can be self-starting, while other countries (the dependent ones) can do this only as a reflection of that expansion, which can have either a positive or negative effect on their immediate development.[4]

A further analysis of the conceptual roots of dependence reveals that dependency is a "conditioning situation." The conditioning process is such that "each change in the interests and in the policy of the metropolitan country has produced and continues to produce a similar process in the inner workings of the dependent society."[5] Furthermore, metropolitan economic interests determine the nature of dependent relations, the social class structure, and political control in the dependent society. Thus, according to this view, it is important to understand that dependence is not merely an "external" economic phenomenon, expressed in terms of economic relations, but it is a political phenomenon "which includes the entire institutional framework of the dependent society."[6]

Historically, Latin America's subordinate relationship to feudal, mercantilist, and capitalist powers—Spain and Portugal in the colonial and early post-independence period; Britain during most of the nineteenth and early part of the twentieth centuries; and the United States since the middle of the twentieth century—in the view of Cockcroft et al. "has resulted in the present economic, social, and political traits of underdevelopment that are internal to Latin American countries."[7] Thus, the post-conquest societies of Latin America were shaped by world capitalism in its mercantile stage and, as a consequence, these societies have ever since been dependent on and penetrated by the international system in general and its dominant center in particular. Therefore, as Murga argues, "underdevelopment cannot be considered in this sense as a stage prior to capitalism, but rather as a consequence of the expansive process of capitalism."[8] Underdevelopment, then, according to the dependency theorists, in its contemporary Latin American context constitutes a particular form of capitalism, namely "dependent capitalism."

The dependency theory views the capitalist system as a global, international system within which national economies of underdeveloped countries constitute subsystems.[9] This means that "Latin America has fulfilled certain definite functions in the 'world economy' or world market, and the domestic development of Latin America has been limited . . . by the needs of the dominant economies within that world market."[10] The world market refers to all flows of goods and services among both developed and underdeveloped countries with capitalist economies. It encompasses all capital transfers—including foreign aid and overseas investment—and all commodity exchanges. But, according to Bodenheimer, it constitutes the core of a broader international system:

> This international system includes not only a network of economic (market) relations, but also the entire complex of political, military, social and cultural international relations organized by and around that market (e.g., the Monroe Doctrine, the Organization of American States, "Free World" defense treaties and organizations, and media and communications networks). The interna-

tional system is the static expression and outcome of a dynamic historical process: the transnational or global expansion of capitalism.[11]

Underdevelopment in Latin America, the dependency theorists argue, is structurally linked to development in the dominant capitalist nations. Accordingly, it is important to understand in this context that although the fact of Latin America's dependence on hegemonic powers has been constant for the past four centuries, the forms of dependency relations in particular countries have changed throughout history. Basic variations in any given historical period have taken place according to (1) the specific characteristics of the international system and (2) the specific functions of the Latin country within that system.[12] These two conditions of dependence are outlined briefly below.[13]

(1) Characteristics of the international system:
    (a) the prevalent form of capitalism (commercial or industrial, corporate or financial);
    (b) the principal needs of the dominant nation(s) in the international system (agricultural commodities, strategic raw materials—minerals and petroleum—cheap labor, commodity markets, capital markets, etc.);
    (c) the degree of concentration of capital in the dominant nation(s) (competitive or monopoly capitalism);
    (d) the degree of international concentration of power (one hegemonic power or rival powers);
    (e) the typical form of world trade (mercantilism, "free trade," protectionism and/or trade within the structure of transnational corporations).
(2) Characteristics of the Latin country within the international system:
    (a) functions primarily as a supplier of raw materials or agricultural products, as a market for manufactured goods, as a supplier of certain manufactured commodities, as an arena for direct foreign investment, or any combination of the preceding;
    (b) the degree of foreign control in the principal economic sectors and consequent decapitalization;
    (c) the degree of relative autonomy (periods of international war or depression vs. "normal" periods of capitalist expansion);
    (d) the close political and economic correspondence between the interests of the national oligarchy and the national bourgeoisie and the structure of the international system.

Following the line of reasoning outlined above, the dependency theorists have argued that it is thus possible to trace certain changes that have taken place in the international system during the historical process of capitalist expansion. And, in the present period, the process of global economic expansion of dominant capitalist nations (particularly the U.S.) is taking place through the extraterritorial operations of transnational corporations.

A closer examination of the operational activities of these corporations, Sunkel notes, reveals a fairly definite pattern:

> first, they export their finished products; then they establish sales organizations abroad; they then proceed to allow foreign producers to use their licenses and patents to manufacture the product locally; finally, they buy off the local producer and establish a partially or wholly owned subsidiary.[14]

This pattern, he argues, illustrates the dynamics of external economic penetration of the national market from within, through the establishment of enterprises located in the country itself. As a result, while previously only the international primary product market was monopolized, a monopoly situation is now also created in the international market in manufactures.[15]

In an article titled "The Changing Structure of Foreign Investment in Latin America," Dos Santos, after examining a large body of data, concludes:

> Our data reveal [that] foreign investment is gradually ceasing to be a colonial-exporting enclave and is changing the old international division of labor: the production of raw materials by underdeveloped countries and the production of manufactured goods by developed countries. Faced with the industrial growth of Latin America in the 1930s and the protectionist measures taken by the governments of that period, foreign capital is turning toward the manufacturing sector, is being integrated with the present economies, and is proceeding to dominate their industrial capitalist sectors. This is what is now happening in Latin America. What effects has this process on the economic structure of Latin America?
>
> In the first place, there are qualitative changes in the size of the enterprises. Corporations are being formed, generally affiliated with North American or European corporations. The possibility of

monopolizing the existing market allows them to increase their profits without opening up new markets. This diminishes the stimulus to development that the enterprises might have given these economies.

In the second place, an intensive integration of the economy of these countries with foreign capital is taking place. Contrary to what is believed by many social scientists, this integration increases the economic dependence of these countries on other countries.[16]

In a follow-up article titled "Foreign Investment and the Large Enterprise in Latin America: The Brazilian Case," Dos Santos goes on to argue that "the changes in the international division of labor during the phase of monopoly capitalism submit the dominated countries to: (a) the predominance of the large enterprise; (b) economic concentration under the rule of large industries, especially international industry; (c) monopoly of the market."[17] After a careful analysis of the Brazilian case, Dos Santos concludes: "foreign capital has intensified its penetration in the past decade; this penetration is basically directed toward the manufacturing sector, particularly toward basic industry; and this penetration requires a high fee in the form of profits, interests, royalties, technical services, etc., and leads the economy into increasing indebtedness."[18] After investigating the nature and structure of foreign capital vis-à-vis Brazil's national economy, Dos Santos states that "we must now study the internal effects of this penetration." He asks: "What type of relationship does it establish within the economy itself?"

In the first place, we must determine the relative importance of foreign capital compared to national capital and the forms of penetration that it uses. The strategy used by foreign capital to gain internal control of the economy, whether by design or because of its own structural character, may be described in the following manner:

(a) The high degree of technological integration of foreign-owned enterprises permits them to confine themselves to specialized sectors of activity in which they control the market, together with national economic groups dispersed in various sectors of activity and without strong monopolistic conditions.

(b) Foreign capital seeks to penetrate sectors in which it can obtain control of the market, establishing conditions of monopolistic competition.

(c) It seeks to maintain financial independence for its enterprises, utilizing local financial sources for secondary purposes. This comes from the character of its investments, which are made largely in the form of transfer of machinery (often obsolete in the country of origin), which do not involve actual disbursements of fixed capital.[19]

According to Bodenheimer, other, more specific characteristics of dependent industrialization include:

1) increasing foreign control over the most dynamic and strategic industrial sectors through direct ownership and control over production, control of marketing and distribution, or control of patents and licenses (in many sectors foreign corporations have been buying out formerly national industries); 2) increasing competitive advantages for (often monopolistic) foreign enterprises over local firms, particularly in industries of scale; 3) as a result of foreign ownership, outflow of capital (profits) abroad; 4) despite some production for the internal market, adaptation of the entire economic structure to the needs of the buyers of Latin exports in the dominant nations; 5) introduction of advanced, capital-intensive foreign technology, without regard to size or composition of the local labor market, and consequent aggravation of unemployment (which in turn results in restriction of the domestic market): in several countries (e.g. Chile, Colombia, Peru) employment in manufacturing industry actually declined as a percentage of total employment between 1925 and 1960; 6) also as a result of foreign control over technology, its restriction to those sectors in which foreign capital has a direct interest; 7) lack of a domestic capital goods industry in most countries, and consequently an increased rather than reduced dependence on imports and rigidities in the composition of imports. In short, dependent industrialization has aggravated rather than resolved such basic problems as balance of payments deficits, unemployment, income disparities, and an insufficient domestic market.[20]

The dependency theorists argue that the relations of economic dependence with external hegemonic powers constitute only one aspect of the phenomenon of dependence. They point out that "dependence is not simply an 'external' relation between Latin America and its world capitalist metropolis but equally an 'internal,' indeed integral, condition of Latin American society" that has penetrated all aspects of their existence—economic, political, social, ideological, and psychological.[21] The emphasis here is on the dynamics of the dependent class structure and the ideological and political alliance among the dominant classes of both the center and the peripheral countries. Cockcroft et al. state that because

> The international system of monopoly capitalism conditions the formation of class structures in Latin America . . . the bourgeoisie maintains itself economically and socially on the basis of capitalism and, in order to maintain itself, has to make political effort to preserve the same exploitative and underdevelopment-generating structure that brought it into existence.[22]

Thus, it is important, the dependency theorists stress, to trace the sociopolitical implications of the dominant classes in dependent countries which serve to perpetuate the prevailing order of "dependent capitalism" that generates profits and wealth for the few while bringing massive poverty and a general condition of underdevelopment to the region as a whole. "The existence of these clientele classes . . . whose interests correspond to those of the dominant classes in the dominant nations," argues Bodenheimer, "is the . . . *sine qua non* of dependency."[23]

Although a dependent country does not have control over the major decisions affecting its own economy, the infrastructure of dependency, it is argued, plays a substantial role in legitimizing the prevailing socioeconomic and political order through institutional means. Hence, the domestic political economy of a particular country may have a profound effect on its external relations vis-à-vis its overall development:

> The fact that a developing country needs to import machinery or technology does not necessarily make it a "dependent" country; what is crucial is the type of political regime which makes the decision on what to import (the global political context), the criteria used in the selection of imports, and the relationship between the current imports and the overall future development project. The decision to import technology by a working class socialist regime is directed toward maximizing social benefits through increases in production, creating the economic and scientific basis for the emergence of indigenous sources of innovation that will, in the future at least, partially surpass the need to import technology. Importation of technology in this context is a transitional phenomenon, a temporary dependence toward relative autonomy. In nonsocialist or dependent capitalist societies, importation of technology (or capital) creates a relatively stable group of institutions

and elites that serve as permanent transmission belts for external penetration, independent of local needs.[24]

Dependency relations, then, according to this theory, take place within the framework of the world capitalist system and are an aspect of (1) economic imperialism (originating in the heart of that system, namely, the advanced capitalist nations in general and the current center of world capitalism, the United States, in particular), (2) the internal dynamics of the dependent society, and (3) the political-economic and ideological alliance of the dominant and dependent countries of the world system. In this context, argues Dos Santos, "the situation of dependence to which Latin American countries are subjected cannot be overcome without a qualitative change in their internal structures and external relations."[25] For this reason, Murga observes, one cannot speak in terms of the possibilities of "autonomous" or "national" development in the dependent societies "while the same dominant traditional classes or modern allies of the dominant metropolitan class continue to exist."[26]

The conclusions reached and the alternatives posed by the dependency theorists lend themselves to a set of choices that are polar opposites: "dependency" or "autonomy;" "exploitation" or "liberation;" "repression" or "revolution." Such analysis tends to indicate that only the revolutionary transformation of the system of structural dependence can break the vicious circle of underdevelopment and generate "authentic" development:

> The only way to obtain this political autonomy and thus to arrive at the real possibilities for development (a phenomenon historically frustrated by the capitalist system) is by means of radical change in the structures that have brought about and maintain underdevelopment and the relations of dependence.[27]

Andre Gunder Frank puts it bluntly:

> this historical process of underdevelopment cannot be reversed and turned into economic and social development for the majority of the Latin American people until they destroy the capitalist class structure through revolution.[28]

Similarly, Brazilian economist Theotonio Dos Santos, assessing the revolutionary potential in Latin America, observes the coming of prolonged crises in these countries:

Everything now indicates that what can be expected is a long process of sharp political and military confrontations and of profound
social radicalization which will lead these countries to a dilemma:
governments of force which open the way to fascism, or popular
revolutionary governments which open the way to socialism.
Intermediate solutions have proved to be, in such a contradictory
reality, empty and utopian.[29]

WORLD SYSTEM THEORY

In response to the criticisms of dependency theory during the
1970s, especially in regard to debates on the nature and causes of underdevelopment in Latin America as having its origins in feudalism or capitalism,[30] Immanuel Wallerstein launched a multivolume study of the
origin and development of "the modern world system" in an effort to
reexamine the transition from feudalism to capitalism in Western
Europe[31] and its subsequent development and expansion to the rest of
the world with its impact on colonial and semicolonial regions of the
Third World. This was followed by Samir Amin's two-volume study of
accumulation on a world scale and Andre Gunder Frank's later historical studies of the world accumulation process from colonial times to the
present.[32] Thus began the formation of an entire school of thought that
eventually came to be known as "world system theory."[33]
    Making the world system his unit of analysis, Immanuel Waller-
stein argued that he

> abandoned the idea altogether of taking either the sovereign state
> or that vaguer concept, the national society, as the unit of analysis.
> I decided that neither one was a social system and that one could
> only speak of social change in social systems. The only social sys-
> tem in this scheme was the world system.[34]

"Once we assume that the unit of analysis is such a world-system and
not the state or the nation or the people," argues Wallerstein, "then
much changes in the outcome of the analysis."

> Most specifically we shift from a concern with the attributive char-
> acteristics of states to concern with the relational characteristics of
> states. We shift from seeing classes (and status groups) as groups
> within a state to seeing them as groups within a world-economy.[35]

This argument is made clear in stronger terms by another world system theorist, Albert Bergesen, who claims that

> The emergence of the modern world-system nullified the internal evolutionary dynamics of autonomous societies as they were one by one incorporated into the emerging world-economy. Autonomous internal societal development, whether by Marxian class struggle or Parsonian structural differentiation, ends when that social formation becomes part of the world-system, for at that point the principal determinant of its development shifts from internal social relations (including class relations) to global social relations particularly the core-periphery class relation).[36]

An essential element in the global analysis of the modern world system is the theory's three-tiered model of "core," "periphery," and "semi-periphery," which divides the world system into three areas or zones that are defined on the basis of a society's level of development and incorporation into the world system, and the political-economic content of such incorporation.[37] This brings up the question of "the network(s) of governance or rule in the area in question."[38] "In this respect," Hopkins and Wallerstein explain, "incorporation entails the expansion of the world-economy's interstate system":

> Interstate relations and the interstate system overall, in part express and in part circumscribe or structure the world-scale accumulation/production process. In short, the relational networks forming the interstate system are integral to, not outside of, the networks constitutive of the social economy defining the scope and reach of the modern world-system. . . .
> Insofar as external areas are incorporated, then—and in the singular development of the modern world-system all have been—the transition period framing incorporation encloses definite directions of change in a once external area's arrangements and processes of rule or governance.[39]

The main feature of the modern world system is, in essence, the transfer of surplus from the periphery to the core of the system, conceptualized in a manner similar to the Frankian "metropolis-satellite" model of domination and exploitation. But, in world system theory the modern world system (dominated by the core) allows, under certain conditions and in the context of certain political-economic processes, the transformation of some peripheral states into semi-peripheral ones. However, such transformation (or mobility) of states along the three-tiered continuum takes place within the context and logic of the system as a whole and as a consequence of the dictates of the dominant (or, capitalist) world system in a given historical period. Thus, the various parts of the system that make up its totality always function within the framework of the relationship of the parts to the whole.

It is for this reason that world system theory rejects the study of internal class structures in isolation, opting instead for a study of the relationship between the three components that make up the modern world system and conceptualize class in world-systemic terms. Thus, in line with this formulation, Samir Amin has developed a parallel argument:

> capitalism has become a world system, and not just a juxtaposition of 'national capitalisms'. The social contradictions characteristic of capitalism are thus on a world scale, that is, the contradiction is not between the bourgeoisie and the proletariat of each country considered in isolation, but between the world bourgeoisie and the world proletariat.[40]

The conceptualization of the problem in such global terms has prompted some critics to observe that in a most fundamental way the world system approach is in fact quite similar to the dependency theory, as both of these perspectives complement each other in attempting to explain the historical development of the structures and dynamics of the capitalist system on a world-systemic level.

Both the dependency theory and the world system perspective have come under strong criticism in Marxist circles on a number of counts. These are discussed in the next chapter in the context of an overview of the Marxist alternative in development studies.

CHAPTER 3

THE CONTROVERSY OVER
IMPERIALISM AND DEVELOPMENT:
THE MARXIST ALTERNATIVE

During the past two decades a new body of literature has emerged in Marxist circles on the imperialist industrialization of the Third World. Based on the analysis of the dynamics of capitalist development and its implications for the expansion of transnational capital to the Third World, these studies have suggested that imperialist expansion, during the period of the internationalization of productive capital, works toward the relative industrialization of the Third World.[1] Whatever form this industrialization may take, the arguments presented in these works are contrary to that of the dependency theory and the world system approach discussed in the previous chapter.

In this chapter, we shall attempt to clarify a number of theoretical and substantive issues related to the interpretation of the dynamics of capitalist development explicated in recent Marxist works and draw from them the political implications of such analysis vis-à-vis the theory of dependency and the world system.

THEORETICAL CONSIDERATIONS

The "imperialist industrialization" thesis, which has gained increasing importance in recent years, is not an entirely new interpretation of the classical Marxist theory of capital accumulation on a world scale.

In writing about the East India Company in 1853, Marx saw Britain as fulfilling "a double mission in India: one destructive, the other regenerating."[2] He projected that the "means of irrigation and of internal communication," "the immediate and current wants of railway locomotion" could be the "forerunner of modern industry."[3] Referring to the impact of British rule on Indian villages, "however much the English may have hibernicized the country," Marx wrote in a letter to Engels, "the breaking up of those stereotyped primitive forms was the *sine qua non* for Europeanization. The tax-gatherer alone could not achieve this. The destruction of their ancient industry was necessary to deprive the villages of their self-supporting character."[4]

Lenin, in his classic work *Imperialism: The Highest Stage of Capitalism*, writes: "The export of capital influences and greatly accelerates the development of capitalism in those countries to which it is exported. While, therefore, the export of capital may tend to a certain extent to arrest development in the capital-exporting countries, it can only do so by expanding and deepening the further development of capitalism throughout the world."[5] Thus, "capitalism is growing with the greatest rapidity in the colonies and in overseas countries."[6]

Marx and Lenin were interested in the contradictions of this capitalist expansionary process above all from the angle of the proletariat and the laboring masses in the colonies and in the colonial centers. "All the English bourgeoisie may be forced to do," Marx wrote in *The Future Results of the British Rule in India*, "will neither emancipate nor materially mend the social condition of the mass of the people [in India]. . . . But what they will not fail to do is to lay down the material premises for both. Has the bourgeoisie ever done more? Has it ever effected a progress without dragging individuals and peoples through blood and dirt, through misery and degradation?"[7] He added: "The Indians will not reap the fruits of the new elements of society scattered among them by the British bourgeoisie, till in Great Britain itself the now ruling classes shall have been supplanted by the industrial proletariat, or till the Hindus themselves shall have grown strong enough to throw off the English yoke altogether."[8]

These concerns are also expressed by Lenin in his book *Imperialism*, where he writes:

> The building of railways seems to be a simple, natural, democratic, cultural and civilizing enterprise; that is what it is in the opinion of bourgeois professors who are paid to depict capitalist slavery in

bright colors, and in the opinion of petty-bourgeois philistines. But as a matter of fact the capitalist threads, which in the thousands of different intercrossings bind these enterprises with private property in means of production in general, have converted this railway construction into an instrument of oppressing *a thousand million* people (in the colonies and semi-colonies), that is, more than half the population of the globe that inhabits the dependent countries, as well as the wage-slaves of capital in the "civilized" countries.[9]

Further on, Lenin explains:

> The description of "British imperialism" in Schulze-Gaevermitz's book reveals the same parasitical traits. . . . While the "merit" of imperialism is that it "trains the Negro to habits of industry" (not without coercion, of course . . .), the "danger" of imperialism lies in that "Europe will shift the burden of physical toil—first agricultural and mining, then the rougher work in industry—on to the colored races, and itself be content with the role of rentier, and in this way, perhaps, pave the way for the economic, and later, the political emancipation of the colored races."[10]

Thus, Lenin concludes: "Imperialism is the eve of the social revolution of the proletariat . . . on a world-wide scale."[11]

In the light of the above observations by Marx and Lenin, we shall argue that the recently ascending imperialist industrialization thesis is at base firmly rooted in the classical Marxist theory of capitalist imperialism.

While both Marxism and the dependency and world system theories contend that they offer a concrete analysis of the capitalist political economy on a world scale, we would argue that in fact only the former offers us a coherent explanation through the formulation of the problem in terms of the laws of motion of the capitalist mode of production in its global manifestations.

While to the dependency and the world system theories the basic units of analysis are "nation states" and the "world system" and the tenet that "exploitation" takes place between these units at the level of circulation resulting in "unequal exchange" (effected through "metropolitan-satellite" or "core-periphery" relations of domination and dependence), Marxism argues that in studying development one must always start with an analysis of social classes and class struggles (at both national and international levels) and that the focus of analysis should be class exploitation rooted in relations of production in specific social formations.[12]

As we shall see shortly, the political implications of the two sets of theories vary sharply when we view the question of imperialist expansion in these divergent terms. Thus, while the dependency theory argues that imperialism "blocks" capitalist development in the Third World and that therefore the dominated countries ought to "break away" from the world system,[13] the Marxist theory concentrates directly on the relations of production under imperialism and focuses on the class nature of imperialist exploitation, moving beyond national/institutional questions such as unequal trade, foreign debt, and technological dependence, to a characterization of imperialism as an extended form of the capitalist mode of appropriation of surplus value from workers on a world scale.[14]

Not grounded in an analysis of the laws of motion of capitalism originating in the imperial centers and its subsequent expansion through various stages to the economically backward areas of the Third World, the dependency/world system theory starts from the subjective-empiricist notion that imperialism exists in a vacuum and, further, that it somehow plays an inherently regressive role vis-à-vis industrialization and development. Thus, while this eclectic conceptualization of imperialism (as a mechanism that blocks national capitalist development) is a major shortcoming of the dependency/world system theory, the Marxist theory provides a cogent analysis of the dynamics of the laws of capitalist development, from which it develops its interpretation of the role of imperialism in the context of the international dimensions of the capitalist mode. Hence, the latter approach, based on its concrete understanding of these laws, is rooted in Marxist political economy, while the dependency theory ends up supplementing an eclectic perspective with a selective and inconsistent use of (neo-) Marxist terminology.[15]

Although it provides an eloquent analysis of the historical underdevelopment of Third World societies, we would argue that dependency theory is essentially incompatible with Marxism, since it takes its starting point from the perspective of the oppressed nations in a subjectivist political formulation, rather than an objective economic one as viewed from the angle of the laws of motion of transnational capital from its inception in the imperial centers.[16] The formulation of the question in these national terms thus leads the dependency theory to a conclusion opposite to that of Marxism in that, while the Marxist theory provides us a dynamic conception of capitalist development, the dependency theory lends itself to a static conception with respect to the internal laws of the changing capitalist mode.[17]

If, as in the dependency approach, the ultimate units of analysis are nations and national institutional structures (and not classes and class struggles), then clearly one is not engaging in class analysis. In instances when classes are discussed by the dependency theorists, they are done so in an eclectic, arbitrary fashion, as the following statement by Andre Gunder Frank indicates:

> Turning to the underdeveloped countries, specifically to those of Latin America, I may hazard the following general observations. The proletariat includes most of the participants in the economic system. It most certainly includes the peasants, "subsistence" peasants included. Also the steadily employed workers, casually employed workers be they urban or rural (in case one doesn't want to call the latter "peasants"), most of the members of the "middle classes," urban and rural.[18]

Marxist theory, on the other hand, grasps the class nature of imperialist expansion in dialectical terms: the reality of its (selective) industrialization of the Third World through industrial/manufacturing investments and its simultaneous exploitation of the working class on a world scale. (We shall return to this point shortly.) Thus, lacking a clear understanding of the nature of class relations—instead, emphasizing the institutional aspects of imperialist domination and "surplus extraction"—the dependency theory ultimately fails to provide a concrete analysis of the social relations of production in the period of the internationalization of capital and capitalist relations as manifested in specific Third World social formations.[19] This mislocation of the source of the problematic leads to erroneous and conflicting political conclusions, as we shall see later.

SUBSTANTIVE ISSUES

The central contribution of the Marxist theory is its objective analysis of the laws of motion of the capitalist mode of production. It views capitalist development as rooted in its own internal contradictions. This means that, as capitalism develops, so do its various forms of exploitation (both within and between specific social formations) and the nature of imperialist exploitation varies in accordance with the nature of the specific class structure of Third World social formations with which imperialism comes into contact. Hence, within this framework, it is possible to substantiate the different stages of capitalist development and the mechanisms that are peculiar to each stage: the period of colonization and primitive accumulation, involving the plunder of economically backward precapitalist areas; the period of the internationalization of the circuit of commodity-capital, involving the blockage of industrialization in the Third World; and the period of the internationalization of the circuit of productive-capital, involving the industrialization of the Third World and the exploitation of wage-labor.[20]

On the other hand, viewing this process within a static (undialectical) framework, the dependency/world system theory has been unable to account for changes in the advanced capitalist economy of the center states or for its development, especially in its expansion across national boundaries, which is, of course, one of numerous but key manifestations of the very dynamics of capital accumulation itself. Instead, it has attempted to explain change in terms of the dynamics of underdevelopment in the Third World from the angle of the less-developed countries, stressing the external dependence of Third World nations on successive European and North American "metropolises" as the main cause of the former's structural underdevelopment. The development of the Third World thus becomes subject to the imperialist mechanisms of economic and political/military control, and changes occur only or mainly in the successive forms of imperialist control, oppression, and exploitation (i.e., from colonialism to imperialism to neocolonialism or neoimperialism) while the substance of that control, underdevelopment and exploitation (defined in national, regional, or global terms), remains constant.[21]

The conceptualization of the problem in these geographic, structural, and institutional terms again leads to the mistaken conclusion of the statics of the system. From the perspective of the dependency/ world system theory, however, which takes the world system and the underdeveloped countries within it as the main units of analysis, dependency relations are viewed as dynamic, whereas imperialism and the center's monopoly capitalist structure are not.[22] This line of reasoning leaves the impression that it is as though capitalism has reached its highest, imperial stage and then suddenly ceased to be in motion, and, because of its monopoly in both the core and the periphery, has rid itself of all contradictions, except that between the metropolis and the satellites in the periphery. It is just such an undialectical and nonclass conceptualization of the problem that has led to confused analysis and distortions of Marxism.[23]

It can be argued that since the central concern in Marxist analysis is the exploitation of labor, there would be little basis for argument among Marxists over formal differences between transnational industrialization ("dependent capitalism") and national industrialization (that led by the national-, petty- or "state"-bourgeoisie) as in fact both are governed by the capitalist law of profit. The distinction, therefore, between transnational capitalist industrialization and national capitalist industrialization (aside from the former's "distorted" nature, vs. the "integrated" and "diversified" nature of local capitalism in the absence of imperial domination) is grossly exaggerated. Both forms of industrialization are subject to the laws of the capitalist mode of production, which accelerate capital accumulation for the transnational and/or the national bourgeoisie and prolong capitalist class rule. Under either form of industrialization the appropriation of surplus value by the capitalist class continues and is increased as more and more peasants and marginal segments of the population are drawn into wage-labor employment. Thus, the de facto dependency emphasis on the "progressive" nature of national (as opposed to transnational) capital, and the claim that therefore the critique of "blockage" by imperialism of the national industrialization process should, in effect, be the focus of analysis, as has been the case in most dependency studies, are, we believe, misconceived and misdirected; in practice they may also lead to wrong (nationalist and class-collaborationist) politics.[24]

It is clear that part of the problem in the disagreement between the two theories stems from the differential definition of the concepts "industrialization" and "development." Industrialization, to the dependency/world system theory, means the material outcome of an integrated and diversified national economy based on the model of classical European capitalist development after the period of primitive accumulation. The "lack" of industrialization in the Third World today, according to this theory, is a manifestation of (1) the unavailability to the Third World bourgeoisie of the conditions of development that were available to European capital at the time of its inception and maturation from the 18th to the 20th century and (2) the imperialist "blockage" of industrialization in the Third World, which "postpones" or "eliminates" the possibility of an independent, diversified national capitalist development. This formulation leads one to the erroneous conclusion that the problem of underdevelopment would be overcome once the "inhibiting" forces of imperialist control are eliminated. Erroneous from the start, this sort of argument, in effect, results in the conclusion that all one needs to do is to fight for a "break with the world system" for "independent, autonomous development." This is certainly the implication of the analysis provided by most dependency and world system theorists, including Frank, Wallerstein, and Amin.[25]

Continuing this line of argument in his most recent book, *Delinking*, Amin advocates a complete break in links with the imperial center in favor of "autonomous," "independent" development.[26] The crucial determinant of the social content of such "delinking," however, is the class nature of the forces leading society and the nature and direction of a particular formation defined by the dominant mode of production, and not "delinking" per se for some unspecified "autonomous" form of development, devoid of any clear conception of class.

Conceptualizing capitalism as a world system, Frank, Wallerstein, and Amin have thus freed themselves from the obligation of adopting a class analysis approach to study social formations and their dominant mode(s) of production within definite societal boundaries. Such reformulation of dependency theory at the world-systemic level has further led to the development of more recent positions that advocate "disengagement" from the world system.[27] In all of these approaches, however, the units of analysis have remained abstract systemic forces that operate on a global level, rather than concrete classes and class struggles that take place in determinate social formations. Such abstract formulations of the world-systemic problem have, in effect, led to idealist, populist conceptualizations of system-wide rebellions and revolutions that never seem to happen on a system-wide basis. Clearly, given the historically specific experiences of societies at different stages of development, one cannot expect a uniform, system-wide, simultaneous response to the forces dominating the world system. Thus, taken together, these approaches have yielded the same net result in terms of their political implications.

Contrary to the abstract notions of "underdevelopment" and "world system," which have failed to mobilize any concrete class forces to challenge them, we would argue that the main problem faced by the laboring people in the Third World is international capitalism, for it exploits wage-labor at global proportions.[28] The class struggle between labor and capital has in this period of the internationalization of capital become the principal contradiction of capitalism on a world scale—in both the imperial centers and the Third World.[29] And the mobilization of class forces around this principal contradiction opens the way for a concrete challenge to the international capitalist system that is both real and possible.

CONCLUSION

It is not dependence, underdevelopment, unequal exchange, blockage, world system, or exploitative relations between the core and the periphery that constitute the primary contradiction of world capitalism today (although all of these factors are important in the comprehensive treatment of the political economy of international capitalism at the present conjuncture). Rather, the primary contradiction of the international capitalist system in this period is rooted in relations of production and exploitation on a world scale, as manifested in class struggles in specific social formations throughout the world.

This means that the working class (and its allies) face exploitation and oppression at both ends of the imperialist capitalist system. Opposition to the monopoly-capitalist bourgeoisie in the imperial center is thus intimately tied to opposition to the same monopoly-capitalist (imperialist) bourgeoisie and its local reactionary allies in the Third World. The Third World workers, then, instead of confronting imperialism as an alien force that manipulates national economies from the "outside," in fact confront it on the very soil of their countries and identify it—much as they do "their own" national bourgeoisie—as an exploiting class that extracts surplus value/profits.

The deeper the imperialist penetration of the Third World, the more numerous, the stronger, and the more organized is the Third World working class—which adopts proletarian ideology and political outlook in forming a genuine challenge to imperialist capitalism. The further the process of the internationalization of productive capital, the sharper become the contradictions between transnational capital and Third World wage-labor. And the more forceful the class struggle in the Third World, the deeper and more pervasive internationally the contradictions of imperialism, which force it to increase its level of exploitation in the center as well, thus leading to increased class struggles and revolutionary conditions throughout the center states. Cornered by a strong and determined working class at both ends, imperialism thus resorts to an all-out reaction and attempts to stifle and block the movement of the international proletariat. By doing so, however, it further accentuates the contradictions between labor and capital at all fronts, thus preparing its own demise on a global scale.

These and other related contradictions of international capitalism are examined in detail in the chapters that follow.

PART II

Paths of Capitalist
Development in the Third World

EXPORT-ORIENTED INDUSTRIALIZATION IN THE THIRD WORLD: ITS NATURE AND CONTRADICTIONS

During the past two decades we have seen the restructuring of the world economy through the emergence of a new international division of labor. This has occurred as a result of the entry of an increasing number of previously raw materials-producing countries in the Third World into the stage of rapid industrialization through massive flows of capital from the advanced capitalist centers, in particular the United States. This transnational, corporate-initiated, capitalist expansion in a select number of countries in the Third World has come to be known as "export-oriented industrialization."

In this chapter we examine the nature and contradictions of export-oriented industrialization in four less-developed countries of the Third World—Brazil, Mexico, South Korea, and Taiwan. After a general analysis of the nature of this mode of development, we focus on the nature of production and the labor force structure of these countries from the early 1950s to the late 1980s. We then venture into an analysis of the struggles of the working class against the prevailing social and economic structures in each of these countries, drawing out the political implications of these developments.

THE NATURE OF EXPORT-ORIENTED INDUSTRIALIZATION

The vagueness of the concept of export-oriented industrialization has created much confusion as to what the basic nature of this mode of economic development actually is. The path of industrialization in the Third World through the expansion of export-oriented industries is supposed to provide solutions to three major problems:

(1) the creation of jobs and the reduction of unemployment;
(2) the training of a skilled industrial labor force and the transfer of technology; and
(3) an increase in foreign-exchange inflows with a resultant easing of balance-of-trade and balance-of-payments crisis.[1]

Export-oriented industrialization, in essence, is industrialization promoted by transnational firms and their subsidiaries for the manufacture of consumer goods for export to markets primarily in the advanced capitalist countries.[2] This process of industrialization, its critics argue, exacerbates the major problems confronting the less-developed countries, while creating a minimum of employment at very low wages, maintaining control over the technology that is transferred into the host country, and draining profits made from the sale of exported goods. Such are the major consequences of a form of industrialization initiated by transnational capital, whose interests are bound up in a worldwide production process linking the different aspects and stages of production in many countries throughout the world with the final disposal of the finished commodities in markets lodged in the advanced capitalist centers. The global nature of transnational production thus dictates the nature of the production process in each country, imposing severe limitations on the type of industrialization to be adopted in the dependent and semidependent countries of the Third World.

THE CONTRADICTIONS OF EXPORT-ORIENTED INDUSTRIALIZATION

The economic, social, and political contradictions of export-oriented industrialization include: the destruction of an integrated national economy and the installation of enclave export zones controlled by transnational firms; the driving into bankruptcy of small and medium-sized businesses and monopolization of the local economy by foreign capital; income inequalities based on an internal market dependent on no more than five percent of the population; low wages leading to a decline in the standard of living of the majority of the population, with its consequences in the areas of diet, housing, health care, education, and other physical and cultural needs of the people; rising unemployment, poverty, malnutrition, and related ills; and social and political repression through the installation of authoritarian states that violate the most basic human rights of the masses. For a society under the grip of foreign capital, these effects are the outcome of a system of relations imposed on the Third World by imperialism.

The main contradiction of imperialism as international capitalism, however, is to be sought in the sphere of the exploitation of wage-labor on a world scale. Once we focus on this point as the major contradiction of transnational capitalist expansion, the political issues in response to it crystallize around the question of struggle between labor and capital throughout the world. The transformation of the existing relations of production thus becomes dependent on changes in the structure of the labor force, leading to the development of the class struggle through various stages, and on the leadership of a revolutionary class (the working class) prepared to carry out such a transformation. For this reason, it is essential to examine changes in the nature of production and in the structure of the labor force in the countries under study.

CHANGES IN THE NATURE OF PRODUCTION

In examining the data on the sectoral distribution of the gross domestic product in Brazil, Mexico, South Korea, and Taiwan during the period 1950-1987, we find that the share of industrial production in the GDPs of these countries has increased, while that of the predominantly precapitalist agricultural sector has declined over the past several decades (see Table 4.1).

Given the capitalist nature of industrialization in these countries, the relative proportionate shift in the GDP from agricultural to industrial production signifies the further development and domination there of capitalism and capitalist relations, as it also indicates a shift in the source of wealth of the dominant classes from agriculture to industry.[3]

Another indicator of capitalist development in these countries would be a rise in the export of manufactured goods, in line with the objectives of export-oriented industrialization,[4] in contrast to economies still specializing in the export of raw materials and agricultural goods. Indeed, when one looks at the export structure of these countries over time, one would find that this is in fact the case in all of the countries

TABLE 4.1
Distribution of GDP, by Sector, 1950-1987
(in percent)

Country	Sector[a,b]	1950[c]	1987[d]
Brazil	Agriculture	17	9
	Industry	36	43
Mexico	Agriculture	19	9
	Industry	30	43
South Korea	Agriculture	45	13
	Industry	15	53
Taiwan	Agriculture	34	5
	Industry	32	54

Notes:
[a]The two sectors do not add up to 100 percent, as other sectors are not included.
[b]Agriculture includes forestry and fishing; Industry includes manufacturing, mining, construction, utilities, transport, and communications, and excludes wholesale and retail trade, finance, insurance, real estate, and business, community, social and personal services.
[c]Data for South Korea are for 1953 and for Taiwan for 1951.
[d]Data for South Korea are for 1986 and for Brazil for 1988.

Sources: United Nations, Economic Survey of Latin America, 1951-52 (New York: UN, 1954); UN, Yearbook of National Accounts Statistics, 1958 and 1986 (New York: UN, 1958 and 1986); UN, Statistical Yearbook for Latin America and the Caribbean, 1988 (New York: UN, 1989); Republic of China, Statistical Yearbook of the Republic of China, 1989 (Executive Yuan: Directorate General of the Budget, 1989); World Bank, World Development Report, 1990 (New York: Oxford University Press, 1990).

under study. The latest data on the composition of exports of these countries show that manufactured goods accounted for 55 percent of all Mexican exports, 75 percent of all Brazilian exports, 92 percent of all Taiwanese exports, and 96 percent of all South Korean exports.[5]

CHANGES IN THE LABOR FORCE STRUCTURE

Data on the sectoral distribution of the labor force in these countries further reinforce the argument above, for these data show that while the proportion of the agricultural labor force has declined over the years, the labor force in industry and services has increased in proportion to the total labor force (see Table 4.2).[6]

TABLE 4.2
Sectoral Distribution of the Labor Force, 1960-1987
(in percent)

Country	Year	Agriculture[a]	Industry[b]	Services[c]	Others[d]
Brazil	1960	58.0	24.8	21.7	3.4
	1986	25.2	29.1	40.5	2.8
Mexico	1960	54.2	22.1	23.0	0.7
	1987	25.8	33.6	39.5	0.5
South Korea	1960	61.9	11.1	20.9	6.1
	1987	21.2	37.5	38.2	3.1
Taiwan	1960	56.1	11.3	24.9	4.7
	1987	15.3	48.1	36.6	—

Notes:
[a]Includes forestry, hunting and fishing.
[b]Includes manufacturing, mining, construction, utilities, transport, storage, and communication.
[c]Includes commerce, wholesale and retail trade, and all types of public, private, and personal services.
[d]Activities not adequately described.

Sources: International Labour Organization, Year Book of Labour Statistics, 1964 and 1988 (Geneva: ILO, 1964 and 1968); UCLA., Latin American Center, Statistical Abstract of Latin America, 1971 and 1984 (Los Angeles: Latin American Center of the University of California, 1971 and 1984); Republic of China, Taiwan Statistical Data Book, 1963 (Executive Yuan: Economic Research Center, 1963); Republic of China, Statistical Yearbook of the Republic of China, 1989 (Executive Yuan: Directorate General of Budget, 1989).

Growth of Wage Labor

In focusing on the size and nature of wage labor, we find that during the past three decades the number of wage earners increased in all of these countries—from 10.9 million in 1960 to 36.7 million in 1986 in Brazil; from 7.3 million in 1960 to 12.1 million in 1987 in Mexico; from 1.6 million in 1960 to 9.2 million in 1987 in South Korea; from 1.5 million in 1960 to 8 million in 1987 in Taiwan (see Table 4.3).

The generally stagnant number of agricultural workers during this period, relative to the increase in the size of the labor force as a whole and that of workers in other sectors of the economy, has meant an overall proportionate shift in the locus of wage-labor employment away from agriculture and toward industry (and services). It should be pointed out, however, that an absolute decline in the size of the agricul-

TABLE 4.3
Wage Earners, by Sector, 1960–1987[a]
(in number and percent)

Country	Year	Total	Agriculture		Industry		Services		Others	
			N	Percentage[b]	N	Percentage[b]	N	Percentage[b]	N	Percentage[b]
Brazil	1960	10,875,854	3,193,933	(29.4)	3,382,092	(31.1)	4,299,829	(39.5)	—	—
	1986	36,650,702	5,621,051	(15.3)	12,527,926	(34.2)	17,211,895	(47.0)	—	—
Mexico	1960	7,261,626	3,296,465	(45.4)	2,110,350	(29.1)	1,781,566	(24.5)	73,245	(1.0)
	1987	12,104,500	1,630,500	(13.5)	4,122,300	(34.1)	2,954,200	(24.4)	3,397,100	(28.1)
S. Korea	1960	1,607,710	279,845	(17.4)	560,400	(34.8)	763,895	(47.5)	3,570	(0.2)
	1986	9,191,000	397,000	(4.3)	5,298,000	(57.6)	3,495,000	(38.0)	—	—
Taiwan	1960	1,471,000	325,200	(22.1)	609,800	(41.5)	533,600	(36.3)	2,400	(0.2)
	1987	8,022,000	1,226,000	(15.3)	3,859,000	(48.1)	2,939,000	(36.6)	—	—

Notes:
[a]Includes salaried employees.
[b]Percent of all wage earners.

Sources: International Labour Organization, *Year Book of Labour Statistics*, various annual issues (Geneva: ILO); Republic of China, *Taiwan Statistical Data Book, 1962 and 1963* (Executive Yuan: Directorate General of Budget, 1962 and 1963); Republic of China, *Statistical Yearbook of the Republic of China, 1989* (Executive Yuan: Directorate General of Budget, 1989).

tural labor force is not essential to signify either the decline of precapitalist relations or the development of capitalism per se. In fact, an increase in the agricultural labor force may even indicate the growth of capitalist relations if the relations of production in the agrarian sector are based primarily on the exploitation of wage labor. Thus, a general decline in the absolute size of the agricultural labor force *in itself* cannot be viewed as an indicator of the transformation of modes of production.

What is crucial, however, is the occurrence of two necessary conditions: (1) a shift in an increasing portion of the GDP toward industry, as this sector is now thoroughly capitalist, and (2) a consistent increase in the proportion of the industrial labor force, as industrial workers are definitely bound up in wage-labor relations under capitalist industrialization. Such trends in the development of Third World economies would signal the further development of capitalism and capitalist relations in these countries; this process would also signal the restructuring of power relations between the various dominant classes and their fractions on the one hand, and between them and the laboring masses on the other. The transfer of wealth toward dominant interests in industry not only strengthens exclusively the capitalist forces within a given formation, it also shifts the source of exploitation in a capitalist direction, where an increasingly homogeneous working class begins to occupy a central place in the production process. The development of a wage-labor force through industrialization is thus central to our argument on capitalist development and its contradictions in the Third World.

Growth of the Industrial Working Class

By examining the data in Table 4.3 we see that the number of industrial workers in Brazil increased from 3.4 million in 1960 to 12.5 million in 1986; in Mexico, from 2.1 million in 1960 to 4.1 million in 1987; in South Korea, from a little over .5 million in 1960 to 5.3 million in 1987; in Taiwan, from just above .6 million in 1960 to nearly 4 million in 1987. These figures represent one-third or more of all wage earners in Brazil and Mexico and one-half or more of all wage earners in South Korea and Taiwan. Thus, by 1987 the number of industrial workers in these countries reached a proportionate level comparable to that of the advanced capitalist countries.[7]

This growth in the size of the industrial working class is also reflected in the manufacturing sector—the sector receiving the bulk of U.S. direct investment in these countries—where the steady growth in numbers of wage earners reached a significant level by the late 1980s: in Brazil, manufacturing workers represented 22 percent of all wage earners; in Mexico, 20 percent; in South Korea, 40 percent; and in Taiwan, 49 percent (see Table 4.4).[8]

TABLE 4.4
Wage Earners in Manufacturing Industry, 1960-1987[a]
(in number and percent)

Country	1960		1987	
	N	%[b]	N	%[b]
Brazil	1,741,248	(16.0)	7,935,918[c]	(21.7)
Mexico	1,267,723	(17.5)	2,474,100[c]	(20.1)
South Korea	304,000	(18.9)	3,675,000	(40.0)
Taiwan	362,000	(24.6)	2,624,358	(49.1)

Notes:
[a]Includes salaried employees.
[b]Percent of all wage earners.
[c]Includes mining; data for Brazil are for 1986.

Sources: International Labour Organization, Year Book of Labour Statistics, 1964 and 1988 (Geneva: ILO, 1964 and 1988); Republic of China, Statistical Yearbook of the Republic of China, 1989 (Executive Yuan: Directorate General of Budget, 1989).

The increase in size of the working class in the manufacturing sector and, more broadly, in all major branches of industry (and services), however, has been accompanied by its exploitation through below-subsistence wages,[9] resulting in an unequal distribution of income, as evidenced in Table 4.5.

These developments, coupled with brutal antilabor legislation effected by repressive regimes propped up by the transnationals in response to growing popular unrest, has created an increasingly volitile situation in these countries and has led to the emergence of bureaucratic authoritarian states.

THE RISE OF THE AUTHORITARIAN STATE

The development of export-oriented industrialization in the Third World, with its accompanying austerity for workers, peasants, and other deprived sectors of society, has given rise to repressive, authoritarian states. Resembling the fascist state in Europe and elsewhere in the world in an earlier period, but distinct in being supported by the transnationals and the imperial state lodged outside their territories, these repressive regimes have found it necessary to wage war against their own people in order to make the externally-directed capital accumulation process possible.[10] Directed by the International Monetary Fund (IMF), the World Bank, and other imperial agencies, these states

TABLE 4.5
Wages and Income Distribution, 1980-1987

Country	Hourly Wages in Manufacturing[a] (1987)	Income Distribution[b] Highest 20%	Lowest 20%
Brazil	1.49	66.6	2.0
Mexico	1.57	57.7	2.9
South Korea	1.79	45.3	5.7
Taiwan	2.19	40.1	6.2

Notes:
[a]Local currency converted into U.S. dollar equivalents on the basis of prevailing exchange rates in 1987.
[b]Early to mid-1970s.

Sources: World Bank, *World Development Report, 1989* (Washington, DC: World Bank, 1989); International Labour Organization, *Year Book of Labour Statistics, 1988* (Geneva: ILO, 1988); UCLA Latin American Center, *Statistical Abstract of Latin America*, Vol. 23 (Los Angeles: Latin American Center, 1984); U.S. Bureau of the Census, *Statistical Abstract of the United States, 1989* (Washington, DC: Government Printing Office, 1989); U.S. Department of Labor, Bureau of Labor Statistics, *Handbook of Labor Statistics* (Washington, DC: Government Printing Office, 1989); Republic of China, *Taiwan Statistical Data Book, 1986* (Executive Yuan: Council for Economic Planning and Development, 1986); Republic of China, *Statistical Yearbook of the Republic of China, 1989* (Executive Yuan: Directorate General of Budget, 1989).

---

have unleashed a massive attack on the social and living conditions of broad segments of the population who have come to suffer immensely from the policies of regimes intent on promoting export-oriented transnational capitalism.[11]

The IMF- and World Bank-imposed austerity measures adopted by these states have resulted in a decline in the standard of living of large segments of the population, causing widespread poverty and hunger, despite the fact that the GDP and food production per capita have been increasing.[12] The disparity in wealth and abundance on the one hand, and poverty and hunger on the other, can only be explained by the maldistribution of national wealth, income, and resources among the population in countries that have chosen the export-oriented capitalist path.

These policies, however, have in turn generated conditions for mass opposition to imperialism and the local collaborating capitalist state. The resulting intensification of the class struggles in these countries has further polarized society and led to political repression perpetrated by the state against the popular masses.

The repressive state policies prevailing in these countries today—most visibly South Korea—are in fact undermining the continuation of export-oriented industrialization, as more and more laboring people join in the mass struggle against imperialism and the local collaborating capitalist state.[13] Given the history of labor struggles and the generally politicized nature of the work force in the Third World, the popular mobilization in these countries has resulted in the creation of conditions leading to large-scale social change.[14]

THE RESPONSE OF THE WORKING CLASS

Strikes and demonstrations initiated by workers have become frequent in most of the countries undergoing export-oriented industrialization. The working people are rising up against the local ruling classes, the state, and the transnational monopolies that have together effected the superexploitation of labor for decades.[15] Strikes and mass protests on the one hand, and the labor-led struggles for national liberation on the other, are two sides of the same process of struggle for a radical transformation of society now underway in many of the countries under the grip of foreign capital.[16]

In Brazil, despite the official ban on strikes, protests, and demonstrations, major work stoppages took place in main industrial centers throughout the 1970s and 1980s, with metalworkers and autoworkers at the forefront. In May 1978 metal, engineering, and textile workers in the industrial belt around São Paulo went on strike. Workers arrived at the factories but refused to turn on the machines. In October of that year, 240,000 workers went on strike in support of a 70 percent pay claim and the right to set up workers' commissions. In March 1979 a strike by 180,000 metalworkers in São Paulo marked a further advance in the development of working class militance and organization. In late 1979, after taking industrial action, the bus drivers of Rio de Janeiro, the construction workers of Belo Horizonte (a city north of Rio de Janeiro), and the sugar plantation workers of northeastern Brazil made significant gains.

Between 1980 and 1986 there were 3,468 officially reported strikes in Brazil, increasing from 81 in 1980 to 312 in 1983 to 1,493 in 1986.[17] In April 1980 a major strike by more than 300,000 workers shut down hundreds of factories in several industries for nearly six weeks, affecting such companies as General Motors, Ford, Mercedes Benz, Fiat, and Pirelli. In May 1982 more than 50,000 autoworkers went on strike in São

Paulo, bringing most automobile production to a halt.

In April 1983, São Paulo was rocked by the militant protests of several thousand unemployed workers as they marched five miles through the streets of the city to the governor's palace. In early July of 1983 over 60,000 metalworkers went on strike, protesting the government's economic policies and IMF-imposed austerity measures. The metalworkers' strike was also aimed at showing solidarity with 4,000 other strikers at Brazil's largest oil refinery. Later that month workers of São Paulo, representing 137 unions and 80 percent of the area's nearly one million industrial workers, struck the government and its capitulation to the austerity demands of the IMF. In Rio de Janeiro 50,000 workers demonstrated against the military regime, as did thousands of other workers in Rio Grande do Sul and several other industrial centers. Demands of the workers included repeal of the wage decree laws and the decree law cutting public employee benefits; debt moratorium; an end to negotiations with the IMF; unemployment benefits; and an end to interventions in the unions, whose leaders had been removed from office in the strikes two weeks earlier. The July general strike was highly successful and effectively paralyzed the major industrial and commercial centers. Mass demonstrations supporting the objectives of the strike occurred in many cities throughout the country. In October 1983 nearly 70,000 people filled the main square in São Paulo to protest against the military junta.

In January 1984 as many as 400,000 protesters jammed São Paulo's Cathedral Plaza to demand immediate presidential elections, a new economic order, and an end to military rule. Most prominent and well-organized among those in the plaza were the outlawed communist parties. The demonstration came just two days prior to the signing of Brazil's recent loan of $6.5 billion from the IMF that was designed to help finance the country's staggering $93 billion foreign debt,[18] which climbed to $130 billion in 1990. The mass demonstration in January followed two others in Curitiba earlier that month, with 30,000 protesters, and one in Salvador, with 15,000 protesters. In February 1984 200,000 people took to the streets of Belo Horizonte to demand the resignation of the military government, which had been ruling the country for 20 years.

In March 1987 the navy took over 30 ports after the labor courts declared a seamen's strike illegal. This was soon followed by the army's occupation, backed by tanks and armored cars, of all state refineries, in a successful bid to prevent a strike of 55,000 workers. A month later a nationwide bankworkers' strike shut down the entire banking system.

In late October of 1988 more than 25,000 steelworkers at Companhia Siderurgica National in Volto Redondo, near Rio de Janeiro, went on strike, demanding, along with workers in civil service, hospitals, utilities, and railroads, that wage increases keep up with the explosive inflation rates that had pushed prices up by 700 percent in the past year. Twelve days into the strike, Brazilian army troops opened fire with machine guns on thousands of steelworkers occupying the plant. Eight workers were killed and 50 injured by gunfire and bayonets. Two days later, on November 11, more than 61,000 workers of the petroleum refining industry joined the steelworkers' strike and the walkout of workers in other branches of industry throughout Brazil.

In Mexico, too, workers have risen in large numbers during the past two decades to protest their superexploitation by the transnational monopolies, effected through the compliant Mexican state. Strikes and demonstrations increased substantially during the 1970s and early 1980s, as the Mexican economy plunged into a depression with over 40 percent unemployment, 100 percent inflation, a massive foreign debt, and a sharp devaluation of the peso. Thus the number of strikes increased from 236 in 1975, to 476 in 1977, to 1,339 in 1980, to 1,925 in 1982; the number of workers involved in these strikes rose from 9,680 in 1975, to 13,411 in 1977, to 42,774 in 1980.[19] While there were only 216 strikes in 1983 and 312 strikes in 1986, the number of workers involved in these strikes rose to 45,949 in 1983 and to 82,833 in 1986.[20]

Responding to government repression of the labor movement, over 20,000 workers demonstrated in Mexico City in 1977. As in earlier years, more than 1.5 million workers marched under their union banners on May Day, 1980, in Mexico City. In March 1982, 12,000 telephone workers struck in support of a demand for a 50 percent wage increase, as did 120,000 primary school teachers later that month. A threatened strike by 27,000 Mexico City electrical workers won a 33 percent wage increase, while the largest settlement was produced by the threat of a general strike by the Mexican Workers Congress (CTM).

In March 1987 workers at the Ford auto plant in Hermosillo (about 50 miles from the U.S. border) went on strike for higher wages. In April, after a 40-day strike, the company was forced to meet the union's demands, including a 35 percent wage increase.

In November 1988 more than 20,000 workers at Mexico's largest university, National Autonomous University, went on strike. Represented by Stunam, the university workers' union, and with over 60,000 supporters joining in, the workers marched through downtown Mexico City and camped in front of the National Palace. Their demands were not only economic—higher pay and benefits—but political in character, challenging the policies of the government and its subservience to the conditions imposed by the IMF.

In April 1989 teachers and educational workers from 15 Mexican states, numbering over 400,000, marched through Mexico City, blocking traffic on all the main arteries for hours before gathering in the Zocalo plaza. They demanded a 100 percent pay hike to counter a decrease of 1000 percent in their buying power over the previous eight years.

In late 1989 some 4,000 workers at the Sicartsa steel plant, in the port city of Lazaro Cardenas, took control of the plant for five weeks until their demands were met. And in early 1990 more than 5,200 workers at the Modelo brewery (the largest in Latin America) went on strike and brought to a halt the around-the-clock production of 20,000 bottles of beer a minute, including the supply of 1.4 million cartons a month of Corona beer for U.S. consumption.

In South Korea, too, mass strikes and demonstrations have grown since the latter half of the 1970s. The number of strikes increased from 52 in 1975, to 206 in 1980, to 3,617 in 1987, and the number of workers involved in these strikes rose from 10,256 in 1975, to 48,970 in 1980, to 934,900 in 1987.[21]

During the spring of 1980, the Chonggye Union led a five-week strike that resulted in an eight-hour day and a 40 percent wage increase for garment workers. In April 1980 coalminers and their families rose up in the province of Kangwon. Demanding a 40 percent wage increase to keep up with inflation, 7,000 miners staged sit-in demonstrations and fought off 600 police sent in to disperse them. According to a dispatch of the Korean Central News Agency in April 1980, on the second day of the uprising the striking miners "seized a police ordinance depot, 290 carbines, more than 470 M-1 rifles, 100,000 rounds of ammunition, and several hand grenades and large quantities of explosives." The entire central part of the city of Sabuk was taken over by the rebelling miners. On May 1, 1980, the *Washington Post* reported: "Sit-down strikes, walkouts, and other labor protests, some of them violent, are spreading across South Korea in a wave of worker uprisings." Strikes are illegal under South Korea's so-called national security law, but this did not stop the steelworkers and others from joining the battle initiated by the miners. On the same day thousands of university students began a wave of militant demonstrations, demanding democratic rights and an end to martial law.

In May 1980, in a popular uprising, more than 200,000 workers and students took control of Kwangju, South Korea's third-largest city, for nearly one week, until it was retaken by 15,000 combat troops through a bloody massacre in which over 2,000 people were killed.

In 1982 two major labor struggles were fought, one at the Wuonpoong textile mill, and the other at the Korean subsidiary of the U.S.-based Control Data Corporation. In Wuonpoong 600 women workers belonging to the Wuonpoong Textile Workers Union began a sit-in hunger strike at the Kukje textile mill, despite a government ban on all strikes. In November 1982 hundreds of unionists and students demonstrated in Seoul against government repression, calling for an end to the fascist dictatorship.

In April 1985 more than 80,000 students from 56 universities defied savage police repression to take part in demonstrations protesting U.S. support of the Chon military dictatorship and the Chon regime's subservience to the interests of U.S. corporations and the Pentagon, which continues to maintain in South Korea over 40,000 U.S. troops at 50 U.S. bases, and more nuclear weapons per square mile than in any other country in the world. The streets of Seoul were transformed into a battlefield for several days and nights as thousands of students fought off club-swinging police with bricks and Molotov cocktails. Later in the month, in the city of Pusan, hundreds of students attacked the U.S. cultural center. Farmers also joined the protests, demanding an end to the massive importation of U.S. agricultural products, which is ruining the South Korean peasantry. On April 22 police prevented farmers from impoverished South Cholla province from holding a rally in Seoul. When the outraged farmers then marched on the United States Embassy, 26 were arrested and brutally beaten. On April 24, in the South Cholla city of Kwangju, police attacked a demonstration of several hundred religious figures marching in support of the farmers' demands. Also in late April 2,000 striking autoworkers in Seoul occupied a factory belonging to the Daewoo Motor Company, which is partially owned by General Motors. The strikers demanded better working conditions and an end to government restrictions on labor unions. The plant was surrounded by 8,000 police, but they were deterred from attacking by the workers' threats to set fire to the company's computer center.

On May 19, 1985, the anniversary of the Kwangju uprising, tens of thousands took to the streets throughout the country, including Kwangju itself, chanting anti-U.S. and anti-Chon slogans. In late September car and bus traffic was brought to a halt in the capital city of Seoul as thousands of anti-government demonstrators clashed with riot police, who blocked roads leading to downtown, firing round after round of tear gas. On November 4 and November 5, nearly 10,000 students demonstrated against the regime and U.S. policies.

According to a report from the House Affairs Committee of the National Assembly, South Korea's nominal parliament, 1,848 student protests took place between March and the end of August 1985, involving

475,000 students from 85 universities—a two-fold increase over the previous year. Even more significant, the number of street demonstrations was 11 times higher than for the same period of the previous year. The solidarity movement of the workers, exemplified by the actions of students at 17 women's colleges in support of women textile workers, was an indication of a most profound shift in the student movement toward worker-student unity in opposition to the Chon Du Hwan dictatorship.

In May 1987, on the seventh anniversary of the Kwangju massacre, 42,000 students protested on 62 campuses, including 10,000 in Kwangju. In June a rebellion against the military regime, which began in Seoul, spread to 20 other cities. Protesters burned seven armored police cars in Taejon. The regime deployed 120,000 police, teargassed nearly a million people in the capital city alone, and arrested more than 6,000 students. The spark that set off the explosion was the installation on June 10 of General Roh Tae Woo as the successor to General Chon Du Hwan. Later that month 200,000 people in Seoul and 13 other cities fought the dictatorship in street battles with the police. In Seoul the protesters overwhelmed riot police and for seven hours controlled several square miles of downtown, while 80,000 protesters in Pusan, South Korea's second-largest city, commandeered 58 city buses to increase their strength in confrontations with riot police, and marched to City Hall. Some 10,000 others tried to attack the offices of the Korean Broadcasting System, considered by many a propaganda instrument of the government. The National Police Headquarters reported that during 2,145 separate demonstrations in June, 351,200 tear gas canisters were fired by the police.

On August 17, 1987, over 300,000 workers in Ulsan battled with South Korean riot police and occupied for a day the factories and the shipyard of Hyundai. (Hyundai, partially owned by BankAmerica, is the largest conglomerate in South Korea.) The next day over 100,000 workers and their families rallied and marched through the streets of Ulsan. Three of the largest automakers, Hyundai Motor Company, Daewoo Motor Company (a partially-owned subsidiary of General Motors), and Kia Motor Corporation (which is connected to Ford Motor Company), as well as two of the largest shipyards, were shut down by the workers. Despite the ban on trade unions, strikes, and demonstrations, the workers have shown great determination to fight back and make known their discontent against the bosses and the repressive police state.

In May 1988 ten thousand students from 70 universities throughout South Korea attended a rally at Korea University in Seoul. Later that month 20,000 workers at the Hyundai Motor Company went on strike in Ulsan, followed by another 2,000 workers at Hyundai Precision and Industry Company, which effectively shut down the company. At the same time some 9,100 workers went on strike at Daewoo Motor Company.

In March 1989 the government ordered 14,000 combat police to storm the massive Hyundai shipyard in Ulsan to put down a 109-day strike. They attacked from land, sea, and helicopters. Although 700 workers were arrested, the strike was not broken. Elsewhere that month hundreds of workers of a U.S.-based company, Pico Products, Inc., occupied the American Chamber of Commerce office in downtown Seoul. They demanded that the chamber help them recover $445,000 in wages and severance pay owed them. Shortly thereafter, however, 300 riot police moved in and forcibly removed them.

In May 1989 some 100,000 students and workers marched through downtown Kwangju. There were similar marches in nine other South Korean cities, and 40,000 students rallied on 87 campuses nationwide. The government sent in 17,000 riot police to block a rally of thousands of people in Seoul called by the National Alliance for Democracy in South Korea. Despite hundreds of arrests, the police were not able to stop the demonstration, which went on for several days.

On May Day 1990, hundreds of thousands of workers and students fought with police in the streets of Seoul and 17 provincial cities across South Korea. Firing volleys of tear gas, 13,000 riot police stormed the world's largest shipyard on April 28 to combat strikers who had occupied the huge Hyundai Heavy Industries Company. According to an Associated Press report from Ulsan on April 29, 1990, "Groups of up to 200 workers attacked police with firebombs, rocks, and other projectiles after grouping in alleyways near the shipyard. 'Down with Roh Tae Woo!' workers shouted as they raised clenched fists into the air." Other workers, wearing red headbands bearing the word "fight," set up roadblocks and burned tires.

On May 19, 1990, more than 25,000 students rallied against the government at Chosun University. The next day 10,000 students surrounded a police station in the center of Kwangju, throwing firebombs at the police. As workers, city residents, and other sympathizers joined in, the ranks of the demonstrators swelled to many more thousands.

With the increasing level of resistance against the U.S.-backed military regime, the workers, peasants, students and other popular segments of South Korean society are waging a heroic struggle to free their country from the grip of the United States and its internal reactionary allies, who are able to maintain power only through brute military force.

In Taiwan, where the ruling Kuomintang (KMT or Chinese Nationalist Party) has been in power since it was driven from the Chinese mainland by the Communists in 1949, strikes and demonstrations were illegal until the KMT lifted martial law in July 1987. With the territory under state of emergency for nearly four decades, the workers and their organizations were severely repressed by the brutal anti-communist authoritarian rule of the KMT.

Despite the lifting of martial law, legislation outside the framework of martial law permits the government to continue limiting civil liberties; censoring opposition periodicals and banning newspapers; outlawing strikes and demonstrations; and requiring private organizations to register. The numerous internal security agencies remain present in most large workplaces and in schools, neighborhoods, and private organizations. The government continues to maintain surveillance over opposition activists and monitors mail and telephone calls. The iron rule of the KMT thus in many ways parallels fascist authoritarian rule in South Korea, but surpasses it in terrorizing the population into submission to its dictates, which have become both routine and swiftly regulated by the National Security Law.

Despite such strict control of the population by the ruling KMT, however, the number of strikes, protests, and demonstrations is growing each year. In 1987 alone some 1,600 strikes were reported. In early 1988, 2,000 textile workers in Hsinchu city went on strike over wages and hours. Later that year there was a 23-day strike by 200 bus drivers in Miaoli county. Other mass protests and demonstrations included rallies outside the KMT headquarters in Taipei city, a protest in March 1988 by thousands of Taipei citizens on the 41st anniversary of the massacre by the KMT troops of the Taiwanese, and a demonstration in May 1988 by 4,000 farmers protesting the government's decision to import U.S. farm products, which was suppressed by 10,000 policemen.[22] Through participation in such actions, the opposition democratic forces, which have rallied around the Democratic Progressive Party (DPP), have been gaining ground in local politics in the last few years. With further development of democratic forces, and the ramifications in Taiwan and other states in the region of the emergence of "people power" in the aftermath of the overthrow of the Marcos dictatorship in the Philippines, the potential exists for Taiwanese workers to mobilize their forces, challenge the power of the KMT rulers, and bring about changes demanded by a growing segment of the population.

CONCLUSION

Export-oriented industrialization in the Third World, though vastly different from the classical capitalist development pattern in terms of its economic impact, leads to a fundamentally similar logic of capitalist expansion, whereby it gives rise to the same central contradictions: the development of a (modified) capitalist class structure effected through an increase in size of the wage-labor force, especially in the manufacturing industries; leading to the development of trade unions, labor-based political parties, and militant political/class struggles.

The logic of international capitalist expansion thus leads to the development and intensification of the deep-seated contradictions of export-oriented industrialization in the Third World. These contradictions point toward a fundamental resolution: the head-on confrontation with the very forces of imperialism and capitalist expansion in the Third World.

CHAPTER 5

THE ROLE OF THE
IMPERIAL STATE IN THE
WORLD POLITICAL ECONOMY

Since the end of the nineteenth century, the modern state in advanced capitalist formations has evolved parallel to the centralization of the capitalist economy in its transition to the higher, monopoly stage. In line with its functions in facilitating the existing mode of production and its attendant superstructure, the political apparatus of modern capitalism has come to reflect the changing structure of the capitalist economy, which increasingly operates on a worldwide scale. With the internationalization of capital, the capitalist state has come to assume a greater responsibility in organizing and leading the international capitalist system, thus adopting the role of an imperial state charged with the control and rationalization of the new international division of labor. It is within this context of the internationalization of the advanced capitalist superstructure that the crisis of the imperial state manifests itself on a world scale.[1]

This chapter examines the role of the imperial state in the context of the world capitalist economy, where the internationalization of capital—through the worldwide expansion of transnational monopolies—has had a decisive effect on the role and functions of the capitalist state, and brought to the fore new and more pervasive contradictions, leading to a crisis of management and legitimacy of capitalism on a world scale. It is argued that this has been the result of developments in the latest stage of capitalist expansion, in which the monopoly fraction of the capitalist class in the advanced capitalist countries has secured a thorough control of the state apparatus to advance fully its interests at home and abroad; the monopoly fraction has meanwhile been blocking the state from fulfilling its role of advancing the broader, long-term interests of capitalism and the capitalist class as a whole.

Debates on the nature and role of the imperial state in the world political economy over the past two decades have contributed much to our understanding of the conflicts and contradictions arising within the modern capitalist state as an outcome of the changing balance of forces, both within the economy and the state apparatus itself.[2] Despite the arguments of some critics to the contrary, what emerged from these debates is the understanding that in the advanced, monopoly stage of capitalism, the capitalist state no longer represents the varied fractional interests of the capitalist class as a whole, as was the case in the last century prior to the rise of the monopolies and the monopoly fraction of the capitalist class.[3]

As capitalism developed from its competitive to monopoly (imperialist) stage, the state increasingly lost its "relative autonomy" vis-à-vis the various fractions of the capitalist class, and became an agent to safeguard and advance the interests of its most powerful fraction, monopoly capital. This has been the case in Europe since the 1880s, and in the United States since the early 1900s, especially since World War II. During this period the monopolies in the advanced capitalist countries have become so powerful, through both national and worldwide economic expansion, that the protection and further advancement of their immense economic wealth at home and abroad has resulted in their outright control of the state apparatus at every conceivable level. The political crisis resulting from this fractional domination and fragmentation has led to a crisis of the advanced capitalist/imperial state.

WORLDWIDE CONTRADICTIONS AND
CRISIS OF THE IMPERIAL STATE

The crisis of the imperial state on the world scene is a manifestation of the contradictions of the world economy, which in the late twentieth century has reached a critical stage in its development.

The massive flow of U.S. transnational investment throughout the world, especially in Western Europe, Japan, and other advanced capitalist regions, has led to the post-World War II reemergence of interimperialist rivalry between the major capitalist powers, while fostering antagonisms between them in the scramble for the peripheral regions of the world capitalist economy—Latin America, Asia, Africa, and the Middle East.

With the integration of the economies of Western Europe into the Common Market (European Economic Community) during the past two decades and the emergence of Japan as a powerful economic force, the position of the United States in the world economy has declined relative both to its own postwar supremacy in the 1940s and 1950s, and to other advanced capitalist economies since that time.[4] Despite the fact that U.S. capital continues to control the biggest share of overseas markets and accounts for the largest volume of international investments, its hold on the world economy has recently been slipping in a manner similar to Britain's earlier in this century. This has, in turn, led the U.S. state to take a more aggressive role in foreign policy to protect U.S. transnational interests abroad. Its most recent deployment in the Middle East translates into an enormous burden on the working people of the United States, who have come to shoulder the colossal cost of maintaining a global empire whose vast military machine encompasses the world.

In the current phase of the crisis of the imperial state the critical problems facing the imperial state are of such magnitude that threaten the very existence of the world capitalist system as a global power bloc. Internal economic and budgetary problems are compounded by ever growing military spending propped up by armed intervention in the Third World (Grenada, Panama, Iraq, and so forth), while a declining economic base at home manifested in the banking crisis, deindustrialization, and a recessionary economy is further complicated by the global rivalry between the major capitalist powers which is not always restricted to the economic field, but has political (and even military) implications that are global in magnitude.

The growing prospects of inter-imperialist rivalry between the major capitalist powers, backed up by their states, are effecting changes in their relations that render the world political economy a more and more unstable character. Competition between the United States, Japan, and European imperial states representing the interests of their own respective capitalist classes are leading them on a collision course for world supremacy, manifested in struggles for markets, raw materials, spheres of influence in geo-political—as well as economic—terms, which may in fact lead to a new balance of forces, and consequently alliances that would have serious political implications in global power-politics. As the continuing economic ascendence of the two major capitalist rivals of the United States—Japan and Germany—take their prominent position in the world economy in a more entrenched, established sense, pressures will build toward the politicization and militarization of these states from within, where the leading class forces bent on dominating the world economy will press forward with the necessary political and military corollary of their growing economic power in the world political economy.

These developments in global economic and geo-political shifts in the balance of forces among the major capitalist powers will bring to the fore new and yet untested international alliances for world supremacy and domination in the post-Cold War era. Such alliances will bring key powers such as the Soviet Union and China into play in a new and complicated relationship that holds the key for the success or failure of the new rising imperial centers that will emerge as the decisive forces in the global economic, political, and military equation at the close of the twentieth century.

While the contradictions and conflicts imbedded in relations between the rival states of the major capitalist powers will surface as an important component of international relations in the balance of this century, the most critical problem facing the advanced capitalist state, however, is the crisis emanating from the restructuring of the international division of labor involving the transfer of the production process to overseas territories, in line with the internationalization of capital on a world scale.[5] The consequent deindustrialization of the capitalist centers, such as the United States,[6] has led to higher unemployment and underemployment in the U.S. and elsewhere and has pressed down wages, while imperial-installed puppet regimes have intensified repression of workers and peasants in the Third World and forced upon them minimum wages to generate super profits for the transnational monopolies. Thus, there exists an inseparable relationship between the internationalization of capital and the new international division of labor on the one hand and the impact of these changes on both the U.S. economy and the Third World on the other. Economic decline in the imperial center (manifested in plant closings, unemployment, and recession) and superexploitation of workers in the Third World (maintained by repressive military regimes) yield the same combined result that has a singular global logic: the accumulation of transnational profits for the capitalist class of the advanced capitalist countries—above all, that of the United States, the current center of world capitalism. It is in this context of the changes that are taking place on a world scale that the imperial state is beginning to confront the current crisis of world capitalism.

The contradictions of the unfolding process of global expansion and accumulation have brought to the fore new political realities—renewed repression at home and abroad to control an increasingly frustrated and angry working class in the imperial heartland; and an increasingly militant and revolutionary mass of workers and peasants in the neocolonial states of the Third World.[7]

It is these inherent contradictions of modern monopoly capital that are making it increasingly difficult for the imperial state to control and manage the world political economy, while at the same time preparing the conditions for international solidarity of workers on a world scale.

CRISIS OF THE CAPITALIST STATE
IN THE THIRD WORLD

The expansion of monopoly capital to the Third World has been accompanied by the rise of the authoritarian state, especially in those formations critical to the profit needs of the transnational monopolies. Thus Brazil, Argentina, Chile, the Philippines, South Korea, Taiwan, Indonesia, Iran, and Turkey, among others, have all experienced the domination of the rightist authoritarian state, often in the form of a neofascist military dictatorship, albeit installed to power by the imperialist forces from outside their geographic boundaries.[8]

The rise to power of right-wing repressive states in the Third World are a by-product of imperialism in its late capitalist stage, which finds itself in a position where its domination can be assured only through brute military force. This is accomplished through the installation of repressive military dictatorships in some countries and—what amounts to the same thing—the installation of right-wing "civilian" authoritarian regimes that violate the most basic human rights of the people. Here, the role of the key institutions of the imperial state—from "intelligence" agencies to para-military units—become the decisive forces that subvert the internal political institutions of Third World states in order to maintain imperial control over the authoritarian regimes installed into power, and to eliminate any opposition to their rule. The local repressive state in the Third World is thus an appendage of the imperial state and operates in accordance with its dictates. It is in this sense that the crisis of the imperial state at the global level translates into a crisis of the capitalist state in the Third World.

With the growth of foreign investment and economic activity in a growing number of Third World countries, there has been a marked increase in the size and strength of the working class, leading to strikes and demonstrations and open defiance of the repressive neocolonial capitalist state. This, in turn, has led to further repression of the masses, while at the same time plunging the state into a deep crisis of legitimacy where order is maintained through the brute force of the army and the police.[9] Such repression has, in turn, led to a further crisis of the authoritarian state and elevated the class struggle to a higher level, at which the masses have succeeded in overthrowing these regimes in a number of countries around the world, such as in Iran, Nicaragua, the Philippines, Argentina, Brazil, and Chile, with South Korea and Turkey next in line.

Added to their economic bankruptcy resulting from mounting foreign debt, double- and triple-digit inflation, and alarming rates of unemployment, the political crisis of the capitalist state in these Third World formations, which has led to military/police repression, has thus fueled the forces of change and revolution.

The logic of transnational expansion on a world scale is such that it leads to the emergence and development of forces in conflict with this expansion. The working class has been in the forefront of these forces; strikes, mass demonstrations, political organizing through party formation, confrontation with the local client state machine, armed insurrection, civil war, and revolutionary upheavals are all part and parcel of the contradictory structure of relations imposed upon the laboring people throughout the world by transnational capital, the imperial state and its client states in the Third World.

RESPONSES TO THE CRISIS OF THE
CAPITALIST STATE ON A WORLD SCALE

The worldwide expansion of international capital during the course of this century, especially since World War II, has led to struggles between labor and capital on a world scale,[10] particularly in regions and countries of the world where international capital has made the greatest headway.

In Latin America these are the relatively more developed and larger countries of Brazil, Mexico, and Argentina, and increasingly Peru, Chile, and a number of countries in Central America and the Caribbean region. These struggles, in the form of strikes, demonstrations, mass protests, and a variety of direct and indirect political actions, have intensified in recent years.

The strong presence of Western, especially U.S., dominance in Asia over a long span of time has prompted a wave of uprisings in recent decades—from Indonesia to Thailand, to Burma, to South Korea, to the Philippines.

In Africa, too, class struggles are unfolding with exceptional speed. The popular forces fighting for national liberation and social revolution are waging a determined struggle to break loose from the neocolonial bondage of the transnational monopolies and the imperial state. From Morocco, Tunisia, and Egypt in the north, to Sudan, Kenya, and Uganda in the east, to Ghana and Nigeria in the west, to South Africa in the south, workers and the oppressed are rising up to take charge of their own destinies. Inspired by the victory of the revolutions in Angola, Mozambique, and Zimbabwe, the African masses are yearning to liberate themselves from imperialism and neocolonialism throughout the continent.

The development of capitalism in the Middle East, both in its neocolonial and state-capitalist forms, has engendered intensified class conflicts and struggles throughout the region in recent decades. In war-torn Lebanon the ongoing civil war and the 1982 Israeli invasion have drawn the political boundaries of the contending class forces. Working-class and popular struggles have intensified also in Egypt, Turkey, Iran, and the Gulf states. The recent crisis in the Persian Gulf, has unleashed the forces of U.S. imperialism into the region once again, and will further fuel the discontent of the masses enough to spark a series of uprisings across the Gulf and beyond, with important implications for the balance of class forces in the entire Middle East.

In the heartland of imperialism—Europe and the United States—millions of workers affected by plant closings and the depression in the auto, steel, and other related industries have taken militant actions against the corporate offensive. Thus, increasingly politicized strikes and demonstrations by U.S. and European workers have been on the rise during the past decade.

Although strikes, protests, and other acts of defiance in and of themselves may not always lead to major political changes in a given country, they may nevertheless be viewed as a necessary first step in advancing the subjective conditions toward greater radicalization and class consciousness among workers, setting the stage for deeper and more lasting social transformations that may follow at a later date. Given the politicized nature of the prevailing economy and social conditions in Latin America and much of Asia, Africa, and the Middle East, as well as parts of Western Europe and, increasingly, the United States, strike actions by organized labor for what seems at first purely economic gains may soon (as has often been the case) turn into political protest against the government, local ruling classes, and imperialism, raising issues far beyond wages and working conditions toward political action to alter the existing neocolonial capitalist order.

When we consider the totality of the political forces at work in the Third World, together with those in Europe and other advanced capitalist regions, including the United States, it is clear that the potential unity of the working class and other laboring sections of society across national boundaries is now much closer to the reality of the unfolding process at work throughout the world than it has been the case until recently. The material conditions that have led to U.S. imperial domination of the world economy up to the present period have now reached a point where broad segments of the masses the world over, under working class leadership, are coming together to challenge it at its very foundations.

If the logic of imperialist expansion is capitalist domination of the world, and if the imperial state is unable to control and contain the growing contradictions of the world capitalist economy, then the process of capitalist exploitation on a world scale is preparing the eventual rise of the working class in the struggle over control of the state throughout the capitalist world.

CHAPTER 6

STATE CAPITALISM IN THE
THIRD WORLD

State capitalism, as one of several alternative paths of development in the Third World, has reemerged as the dominant social-economic form in a growing number of countries in Asia, Africa, Latin America, and the Middle East during the past few decades.

This chapter attempts to provide a general theory of state capitalism in the Third World.[1] After a brief discussion and critique of the three major positions on this issue, an alternative formulation that would more closely correspond to the actual characteristics of Third World state-capitalist regimes is proposed. Though critical of each of these formulations as they stand, the proposed alternative constitutes a synthesis of them. The chapter subsequently examines the relative achievements (and failures) of the state in carrying out social and economic transformations in terms of the unfolding internal and external contradictions confronting state-capitalist regimes, and assesses the long-term viability of this form of capitalist accumulation in the Third World in terms of the strengths and weaknesses of contending class forces pressuring the state—forces that ultimately determine the course of development of social formations embarked on this path.

THE EMERGENCE OF STATE CAPITALISM

The recent reemergence of state capitalism in the Third World can be traced back to the period following the Great Depression, when a number of countries, among them Turkey, Mexico, and Brazil, embarked on the nationalist, state-capitalist road of independent economic development;[2] later, in the 1950s and 1960s, other countries (India, Egypt, Algeria, Iraq, Ghana, Tanzania, and Peru) followed suit, establishing the state as the central institution in charge of national industrialization.[3] As specific case studies show,[4] however, the class forces holding state power in these countries, faced with limited internal resources and the impact of changes in the global economic structure, and internal social developments leading to the sharpening of class struggles between main antagonistic classes, were forced to select one or the other of two alternative paths: a move to the left, integrating their economies into the socialist bloc externally and making concessions to workers and peasants in the control of state power internally; or a move to the right, making concessions to traditional class forces and to transnational monopolies, eventually leading to a return to neocolonial relations. Although the final outcome of the state's struggle to maintain its "autonomous" position in these countries was dependent upon the relative strengths and weaknesses of different class forces pressuring the state, the key factors that led these states toward reintegration into the capitalist bloc and the reestablishment of their ties with the advanced capitalist centers, especially the United States, were the recovery of the developed capitalist countries from the severe crisis of worldwide depression in the 1930s, and the post-World War II emergence of the United States as the leading center of the world capitalist system (with its subsequent economic expansion to the Third World in the 1950s).

To understand the causes of the emergence of state capitalism in the Third World, we will first need briefly to outline the social and class structures of Third World social formations subjected to neocolonial rule.

The Class Structure under Neocolonialism and the Emergence of State Capitalism

The class structures of most postcolonial/neocolonial Third World social formations have this in common: the presence of a small, weak, and constantly threatened national bourgeoisie.[5] The working classes are small because of the low level of development of the productive forces. On the other hand, there exists a large agricultural sector: peasants, who work their own small plots of land for subsistence, along with landless peasants (or agricultural laborers), who work for and are tied to the feudal landlord class and/or agrarian capitalists (depending on the country), constitute the bulk of the population.

Despite formal independence from former colonial centers, local industries remain largely under the monopoly control of transnational capital. Within this neocolonial framework, in postcolonial societies the state is controlled by a coalition of political parties (or a single party) that represent the class interests of the comprador bourgeoisie, the big landlords, and the transnational monopolies.[6] While this "triple alliance" in the holding of state power immensely benefits the diverse (yet complementary) interests of each of the classes making up this ruling class coalition, the persistence of such rule means the continued exploitation and/or oppression of the working class, the peasantry, and the petty bourgeoisie. It is in this economic and political context that we see the emergence of state capitalism, led by segments of the petty bourgeoisie connected with the state bureaucracy. This nationalist, anti-imperialist intervention by the petty bourgeoisie does not, of course, occur automatically, but rather becomes materialized only under certain local and international circumstances that are historically determined.

Given that transnational capital dominates and monopolizes the local market and local production in the Third World, and that its interests conflict with those of local/national capitalists who themselves want to increase their capital accumulation, the latter benefits by transforming the transnational-controlled and internally- (landlord-comprador) supported neocolonial system. But given the overwhelming strength of the transnational bourgeoisie, both economically and militarily, the national and petty bourgeois classes, as a rule, have seldom waged effective battles to come to power and consolidate their base during "normal" periods of international economic expansion and overseas control;[7] such attempts have mainly succeeded during periods of global economic crisis and world war, when the imperialist powers are adversely affected. Of course, such conditions do not put Third World regimes on a favorable footing either, but they do nonetheless give the impetus for the national bourgeoisie to develop an independent industrial base. Indeed, during such periods a considerable number of postcolonial nations have embarked on a nationalist, state-capitalist path of development.

Global Crises and the Bourgeois Response in the Third World

The transition from neocolonial to national, state-capitalist development in the Third World occurred in more-developed countries (Argentina, Brazil, and Mexico),[8] particularly after the world depression of the

1930s. "Up until then," writes Celso Furtado, "the development of the industrial sector was a reflection of exports; afterwards, industrialization would be induced mainly by structural tensions provoked by the decline or the insufficient growth of the exporting sector."[9] Throughout the decade following the 1929 crisis, Latin America's capacity to import was severely curtailed, its exports were limited and, most important of all, its terms of trade had deteriorated. Thus, the collapse of the global economic system was primarily responsible for the development of national industrialization in several of the major Latin American countries. This process of domestic industrialization undertaken by the national bourgeoisie was directed toward the diversification of the internal productive structure.

Similar developments took place elsewhere in the Third World during this period. Of these, Turkey is a prime example of a nationalist, state-capitalist regime in the Middle East during and immediately following the Great Depression.[10]

World War II and the Korean War provided another opportunity for a similar wave of nationalist movements in the Third World that brought to power national- and petty-bourgeois elements in a number of countries in Asia, Africa, and Latin America—among them, India, Egypt, Syria, Iran, Guatemala, and later Algeria.

Following the relatively stable late 1950s and early 1960s, the preoccupation of the center states (especially the United States) with the Vietnam War in the mid- and late 1960s opened the way for countries such as Peru to follow a nationalist, state-capitalist path. And again, from the late 1960s to the mid-1970s, the gravest economic crisis since the Depression—coupled with the "oil crisis" and the continuing Vietnam War—brought another cycle of anti-imperialist challenge from a number of countries in the Third World. Peru, Panama, Tanzania, Libya, and Ethiopia are notable examples of the emergence of radical petty-bourgeois regimes during this period.[11]

THEORIES OF STATE CAPITALISM IN THE THIRD WORLD: AN OVERVIEW OF THREE MAJOR POSITIONS

There are three major positions on the nature of state capitalism in the Third World:

(1) Under conditions of worldwide imperialist hegemony and neocolonial rule, no country can expect to become independent and pursue an independent development policy free of external control and dom-

ination without going through a mass-based socialist revolution.
(2) The development path in the Third World is not limited to the alternatives of neocolonialism and socialism; a third path (neither capitalist
nor socialist) is indeed possible, that of "non-capitalist development."
(3) While an independent, national state-capitalist path is not possible
under conditions of foreign domination, it does become possible during periods of worldwide crisis and imperial decline, when its viability becomes dependent on successful struggle with the center states.

In the following analysis of each of these positions, we shall refer
to them as Theories I, II, and III.

The central argument set forth in Theory I is the inevitability of
neocolonial exploitation in the epoch of world imperialism. In the present world situation, the argument goes, Third World countries are
under the domination of (and are oppressed by) one or another of the
major imperialist powers, which strive to subject these countries to their
own imperial interests. Thus, under these conditions (and given the vast
economic and military strength of the imperialist system), Third World
countries cannot be expected to develop independently of (and in opposition to) centers of world imperialism. Those that initially escape such
domination would, in the absence of a complete break with the imperialist system, mass mobilization, and self-reliant development, inevitably
return to neocolonial rule and imperialist oppression.[12] Thus, according
to this theory, state-capitalism is not viable and cannot develop toward
anything but a restoration of neocolonialism; only a worker-led mass
socialist revolution could counteract this tendency and carry forward a
dynamic program of national development that would serve the needs
of the masses. Hence, at the political level, state capitalism is not only a
long-term impossibility, but also undesirable, because it represents a
new form of exploitation—by the bureaucratic "state bourgeoisie."[13]

In contradistinction to the propositions set forth in Theory I, Theory II postulates that the main trend in the Third World today is that of
"noncapitalist development."[14] This trend has emerged in response to
(and is in turn reinforced by) the worldwide decline of imperialism and
the ascent of socialism in this century. In the words of two of the theory's proponents: "the national-democratic revolution and its development into a socialist revolution is the way that permits countries that
have shaken off the colonial yoke to carry out the transition to socialism."[15] Accordingly, "non-capitalist development is a whole transitional
stage in itself, a multistage progressive revolutionary process of carrying out anti-imperialist and democratic transformations that step by
step bring a country up to the point of building a socialist society."[16] It

is by this process that Third World nationalist regimes would evolve into socialism. The countries that have embarked upon the noncapitalist path, therefore, are viewed as being "oriented towards socialism" and are thus "necessarily" moving "in the direction of socialism."[17] As one of its proponents puts it:

> the unique position of the former colonial countries who won independence in an era when socialism had become the main force of world development . . . opens up to the so-called Third World new and as yet historically untried possibilities for social progress. The attempt to unconditionally reduce the contradictory development of young states to either capitalism or socialism ignores the great diversity of transitional steps and stages which, while lacking complete qualitative definiteness, are capable of creating the possibilities and prerequisites for socialist transformations.[18]

In contrast to Theory I, then (which sees the inevitable return of Third World state-capitalist regimes to neocolonialism), Theory II postulates the inevitability of the evolution of "noncapitalist" (state-capitalist) regimes into "socialism." This, in essence, is the theory of "non-capitalist development"—the Soviet conception of state-capitalist development in the Third World.

Theory III, while it agrees with the notion of the long-term impossibility of independent state-capitalist development during "normal" periods of imperialist control and domination, it also sees the possibility of such development during periods of worldwide crises and imperial decline. To back up this position, the theory points to the coming to power of state-capitalist regimes during and immediately following the First and Second World Wars and the depression of the 1930s, as well as in the period since the late 1960s.[19] Thus the process of independent national development is seen in terms of institutional structures (often external) that impede national capitalist development, and that the nature and intensity of external imperialist pressure is viewed as determining the prospects of state-capitalist regimes once they come to power.

THEORIES OF STATE CAPITALISM: A CRITIQUE

It must be pointed out at the outset that all three of the positions outlined above fall short of a complete analysis of the nature and dynamics of state capitalism in the Third World.

The major problem with Theory I is its tendency to preclude, a priori, the possibility of the emergence and current existence of state-capitalist regimes in the Third World. While it is true that, given the immense contradictions these regimes face, state capitalism is not a viable form of development in the Third World, and that workers still face an intense exploitation by the state and national bourgeoisie, it cannot be ignored that there are today a growing number of such regimes throughout the Third World. Necessary to understand the nature of these regimes is a concrete analysis of their dynamics and contradictions, which will delineate (a) their class character and class contradictions, (b) their exact relationship with the masses, and (c) the nature and degree of their ideological influence over mass consciousness. In this regard, it would be correct to say that such regimes are characterized by capitalist relations of production, which involve the exploitation of labor, as well as subsequent compromise with imperialism and local propertied classes, repression of the working class and the peasant masses, and control and later dismantling of independent trade-union and peasant organizations.

The problems associated with Theory II lie first and foremost in the lack of class analysis of the nature and especially the policies of the leadership holding state power in these countries. The main question that needs to be raised here is: Which class, or alliance of classes, holds state power? The reply, "revolutionary democrats," is unacceptable, since revolutionary democrats (characterized by their political/ideological stance) do not constitute a distinct class, but are individuals who come from a preexisting class and serve the interests of a particular class (or a number of classes).[20] The question then, is: Which classes benefit from their policies and which classes lose?

Theory III, on the other hand, while providing a useful account of historical developments in the Third World in relation to changes in the imperial centers, has developed in the context of institutional analysis, with the resultant neglect of social classes as rooted in relations of production. Such an approach, therefore, overemphasizes external domination and obscures a clear conception of the internal class contradictions of regimes embarked on the state-capitalist path. Consequently, once such external relations are transformed by radical-nationalist, state-capitalist regimes (who expel imperialism and gain a degree of independence), the theory is hard put to explain the class nature and contradictions of such regimes, as it lacks a class conception of developments on this path. Conceiving of the problem in such national and external terms also leads the theory toward populist responses in politics, as the question of liberation becomes national or regional, rather than one of class—the working class. As a result, theorists in this tradition have been preoccupied with developing strategies to overcome subordination to imperial centers and to promote national, autonomous development.[21]

All three of the theories presented and critiqued here have given at best a partial and generally incomplete analysis of the nature of Third World radical-nationalist regimes.

TOWARD A GENERAL THEORY OF STATE CAPITALISM IN THE THIRD WORLD: AN ALTERNATIVE FORMULATION

At the heart of our analysis of the nature of state capitalism in the Third World lies the question of the state. And the role of the state in national economic development is related to the political structure of a particular regime. "When talking about the state in any society," says R. B. Sutcliffe, "we have to ask several questions: firstly, who (what social class, group or alliance of classes) controls or wrestles for the power of the state? This depends upon how powerful are the groups or classes which control it; if their position is weak in society they will not be able to use state power against other interests."[22]

We contend that, under state capitalism in the Third World, the state is dominated and controlled by the petty bourgeoisie led by the military and civilian sectors of the state bureaucracy which incorporates sections of the intermediate, professional strata. When we refer to the military and civilian sectors of the state bureaucracy as petty bourgeois, it is not because the bureaucracy in itself occupies an intermediate position within class society, but because in most postcolonial/neocolonial Third World societies officers in both of these sectors (especially junior officers in the Army, who are often the main leaders inciting anti-imperialist military coups) are drawn from the ranks of the petty bourgeoisie who bring petty-bourgeois ideals into the state apparatus.

While progressive Third World intellectuals educated in the West develop a sympathetic attitude toward bourgeois conceptions, their petty-bourgeois origins and nationalist ideology set them against their ex-colonial masters, who are engaged in the plunder of "their" nations. It is this contradiction that defines the postindependence policies of the petty-bourgeois bureaucratic leaders under state-capitalist regimes, as these policies are both procapitalist *and* anti-imperialist. Their main goal is to replicate the Western (capitalist) model to harvest the fruits of capitalist development nationally. But their actions on this path bring them into sharp conflict with those interests who prospered precisely through the plunder of these countries. The recognition of this point draws the petty-bourgeois leaders to the side of the national bourgeoisie, who develop great hopes for the latter's potential for national industrialization under the new nationalist, anti-imperialist regime.

Given the previously weak and inferior position of the national and petty bourgeoisies in postcolonial societies, the petty-bourgeois controlled and directed state attempts to strengthen the position of the national bourgeoisie as well as of its own class under the new nationalist regime. The state gradually acquires the ownership of the major means of production and distribution because the national bourgeoisie is not in a position to develop these sectors of the economy. Initially, the state is not so much interested in the task of capital accumulation per se (or to take on the role of entrepreneur), but rather serves an important function by aiding the national bourgeoisie to build and strengthen the latter's industrial base.[23] Only after the failure of this initial stage does the state step in to take over the production process and, in its own right, become an agent of capital accumulation, whose top bureaucratic leaders can now be seen as a "state bourgeoisie."[24]

It is at this point that the state begins to move against individual capitalists (but not the capitalist class as a whole) in sectors of the economy it believes threaten the long-term development of national capitalism and capitalist industrialization. Contradictions and conflicts develop between the state and individual capitalists not living up to the state's expectations of national economic development. The state thus feels obliged to take up the task of industrialization and in the process alienates more and more sections of national capital. Although it acts in the long-term interests of the capitalist class as a whole (by promoting capital accumulation within the framework of the existing social order), its short-term policies do nonetheless come into conflict with those of individual capitalist enterprises.

In line with its development scheme, the state-capitalist regime "borrows 'socialist forms'—political (one party state, socialist rhetoric, etc.) and economic (state ownership, planning, etc.)—to accomplish capitalist ends—the realization of profit within a class society."[25] Consequently, the petty-bourgeois state takes upon itself the responsibility (in the short run) of providing the necessary capital to develop vital resources (such as petroleum and mining), in addition to its role in industrial production and in meeting public necessities (e.g., transportation and utilities), in a country where the bourgeoisie has not developed sufficiently to assume ownership of these sectors. Hence, the state plays a major role in the realization of the long-term interests of the developmental agency in capitalist accumulation—the national bourgeoisie. But because of the undeveloped and distorted nature of the local economy, many of the tasks traditionally assumed by private national capital are now taken up by the state, which, in turn, provides a leadership role in the development of the productive forces and in the accumulation of capital. Thus:

> State capitalism here has basically *national* tasks to perform aimed at creating an independent national economy, and is, sooner or later, necessarily directed against foreign capital. . . . Apart from foreign capital and . . . comprador private capital, *national* capital is interested in the fulfillment of these tasks.[26]

In addition to its active role in the development of the productive forces, the state attempts to eliminate the remnants of precapitalist relations in the agrarian sector through a series of agrarian reform measures, and expropriates large tracts of land "belonging" to big landowners. Such land is then transferred to the middle- and small-holding peasantry, along with agricultural implements, credits, irrigation works, etc., in order to incorporate the peasantry into the cooperative movement in the rural sector. At the same time, the state nationalizes the major means of production and restricts or expels foreign capital (often with compensation). Parallel to this is the development and implementation of a broad-based industrialization program with high levels of state investment in heavy industry as well as in consumer goods production. The regulation of commerce is brought under state control and special organs such as state banks and development corporations are created to assist the industrialization process.

The Class Contradictions Under
State Capitalism

While the development process forges ahead under the state-capitalist regime, so, too, the contradictions between the state and various classes hostile to it sharpen. These are: the landlords vs. the state; the state vs. the comprador bourgeoisie; the landlords vs. the peasantry; and the workers vs. the state and national bourgeoisie.

At the center of the conflict between the state and the landlords lies the question of land reform and its implementation. The state attempts to eliminate the entrenched power of landlords by expropriating large tracts of land in the hands of big landowners in order to redistribute such land to small-holding and landless peasants.[27] But, given the immense power and resistance of landlords in the countryside, the petty-bourgeois state is not always successful in implementing its plans in the agrarian sector, and a failure on this front may well lead to the restoration of neocolonialism.

Elsewhere in the economy, the state takes decisive steps against the urban comprador bourgeoisie in order to curb their power and interests vested in international trade. In the initial period of the development process under state capitalism, the state attempts to transform the comprador elements into industrial capitalists. Yet this effort, for various reasons—above all, the reluctance of compradors to give up their parasitic position in import-export trade, which links them to foreign capital and the imperial centers—often results in failure. It is largely in response to that failure, as well as to counteract the adverse effects of international crises on the national economy, that the state begins to take an active role in the regulation of commerce and industry, adopting measures decidedly antagonistic to the interests of the comprador bourgeoisie.

While the struggle between different factions of the dominant classes continues throughout the state-capitalist period, the superexploitation of the laboring masses, in both the city and the countryside, persists under the nationalist regime. The peasants continue to be exploited by the landlords, while workers continue to generate high rates of surplus value, which in turn is appropriated by the state and the national industrial bourgeoisie, resulting in the enrichment of the state and local capitalists at the expense of the masses of the laboring people.

The struggle between the state and various antagonistic classes (primarily the landlords and the comprador bourgeoisie) significantly weakens the nationalist regime and makes it susceptible to external penetration. Also, with the recovery of the imperial centers from global economic and military crises and the reestablishment of world market relations, the position of the national economy vis-à-vis the world market begins to deteriorate: export prices begin to drop, while prices of foreign-supplied capital goods or technology, crucial for the internal industrialization process, begin to rise. Faced with this situation, the state (still controlled by the petty-bourgeois bureaucratic stratum) makes appeals to the workers for increased production, while at the same time pressing for wage cuts, reducing social spending, and continuing to resort to inflationary measures. The more this continues the more the contradictions become sharpened. But, being a petty-bourgeois state, it governs at a level of delicate equilibrium between pressures from above (landlords and compradors, and foreign capital) and pressures from below (primarily the working class). The regime thus loses most of its initially established stable character based on "patriotism" and "nationalism" that it had propagated immediately after its inception to power. From here on the petty-bourgeois leadership takes on its real class character—vacillating, spontaneous, authoritarian and repressive.[28]

It is precisely this contradictory position of the postcolonial petty-bourgeois state that provides the key to an understanding of the dynamics and contradictions of state capitalism in the Third World. Generally, the greater the pressures from imperialism and landlord-comprador interests (in the relative absence of pressures from the working class and the left), the greater the tendency for the regime to move to the left; conversely, the greater the pressures from the working class and the left (in the relative absence of pressures from imperialism and local reactionary classes), the greater the tendency for the regime to move to the right. What must be remembered, however, is that such moves are almost always temporary, and are made under extremely difficult conditions which threaten the survival of the regime. The preferred course that these regimes would like to follow (given the class interests of those who hold state power) is an independent, national-capitalist path, arrived at by playing the socialist states and the advanced capitalist states against one another.[29]

In short, because of the highly unstable nature of this form of capitalist accumulation in the Third World in the era of global imperialism, the direction of the further development of these state-capitalist regimes is determined by the nature, intensity, and outcome of the internal class struggle. As state capitalism develops further and reaches a state of maturity, the main antagonism in this struggle increasingly becomes the petty-bourgeois state vs. the working class, and the final outcome of this struggle rests on the successful coalition of social forces through class alliances in order to capture or sustain state power.

CONCLUSION

Several points lie at the center of our analysis of state capitalism in the Third World. In summary:

(1) State-capitalist regimes emerge (a) in response to colonialism and imperialism/neocolonialism, or (b) during periods of international crises, or (c) in reaction to internal developments (the growing power of the working class and its organizations and/or the continuation of the domination of the landlords and compradors in national politics).

(2) State capitalism is not a distinct mode of production, but a variant of the capitalist mode of production, which becomes materialized in

the Third World under certain historically determined conditions within the world economy. By "state capitalism" is meant the introduction and institution of the capitalist mode of production (through direct state intervention) by the petty bourgeoisie. Because the contemporary world economy is dominated by a handful of advanced capitalist states, this makes it difficult or impossible for Third World capitalists to develop along the classical lines of capitalist development, as it took place in Europe in the previous century, without the direct role of the state in capital accumulation; hence the necessity for the procapitalist sectors within the bureaucracy fully to utilize the powers of the state to engage it in the productive sphere in order to facilitate capital accumulation in a way that would promote the long-term interests of the local, national bourgeoisie.

(3) While these regimes must, of necessity (given our model), be strongly anti-feudal and anti-imperialist, this is not always the case. Such cases must therefore be examined carefully in direct relationship to the level and intensity of the class struggle and the pressures put on the petty-bourgeois state by contending class forces in their struggle to capture or recapture state power. The degree of anti-feudalism and anti-imperialism of such regimes is thus a direct function of the nature and intensity of the class struggle during their tenure.

(4) State-capitalist regimes have two important aspects: (a) the positive, "progressive" side (the development of the productive forces and, as a result of their anti-imperialism—necessitated by the drive to facilitate national capital accumulation—the weakening of imperialism internationally); and (b) the negative, reactionary side (continuation of capitalist exploitation as a result of the persistence of capitalist relations of production—albeit in a somewhat different, "statist" form).

(5) Under state capitalism it is the petty bourgeoisie that holds state power. This develops in the context of the colonial or the neocolonial situation and is dependent on the forging of successful class alliances under the leadership of the petty bourgeoisie. This is why we often find a struggle within national liberation movements that takes place between the petty bourgeoisie and the working class over the leadership of the movement. The aim of the petty bourgeoisie in this context is to control the working class and its political organizations and prevent its leadership from coming to dominate this movement. The success in this struggle of the petty bourgeoisie marks the emergence in these countries of state capitalism.

Given this general theoretical framework, what is now necessary to evaluate the propositions advanced in this chapter are empirical studies of social formations embarked on the state-capitalist path in the Third World—a task we undertake in the next several chapters.

PART III

Case Studies of the
State and Development
in the Third World

CHAPTER 7

CLASS, STATE, AND DEVELOPMENT IN THE MIDDLE EAST: THE CASE OF TURKEY

Until the beginning of the twentieth century, the Ottoman Empire was the major political force in the Middle East. The predominant mode of production in the Ottoman formation was for seven centuries the Asiatic mode. Although it came in contact with many different modes of production and exchange, the Ottoman formation retained its powerful despotic state until its collapse early in this century.

In this chapter a brief analysis of the factors contributing to the collapse of the Ottoman Empire and its impact on the formation and development of the modern Turkish state is followed by an extended analysis of the political economy of Turkish development during the 1920s and 1930s. After drawing some important conclusions as to the nature and contradictions of Turkey's development process under state capitalism during this period, it examines the post-World War II reintegration of Turkey into the world economy and the development of a neocolonial political-economic order in the postwar period to the present.

THE OTTOMAN LEGACY

Interaction between Ottoman and Byzantine society developed after the invasion of Constantinople by Ottoman forces in 1453. This, together with interaction with other European formations following the Ottoman expansion into Europe in the fifteenth and sixteenth centuries and the state's land-allocation system (*timar*),[1] eventually led to feudal forms in Ottoman agriculture (*iltizam*, or tax farming). Over time, large-scale private property in land (*çiftlik*) acquired increasing importance, transferring a higher proportion of the land to a few owners.[2] This transformation of the agrarian structure took place during the seventeenth and eighteenth centuries; as a result, a landed gentry (*ayan*) developed, displacing the *sipahis* as intermediaries between the state and producers. By the end of the eighteenth and beginning of the nineteenth centuries, the *ayan* was a fully developed feudal landowning class that began to challenge the authority of the central state by equipping its own armies. But the *ayan* never became powerful enough to overthrow the central state.[3]

While the introduction of tax farming initiated by the state strengthened the position of landlords, interaction with Europe also facilitated the expansion of European commercial capital into the empire, leading to the development of a comprador class tied to European imperialism. Nevertheless, the development of feudalism in agriculture and, later, capitalism in commerce and industry, took place within the confines of a society dominated by the Asiatic state, which permitted the coexistence of these diverse modes.

The collapse of the Ottoman Empire came gradually. After centuries of expansion and conquest, the Ottoman state began to lose ground to rival forces in Europe during the eighteenth and nineteenth centuries and became vulnerable to pressures from the West.

While the Ottoman state was becoming rapidly weaker and its influence in the Mediterranean suffering continual erosion, Europe had completed its transition from feudalism to capitalism.[4] Thus, by the late eighteenth century Europe's old (feudal) economy had been transformed by the expanding capitalist mode, which spread with increasing vigor to the Mediterranean region and elsewhere in pursuit of raw materials and new markets. Growing trade between Western Europe and Ottoman Turkey during this period began to have adverse effects on local, small-scale Ottoman industry. Faced with rising costs and operating under strict price regulations, the Ottoman guilds were unable to provide goods at prices low enough to compete with the cheap European-manufactured goods that entered the Empire without restriction due to the Capitulation Agreements.[5] Consequently, traditional Ottoman industry entered a period of rapid decline and the Empire became more and more dependent on the European economies.

As European capital began to expand, there was no longer a need to depend on imports of manufactured goods from the East, as had been the case earlier. In fact, the growing capitalist economy in Europe, now able to take full advantage of the favorable terms provided by the Capitulations, was in a position to bring about a complete reversal in international trade. Whereas England was previously an importer of textiles from the East, it now became an exporter of textiles.[6] The process of British (and other European) expansion into the Ottoman economy accelerated following the Anglo-Turkish Commercial Convention of 1838, for it extended extra-territorial privileges to all foreign traders and abolished the state's protective tariffs and monopolies. This resulted in a reversal of the import-export structure of the Empire and led to the destruction of the textile industry in Ottoman Turkey. Soon many other branches of Ottoman industry became affected and by the late 1800s the whole of Ottoman industry was on the verge of collapse.[7] These developments thus marked the end of industrialization via the manufacturing sector and the Empire was instead relegated to raw materials production geared to the needs of the European-dominated world economy. With its native industry destroyed, the Ottoman Empire gradually became transformed into an agrarian reserve of the expanding European capitalist economies.[8]

By the late nineteenth century, then, Ottoman Turkey had for all practical purposes become a semicolony of the expanding European powers. Its economy was mortgaged to foreign capitalists and their states; widespread revolts and rebellions had occurred throughout its conquered territories; and new social groups had emerged which began to pose problems for its continued, if ill-fated, existence under the rule of the Sultans and the Palace bureaucracy.

The European powers, taking advantage of all these problems, found their way in through direct economic controls and later military occupation of large parts of Ottoman territory at the end of the nineteenth and beginning of the twentieth centuries, which culminated in the occupation of virtually every corner of the Empire during World War I.

Following the collapse of the Ottoman Empire at the end of the war, Britain, France, Italy, and other European countries colonized its territories and remained in control of its various provinces for several decades. From the Persian Gulf to Palestine, to the Suez Canal, down to the Arabian peninsula, and across North Africa, much of the territories of the Empire came under the jurisdiction of Britain and France, who divided up these territories to secure trade routes, raw materials, and new markets for the expanding European-controlled world economy.

In time, local populations resented foreign domination and attempted to oust the Europeans from their lands. After long struggles for national liberation, some colonized regions of the Empire gained political independence and set up a series of nation-states, notably Turkey, Egypt, Syria, Lebanon, Iraq, and Algeria.

The independence movement in Turkey and the origins of the modern Turkish state go back to the Young Turk Revolution of 1908. The Committee of Union and Progress, which led the 1908 revolution, was mainly composed of Turkish intellectuals greatly influenced by European nationalist thought.[9] Their ideology brought them in line with their main allies, the *esnaf* (artisans) and *tüccar* (merchants) of the towns—the class out of which they sought to forge a Turkish bourgeoisie.[10] In this context, and after massive territorial losses following the two Balkan wars (1912-13) and the failure of the ruling Young Turk government to safeguard Turkey from imperialist occupation forces during World War I, the stage was set for Mustafa Kemal and the Kemalists to assume the leadership of the liberation forces and secure a nationalist victory. With the coming to power of the bourgeois nationalist forces, Turkey embarked on a path of national capitalist development under the guidance and control of the state and the military-civilian bureaucracy.

THE ROLE OF THE TURKISH STATE IN THE DEVELOPMENT PROCESS IN THE 1920S

The state's role in the economy in the 1920s expanded into local industry to develop the infrastructure, establish banks, and regulate commerce. Among the most notable activities of the state were the development and expansion of state-owned and controlled enterprises and the establishment of several major industrial and commercial banks. The state also acquired full ownership and control of major sectors of the economy, including raw materials and petroleum, railways, major seaport facilities, and a number of enterprises in mining and extractive industries.

In addition to the direct role played by various state banks and credit institutions in encouraging the expansion of national industry, many special laws were passed by the Grand National Assembly granting major concessions to private capital. Important legislation to encourage industrialization through private capital was effected by the passage of the Law for the Encouragement of Industry in 1927.

Despite the extraordinary advantages provided by the state to private capital, however, the Turkish bourgeoisie during this period lagged far behind the state's expectations of rapid industrialization. This prompted the state to take measures to strengthen the public sector in order to accomplish this task. With the increase in the number of enterprises supported by the state—from 470 in 1927 to 1,473 in 1933[11]—the state at the end of the 1920s and during the 1930s began to assume an even greater role in and more complete control over the national economy, as we shall see later.

Parallel to these developments in industry, steps were taken by the state to accelerate capital accumulation in the countryside. Among these were the abolition of the *öşür* (tithe tax) in 1925 and the distribution of land to landless peasants in 1927 and 1929.[12]

Although a thorough transformation of the agrarian structure was not carried out during these initial years, the state

> did, however, attempt to increase production by establishing experimental stations, agricultural schools, and modern demonstration (state-owned) farms. Improved seed was provided and instructors were sent to villages to show new ways of cultivation.[13]

The regime envisioned that the introduction of capitalist methods in agriculture would, with state aid in the supply of credit, means of production, and distribution, increase efficiency, productivity and the accumulation of capital in the countryside, a process that would parallel and supplement developments in the urban industrial sector.

However, because existing relations of production were kept intact in the countryside, and the economic, political, and socioreligious strength of the landlords and their domination over local branches of the state-initiated credit unions and producer cooperatives continued, the financial resources provided by the state directed toward the peasants were all diverted to the landlords' own private accounts. Thus, while in this way the landlords were able to expand their fortunes and further enrich themselves, landless peasants and small producers continued as in the past to be enslaved to them.

The landlords' control over the mechanism of state aid to the agricultural sector did, nevertheless, expand the growth of output in some sectors of the rural economy. And while this growth was sufficient to divert the state's attention to other areas of the national economy, the increased revenues accruing to the landlords further strengthened their material position in relation to other propertied classes such that the possibility of a genuine agrarian reform was to become very remote after the 1920s.

Despite the extensive efforts of the state to aid the development of Turkish industry during the 1920s, capitalist development failed to achieve the results envisaged by the state in trying to elevate Turkey to a full-fledged capitalist nation. Of the numerous obstacles to the industrialization of the country during this period, two were decisive: the resistance of landlords in areas where their interests were threatened by industrial expansion, and the failure of the expected transformation of Turkish compradors into industrial capitalists.

Internal reaction, led by the landlord-clergy coalition, who viewed the state's industrialization efforts as part of the process of modernization that challenged their control over the countryside, succeeded in blocking the expansion of indigenous industry into the rural interior, leaving control over vast sections of Anatolia exclusively in the hands of big landowners. As a result, the limited transformation that did take place in the agrarian sector was almost exclusively in the sphere of agricultural production; this did not alter the conditions prevailing there in favor of industrialization.

The comprador bourgeoisie was reluctant to expand into the industrial sector, despite the state's consistent encouragement through the offer of credit, grants, and numerous concessions. Rather than employ the loans, credits, and supplies provided by the state to expand production, most of them simply failed to take advantage of these concessions. Instead

> the majority of the so-called entrepreneurs initiated "paper" businesses, claimed the bonuses offered by the government, bought the products of the state factories well under their market prices, and sold them to other operators. After making exorbitant profits, they closed their "enterprises" before they even started them. Even heavy machinery imported for the establishment of new industries was exported to other countries after their registration at Turkish ports of entry.[14]

Thus the profits made by the big merchants were generally employed in usury and commerce, not industrial production.

Although further efforts were made by the nationalist leadership to accelerate industrialization by providing domestic finance and a guarded acceptance of foreign capital in various branches of the national economy, Turkey remained a part of the imperialist-controlled capitalist world economy until the end of the 1920s. Turkey's continued role as supplier of raw materials and agricultural products and an importer of finished manufactured goods was determined by forces at work at the global level—forces that subjected Turkey to the dynamics of development at the center of the world capitalist economy. It is for this reason that the Great Depression had an immense impact on the Turkish economy.

The financial collapse in the imperial centers in 1929, lasting until the mid-1930s, affected the Turkish economy largely through the severance of commercial ties between Turkey and the center states. This meant not only a major cut in the supply of manufactured goods to Turkey, but also a drastic drop in foreign demand for Turkey's exports of raw materials and agricultural produce—the largest categories of Turkish exports. The resulting drop in the value of the Turkish lira led to a major decline in the prices of agricultural products,[15] affecting the balance of trade, agricultural revenues, and ultimately the state treasury. With the coming of the Depression, then, Turkey began to experience considerable difficulty in continuing its industrialization through dependence on the world market;[16] the wide-ranging expansion of the state into all branches of the national economy during the 1930s was in large measure a direct response to the adverse conditions created by the financial collapse in the imperial centers.

With the state beginning to assume the commanding heights of the economy in the early 1930s, Turkey thus entered a period of capitalist development later called *devletcilik*, or statism, which marked the beginning of the period of consolidation of state capitalism in postindependence Turkey.

STATE CAPITALISM IN TURKEY IN THE 1930S

The adverse conditions brought by world economic crisis made it necessary for the Turkish state to take an even more direct role in the national economy. In the future the state would play a central role in the industrialization and capital accumulation process by replacing the small, weak, and incapacitated national industrial bourgeoisie.

The consolidation of the state's role in the national industrialization process in the early 1930s occurred after Turkey had gained control over its customs and established a protectionist customs policy designed to encourage domestic production. The state's long-term objective was to establish and manage state-owned enterprises that would form the basis of the nation's industrial economy. This would put the state in the forefront of planning and implementing a program to accelerate the development of capitalism in Turkey—a process that had failed in the initial postindependence period in the 1920s.

Several parallel developments complemented Turkish industrialization efforts during the 1930s: the nationalization of foreign firms; the First and Second Five-Year Development Plans; and the establishment of new state banks and agencies to finance and carry out development projects to meet the objectives of these plans.

In an effort to resolve Turkey's balance of payments crisis, resulting from the deteriorating terms of trade following the Depression, the state launched an all-out campaign of nationalization of foreign firms. The first signs of a broad-based nationalization policy came with the state takeover of the main railways, utilities, transportation, and port facilities in the early 1930s. This was followed by the nationalization of dozens of mines and factories owned by foreign capital in the latter half of the decade and early 1940s.[17]

The nationalization policy of the state during this period played a significant role in strengthening the Turkish economy. It virtually ended the outflow of capital, hence improving the country's balance of payments, and with the expansion of the state into different branches of the nation's industrial economy, it opened the way to state planning to increase production and to accelerate the process of independent capitalist industrialization. In light of the significant achievements of planned development in Turkey's northern neighbor, the Soviet Union, coupled with the considerable aid and protection the Soviets provided Turkey during this period, the state began to formulate, and soon thereafter implement, the First and Second Five-Year Industrial Development Plans during the 1930s. These plans enabled the state to make significant progress in national industrialization.

Throughout the 1930s the state placed major importance on the rapid development of industry, giving less attention to agriculture. Consequently, the industrialization drive significantly limited the development of Turkish agriculture, relative to industrial expansion. The agricultural sector, given the resistance of powerful landlords, never became successfully incorporated into the Five-Year Plans and remained on the periphery of the industrialization process. Nevertheless, despite its marginal role, the agricultural sector did make a substantial contribution to the national economy through increased production. This was achieved through a certain degree of modernization of the productive forces throughout the countryside made possible by extensive state aid.

The mechanization of the countryside, and the consequent increases in agricultural productivity contributed to the development of Turkey's agricultural sector. The state expanded its activities in rural areas by setting up model farms, encouraging peasants, through the use of new implements and machinery in state-operated agricultural schools and stations, to adopt modern and more efficient techniques of production, and providing them with the means to purchase machinery. Farm machinery was imported through the Ministry of Agriculture and sold to peasants by way of loans and credits provided by the Agricultural Bank.

Despite the concerted efforts of the state bureaucracy to implement these projects, many of the programs outlined here never fully materialized—because of both the strong resistance of local landlords to land reform and projects connected with it, and the outbreak of World War II, which compelled the state to adopt a war economy. Consequently, a large number of these projects remained on paper, and though others were completed they did not substantially alter the structure of the rural economy or accelerate rapidly the modernization process in the agricultural sector.

The state's moderate accomplishments in agriculture during this period were achieved not through the breakup of predominantly feudal relations in the countryside and the latter's transformation into capitalism; what little progress was made in this direction came in spite of the continuing, overwhelming power and dominance of the landlord class, which the bureaucracy had earlier attempted but failed to destroy because of its reluctance to mobilize the peasant masses from below. The regime's distrust of the masses—a characteristic of petty-bourgeois bureaucratic regimes the world over—later resulted in the loss of support of the peasant masses and set the stage for the coming to power by the end of the 1940s of a coalition of landlords and compradors.

The industrialization drive of the 1930s, coupled with increased agricultural production during the same period, had a significant impact on national trade. In 1930 Turkey began to register a trade surplus, which continued throughout the decade and into the 1940s. This surplus helped increase the country's foreign exchange earnings and with it the balance of payments improved considerably.

While the state-induced capitalist development of the 1930s significantly improved Turkey's overall economic position and placed the country on a favorable footing with respect to industrialization, it sharpened the contradictions inherent in the system.

THE CONTRADICTIONS OF STATE CAPITALISM IN TURKEY

The accumulation of capital under the state-capitalist regime in Turkey during the 1930s and early 1940s was achieved mainly through an intensified exploitation of wage labor in both public and private industries. In this sense, the primary contradiction in Turkey was between state or private capital and wage labor. At the same time, other internal and external problems contributed to increased conflict between the state and various social classes within the country. Together, these contradictions played a major role in shaping the direction of the state-capitalist regime in Turkey.

The State and the Landlords

The most decisive contradiction proved to be that between the state and the landlords and compradors allied with imperialism, centered in the question of land reform. Because of effective landlord resistance, all the attempts made by the state to redistribute land to smallholders and landless peasants failed. Other measures to improve the condition of the impoverished peasantry and to modernize the agricultural sector were taken without encroaching on the interests of local landlords.[18]

The first major effort to alter the traditional land tenure system in Turkey was made in 1934 with the Settlement and Land Bill proposal. In line with the land reform legislation, sections of the 1924 Constitution (regarding the confiscation by the state of privately owned land) were altered in order to strengthen the state's position vis-à-vis the landlords. It was also in this period that the state initiated measures to establish agricultural cooperatives and village institutes.

While these were important steps toward the realization of an effective land reform policy, Kemal's death in 1938 and the outbreak of World War II virtually halted these efforts. It was not until the mid-1940s that the state was again able to take up the fight against the landlords and impose a land reform policy.

The decisive move against the landlords came in 1945, when the ruling People's Party introduced a Land Reform Bill. Debate on the bill lasted five months; by the time it was finally passed and became law it had been substantially weakened. Still, it contained a provision that all privately-held land in excess of 500 dönüms (124 acres) would be nationalized. It was this key provision of the law that posed the greatest threat to the landlords. The passage of the law, even in its severely distorted form, thus raised the class struggle between the state (dominated by the national and petty bourgeoisies) and the landlords (with their allies, the rural and urban commercial interests and local Islamic clergy) to its highest level since the early 1920s.

The first signs of the impending confrontation came with the split within the ruling Republican People's Party (RPP) in early 1946, when the opposition forces representing landed interests within the bureaucracy left the RPP to form the Democrat Party (DP). The subsequent national elections in July 1946 resulted in a significant change in the composition of Parliament in favor of the landlords. This, in turn, substantially weakened the Kemalists' power base in Parliament and led to a series of changes, including the replacement of the Minister of Agriculture by a big landowner. The confrontation between the two contending forces—the state vs. the landlords—ended in favor of the landlords, who further weakened the Land Reform Bill. Thus, at the close of the 1940s, the "nationalization limit was raised from 500 to 5,000 *dönüms*. The distribution began in 1947 . . . and by 1950 only a few score thousand *dönüms* had been distributed."[19] To further strengthen the position of the landlords vis-à-vis the state, the Democrat Party launched a major nationwide campaign in the late 1940s to attract large sections of the population. By identifying the state bureaucracy as the main target of mass discontent, the DP's landlord-comprador leadership began to build up the balance of forces in their favor, which later brought them to power in national elections in 1950.

The State and the Comprador Bourgeoisie

In the initial period of the development process, the state made a major effort to transform Turkish compradors into industrial capitalists. This effort, which extended over a period of several years following independence, was a total failure. In view of this failure, and in order to counteract the adverse effects of the worldwide economic crisis on the Turkish economy, the state began to take an active role in regulating commerce and industry, adopting measures that were decidedly antagonistic to the interests of the Turkish comprador bourgeoisie. It assumed increasing control over foreign trade and attempted to integrate the comprador class into the national, state-capitalist economy. Throughout this period, however, a large part of international trade continued to be in private hands. Because the compradors were engaged in the process of exchange, and not of production, they were relegated to a secondary, peripheral role in the industrialization process—so much so that the state could envisage itself assuming the basic functions of trade without their assistance.[20]

In the early 1940s the Kemalist forces in Parliament introduced a capital tax *(varlik vergisi)*, aimed at the exorbitant wartime profits made by the compradors and big landlords. This was to open up a new source of revenue to the state treasury, which could be used to further the industrialization process, as well as to maintain the large wartime military machine.[21]

The compradors and landlords put up strong resistance, however, and in Parliament their protests effectively blocked the Kemalists in their attempts to implement the tax across the board. Consequently, the capital tax never accomplished its objective, but was used instead against the minority (Greek, Armenian, and Jewish) compradors to further reduce their economic power and to ensure the dominance of the Turkish comprador bourgeoisie.[22]

In addition to their opposition to the capital tax and their largely successful efforts to avoid paying taxes on their wartime fortunes, the Turkish compradors presented broader demands in the form of deregulation of trade, the reestablishment of close relations with the West in order to broaden the scope of their import-export activities, and the driving out of, or monopoly control over, the competing minority comprador groups.

The natural alliance of the compradors and large landowners challenged the rule of the predominantly Kemalist state in order to expand their own class interests and to further consolidate their power. This alliance, which had found outward expression in the establishment of the Democrat Party, subsequently took state power in 1950, marking the triumph of landlords and compradors over the national and bureaucratic/petty bourgeoisie.

While the struggle between different factions of the dominant classes continued throughout the state-capitalist period and intensified in the 1940s, under the Kemalist regime the superexploitation of the working people in the cities and the rural areas persisted. The peasants were exploited by the landlords, while workers continued to generate high rates of surplus value which was appropriated by the state and the national industrial bourgeoisie, resulting in their enrichment at the expense of the masses, who lived in extreme poverty.

The Turkish Peasantry under the Rule of the Landlords

The failure of the Kemalist bureaucrats to break the power of the landlords and to transform the precapitalist relations of production prevailing throughout the Turkish countryside meant that during the state-capitalist period semifeudal production relations remained intact, perpetuating the traditional socioeconomic structures under which the peasantry was exploited by the big landowners.

The basis of the contradiction between the landlords and the peasants was the exceptionally uneven distribution of land. The first agricultural census conducted by the Turkish government showed that in 1927,

1,751,239 family farmers had average holdings of only six acres. In 1933-34 a report by a group of U.S. agricultural specialists estimated that there were some two million farms of similar size.

Throughout the 1930s two million impoverished peasant families were dominated by a few hundred very wealthy landowning families with average holdings of 4,000 acres each. The fortunes of the latter were so immense that, in addition to their own large landholdings, they claimed ownership over entire villages. A landowner named Seyit Riza, for example, owned 230 villages, while another, Haci Musa, owned a substantial portion of the entire Mus Valley, even collecting tribute from those traveling through "his" valley.[23] This vast inequality in the ownership and control of land enabled the large landowners to dominate the rural socioeconomic structure and, in collusion with the religious hierarchy, to impose their rule over the masses of the Turkish peasantry.

As the main exploited class in the predominantly precapitalist rural economy, the peasants shouldered much of the burden of development—largely through taxation and appropriation by the landlords of a large part of the surplus produced by the peasants. The smallholding peasant, who in addition to cultivating his own small plot of land also had to work for the landlords in order to maintain a bare subsistence, was thus the main source of agricultural revenue accruing to the state and to the big landlords.

The vast majority of peasants—in the midst of immense feudal wealth—lived under conditions of extreme poverty and destitution that caused much misery and suffering. Their standard of living was extremely low: in 1935 average per capita annual income for the entire rural population (*including* the big landlords) was 32 Turkish lira (25 dollars).[24] The even lower real level—excluding the landlord's share from the national average—condemned millions of peasants to perpetual hunger and poverty. The then mayor of Erzincan, Ali Kemali Bey, said: "the peasant has no home of his own, nor even a small patch of land. His possessions amount to nothing more than a worn-out blanket, a broken jug, and a few pieces of firewood. His stomach is often empty, and he labors naked and hungry."[25]

The findings of the 1936 Survey of Agricultural Production conducted by the Ministry of Economy showed that the main source of food for the broad masses of the agricultural population was a plain loaf of bread. The average consumption of bread for each "consuming unit" was 440 kg per year; meat consumption averaged only 5 kg per year. This diet was supplemented by some fruit, vegetables, and dairy products. The statistics were for the rural population as a whole, however, and it may be assumed that most, if not all, of the meat and supplementary food sources were consumed by the landlords and rich and middle peasants.

Exploitation of the peasant masses intensified with the coming of World War II, when they were "made to shoulder much of the burden of the wartime difficulties . . . half of the Turkish peasantry sank to below-subsistence level in the course of the war, and some in fact starved."[26]

For the peasants, accustomed as they were to paternalistic relations with the landlord-usurers and influenced by religious beliefs and practices, their dependence on the landlords prevented them from forming mass movements that could have helped raise their class consciousness. Instead, by submitting to the authority of the landlords and the clergy, they perpetuated their subordination to and exploitation by the rich landowning class throughout rural Turkey.

The Workers and the State and National Bourgeoisie

Given the limited scope of industrialization in Ottoman Turkey, workers in manufacturing industry comprised only a small segment of the population, not exceeding 14,000 in 1915.[27] Even in 1927, four years after independence, those employed in factories with ten or more workers totaled only 60,000 for the entire country. With the development of state capitalism, however, especially after the mid-1930s, the size of the manufacturing work force grew rapidly, reaching 427,000 by the late 1940s.[28]

One of the major aims of the state throughout the 1930s and 1940s was to maintain a docile labor force in order to increase production. To achieve this, workers were forced to labor long hours for little pay under unsafe conditions, while unions were outlawed and strikes banned.[29]

Statistics compiled by the government for the period 1935-39 do not include wages or numbers of workers employed in different branches of industry; it is thus impossible to calculate average wage levels for that period.[30] The data available for the 1939-43 period, however, confirm the declining trend in wages for workers at Eti and Sumer Banks, the two major state-owned financial institutions operating dozens of mines, factories, and plants in many branches of industry. The data show that Sumer Bank workers received far lower wages in 1943 than in 1939, while the wages of Eti Bank workers (mainly miners and power workers) were reduced by more than half in the course of a single year (1942-43), from 48.5 kurus per day to 23.9 kurus (or 19.1 U.S.

cents).[31] Wages dropped sharply during this period; workers were sub-jected to speed-ups and forced to put in more hours with the introduc-tion of the 11-hour day.[32]

Turkish workers eventually achieved partial success when, after repeated delays, a labor law was passed in 1936. The law proved to be more a mechanism to keep labor under control, however, than one to bring benefits to workers. Though it did not legalize unions, the right to strike or to assemble in public, or minimum wages, it did establish a 56-hour week in many branches of industry.[33]

Given the extremely low level of wages and the long hours of work, the surplus value extracted by the state and the national bour-geoisie increased dramatically during this period, intensifying the exploitation of wage labor. Even the generally conservative figures pro-vided by the state attest to this fact: "According to our calculations," an important publication of the State Institute of Statistics concludes, "the rate of value added has increased very rapidly in this period [1935-41], such that while this rate was 172 percent in 1932, it has risen to 318.2 percent in 1939."[34]

Although wages continued to stagnate throughout much of the 1930s and actually fell during the war years, prices rose consistently, causing sharp increases in the cost of living index for successive years. According to the State Institute of Statistics, between 1938 and 1944 the cost of living index in Turkey's two largest cities increased by 330 per-cent (Ankara) and 339 percent (Istanbul).[35] Thus, the workers' purchas-ing power even for such bare essentials as food was significantly reduced, and the consumption of many basic food items dropped sharply.

According to Rozaliev, Turkish workers were able to purchase only the equivalent of 2,180 calories in food per day, whereas the mini-mum amount of energy expended by workers in industry is between 4,000 and 5,000 calories, depending on the type of work. Thus, no mat-ter how inflated the official figures on "the minimum standard of liv-ing," says Rozaliev, the Turkish worker clearly consumed only half the calorie intake that is required to maintain normal functioning.[36] Under these most desperate conditions the workers struggled to survive. There was widespread malnutrition; many faced the daily threat of starvation that often resulted in early death.

Not only was industrialization under the state-capitalist regime achieved through the superexploitation of wage labor (by means of the appropriation of surplus value from workers by the state and private capital), but a very substantial portion of the state's revenues was also derived, through taxation, from workers and peasants. Corporate, inheritance, excise, and other taxes paid by the rich dropped from 46.3 million Turkish lira in 1923 to 43.7 million 1939, but taxes paid by the laboring masses (mainly income and consumption taxes) increased more than fivefold from 25.9 million in 1923 to 140.6 million in 1939.[37] Coupled with rising prices and declining wages, this burden further accelerated the impoverishment of workers, more of whom sank into destitution.

Turkish workers remained weak and largely unorganized because of the repressive nature of the state against labor organizations and agitation. Attempts to bring together broad sections of the workers under a national confederation of trade unions and labor organizations were unsuccessful; those that did succeed somewhat were soon brought under state control and supervision. The political strength of the proletariat, under the repressive rule of the regime, was insufficient to challenge the dominance of the state and private capital in order to advance its own class interests. It was not until the 1960s, and especially during the 1970s, that labor became an organized force that could play an important role in Turkish politics.

External Contradictions

Although Turkey's state-directed economic expansion took place within the framework of a semi-independent national economy, it did receive some aid from external sources to assist its development during the 1930s. Before World War II an antagonism between the state and foreign interests over the policy of nationalization of foreign firms could have developed, but in most cases full compensation was paid at the time of nationalization. Nor did external economic aid pose any significant problem to the Kemalist regime in the prewar period, largely because such aid, though valuable at the time, made up only a small portion of the national budget allocated to industrial development, and the terms of the aid provided by the Soviet Union (the main source of external aid to Turkey at the time) were very favorable to Turkish industrialization.

Beginning in 1934 Turkey's relations with Germany substantially improved, leading to the granting of credits by German firms and increased trade between the two countries. With the increase in trade (which accounted for up to 50 percent of total Turkish foreign trade in the 1930s), Germany was in a favorable position to influence Turkish economic policies.[38] In 1938, just before the outbreak of World War II, a preliminary agreement for a German credit of 150 million German marks was reached, although because of the war it never went into effect.[39]

Despite close relations with various countries, the Kemalist regime throughout the 1930s maintained a policy of nonalignment, which protected its independence and enabled it to implement its development project. With the outbreak of World War II, however, Turkey increasingly fell subject to outside pressures—pressures that would threaten its independence, put a halt to its industrialization program, and impose the adoption of a war economy.

The danger to Turkey's continued state-capitalist development immediately following the war came from those external forces which had emerged victorious, in particular the United States. It was the latter's worldwide expansion in the postwar period that brought about the incorporation of Turkey into the Western orbit as a strategic ally against communism and national liberation struggles in the Middle East.

The first sign of long-term U.S. involvement in Turkey came in 1946 with the granting of a loan, the first installment of which was $25 million. By 1949 U.S. economic "aid" to Turkey reached $181.7 million, and by 1952 it totaled $351.7 million.[40] The United States further strengthened its ties with Turkey by extending military "aid" through the Truman Doctrine, signed into law in mid-1947. The initial $100 million of military aid in 1948 reached $447 million by 1951 and $687 million by 1952.[41] During the whole period 1948-52 total U.S. aid to Turkey topped $1 billion.

Overall, the late 1940s marked a new stage in Turkey's postwar political economy. This period witnessed the final phase of the struggle between the Kemalist bureaucracy and the landlord-comprador interests who, with increased financial and political support provided by the United States, managed to capture state power.

With the coming to power of the landlord-comprador-controlled Democrat Party in 1950, Turkey embarked on a path of development qualitatively different from the one it had followed earlier under the state-capitalist regime. During the decade of the 1950s, the new regime, through its tightening connection with the United States, consolidated Turkey's place in the world capitalist system, thus marking the beginning of an era of Turkish dependence as a satellite of the United States.

POSTWAR REINTEGRATION OF TURKEY INTO THE WORLD ECONOMY

Shortly after the Democrat Party took office in 1950, the new regime began a process of dismantling the national economy built up during the 1930s. Its main objective was to transfer state enterprises to the private sector. Thus, many state enterprises were put up for sale, with their services, raw materials, power plants, and transportation facilities offered to private entrepreneurs at less than the market price.[42]

Despite extensive state subsidies to private capital, however, "Turkish entrepreneurs did not invest in heavy technologically sophisticated industries."[43] Partly in response to the limited growth of local private capital in industry, but largely because of its close links with foreign capital, the DP regime drew up a foreign investment law so favorable to overseas capital that it was later to throw many of the key branches of Turkish industry into the hands of the transnational monopolies.[44]

The penetration of foreign capital into Turkey and its close relations with Turkish capital in a number of key industries meant the gradual integration of the newly emergent industrial bourgeoisie into the worldwide production process. Foreign capital was concentrated in the raw materials (petroleum) sector; the United States accounted for most of these investments. The amount of foreign investment in Turkey from 1951 to 1963 stood at 1.9 billion Turkish lira; the United States accounted for 64.5 percent of the total, Britain for 24 percent. Petroleum investments alone during an even shorter timespan (1954-63) totaled more than 1.5 billion lira—four times the amount of all other investments combined—with the United States accounting for 70 percent of the total and Britain for 28.8 percent.[45] The concentration of foreign investment in the petroleum industry accelerated the denationalization process by transferring this vital sector of the economy from state ownership to private (foreign) capital. As a result, Mobil, Shell, Esso, Caltex, and a number of other major oil companies came to own large shares in the Turkish petroleum industry.[46] This was also the case in a number of other key industries, such as rubber and tires, fertilizers, chemicals, electrical goods, food processing, and assembly.

During the 1960s foreign investment in Turkey grew at a much more rapid pace than it had during the previous decade; from 1960 to 1968 it amounted to 551,920,845 lira, and the profits transferred abroad by foreign corporations between 1965 and 1969 alone totaled 232,598,315 lira.[47] Throughout the 1960s and beyond, government policy reflected the interests of foreign capital and of local landlord-comprador interests who had consolidated their economic and political power during the previous decade. Thus, denationalization of the Turkish economy continued unabated. Major state enterprises continued to be transferred to foreign and local private hands. This process accelerated the expansion of foreign and local private capital. The most important of these transfers were in mining (especially chromium), iron and steel, manufacturing, and raw material processing. While in the 1930s the extraction of Turkey's minerals wealth had been monopolized exclusively by the state, by the mid-1950s—and especially after 1960—foreign and local private capital were allowed and encouraged to enter this field.

The process of foreign penetration into Turkish industry in the 1960s was further accelerated through joint ventures with local private and state enterprises, as the neocolonial rulers in Turkey "acceded to the demand that foreign capital in the mixed companies should be 60-70 percent and more, instead of the 49 percent stipulated by Turkish law."[48] This meant a more thorough integration of a large section of the national industrial bourgeoisie into the dependent economy, and a gradual transformation of a section of the traditional compradors into a dependent industrial class with direct ties to the transnational monopolies. The Turkish economy had effectively been turned into an appendage of the transnational-controlled world capitalist economy.

Foreign capital was not the sole beneficiary of the open-door policy pursued by the neocolonial regime. The 1950s was also a period of local capitalist expansion in commerce, industry, and agriculture.[49] This expansion, however, took place within the framework of an economy dependent on the West. Its beneficiaries were, first, the Turkish compradors, who in addition to their traditional role as agents of foreign capital were increasingly turning to industry through joint ventures with transnational monopolies; and second, the big landowners, who through the mechanization of the agrarian sector became part of the process of capitalist transformation in Turkish agriculture. In some regions of the country the exploitation of wage labor thus increasingly became the dominant form of surplus extraction.[50]

The 1950s was a period of the most unprecedented expansion in business activity in recent Turkish history. Prominent Turkish capitalists like Vehbi Koc, Danis Koper, Uzeyir Avunduk, and Y. Selek built their fortunes during this period. Free from government regulations and national obligations to which they had generally been subjected during the planned economy phase of the earlier period, the Turkish compradors now had free reign to increase their wealth through industrial production. Now in the hands of comprador interests tied to foreign capital, the state was no longer an agency committed to the protection of national capital against the transnational monopolies. Thus, sections of the local capitalist class whose interests were antagonistic to those of foreign capital either went bankrupt and became incorporated into the dependent economy, or were driven to the margin of existing native industry.

This was also the case in the agrarian sector. Whereas earlier credits provided by the state were officially at least intended to reach the small farmers, now, with the outright control of state power by compradors and landed interests, large sums of money and credits were channeled directly to the big landowners. As a result, thousands of middle and small farmers were driven to bankruptcy, losing their land to big landowners and joining the ranks of the rural unemployed and underemployed or migrating to urban centers in search of work. This meant that an even larger area of cultivable land came under the control of big landowners who were able to further increase their wealth.

The deep-seated contradictions of the neocolonial regime in Turkey began to unfold after the mid-1950s. While the externally-financed dependent economy had brought enormous wealth to a handful of landlords and compradors, it had brought misery and ruin to the great mass of the people. Small and medium businesses were driven to bankruptcy; peasants lost their lands and filled the ranks of the unemployed and underemployed; and workers were exploited, paid below-subsistence wages, and driven to the depths of poverty. Rampant inflation, growing unemployment and the burden of ever-increasing taxes further reduced the purchasing power of the masses during the latter half of the decade.[51]

With the general stagnation of the economy and enormous military expenditure, the burden of debt, the continuous trade deficit, and the resultant balance of payments crisis, as well as the adoption of austerity measures imposed by the IMF, Turkey entered a period of deep economic crisis.[52] The government's IMF-engineered "anti-inflationary" policy, which enforced the devaluation of the currency, further worsened the balance of trade and the balance of payments. In the absence of any favorable change in the relative prices of imports and exports, the devaluation of the lira meant that Turkey would now pay more for its imports, receive less for its exports, and fall deeper into debt.[53]

The economic situation continued to worsen throughout the latter part of the 1950s; from 1958 on it began to affect large segments of the population, especially in the cities. Inflation had not only eroded the small gains made by workers over many years, but also lowered the standard of living of those on fixed income.[54] In addition, the unemployment situation had worsened and shortages had become widespread.

Faced with an economic crisis that was rapidly turning into a social and political one, the regime resorted to repressive measures to remain in power. As the criticism against the government increased, so did the level of repression. Mass arrests; shutdowns of newspapers and publishing houses; banning of political parties, meetings, public assembly, and demonstrations; and the declaration of martial law, did not stop thousands of workers and students from demonstrating against the government. The stage was thus set for the military to move in and, in a last-ditch effort, to preserve and protect the neocolonial capitalist order. Thus, a military coup on May 27, 1960, brought to an end a decade of civilian rule under the Democrat Party, which was no longer able to contain and diffuse mass discontent engendered by the contradictions of the neocolonial political and class structure.

The maintenance by the generals of the existing social order on behalf of the dominant classes thus meant the continuation and eventual worsening of the economic crisis throughout the 1960s. The Turkish economy found itself in a more critical situation at the end of the 1960s than in any previous decade. As denationalization continued, it came to serve the interests of expanding foreign and local private capital; deficits in trade, increased military spending, and the resultant budget deficits led to a crisis in the balance of payments. This, in turn, led to more external borrowing, which exacerbated the problem of foreign debt and debt servicing.[55]

These problems, coupled with the worsening inflation and unemployment situation, led to a general crisis in the economy, which soon began to affect most severely the condition of the working class and the peasantry—in a word, the laboring population.

The role of the workers in the downfall of the neocolonial regime of the 1950s was sufficiently important to win them concessions from the military commanders who overthrew it in May 1960. These concessions, such as the right to strike, were written into the new constitution. Using their newly attained rights, workers began to form many new trade unions and pressed their demands for the implementation of the reforms promised under the new constitution.[56] Two hundred new trade unions were formed in the early 1960s, bringing the total number of unions to 432 in 1960, and to 737 in 1970. While union membership stood at 283,000 in 1960, it increased to 2,088,219 in 1970.[57]

Workers' struggles grew and intensified throughout the 1960s as the level of organization and consciousness of the working class reached new heights. A new stage in the development of the workers' movement began at the end of 1961, when 200,000 workers demonstrated in Istanbul, demanding an end to unemployment, the right to strike, and a law on collective bargaining. This demonstration, which included union delegates from 29 provinces, was the biggest ever in the 40-year history of the Republic. In 1965 more than 6,000 miners went on strike and staged demonstrations in Zonguldak. In 1966 textile workers in Izmir went on strike for two months. In 1968 workers at the Derby rubber factory carried out the first factory occupation in Turkey.[58] Founded in the early 1960s by twelve independent trade unionists, the Workers Party of Turkey (WPT) played an important role in these strikes and demonstrations, and through its links with numerous independent unions helped elevate these struggles to a more political level. The WPT-initiated fight against yellow trade unionism resulted in victory with the establishment in 1967 of the Confederation of Revolutionary Trade Unions (DISK), which became a rallying point for class-conscious workers and trade unionists and progressive organizations throughout Turkey.

In June 1970 more than 100,000 workers in Istanbul and Kocaeli stopped work in 135 factories, protesting an attempt to amend the law governing unions so as to weaken the trade union movement. In the demonstrations that followed, bloody clashes took place between the workers, the Army, and police throughout Istanbul. The right-wing government of Demirel was able to control the situation only by declaring martial law.[59]

The economic and social crises of the late 1960s and early 1970s, which led to a renewed crisis of the state, in effect constituted a new phase in the prolonged crisis of the neocolonial system installed in Turkey in the early 1950s and reinforced following the military coup in 1960. With the increase in the level and intensity of the urban class struggle during the 1960s, and especially toward the end of the decade, the working class and the popular forces came to threaten openly the rule of the neocolonial state with massive social insurrection.[60] Seeing its interests threatened by the developing revolutionary situation, the Turkish capitalists—acting with the support and backing of the Western powers—moved to block this process with renewed military intervention. Thus, in March 1971, in a period of economic and political crisis and social unrest that threatened the survival of the neocolonial state, the generals took full control of the state apparatus in a second military coup.[61]

During the 1970s the condition of the working class worsened, as the rate of exploitation by the mid-1970s increased to over 400 percent. Real wages dropped by more than 56 percent between 1977 and 1980. Unemployment, too, reached disastrous levels during the 1970s, especially toward the end of the decade; by 1978, it had reached 3.5 million, or 20 percent of the labor force, according to the Organization for Economic Cooperation and Development, while official Turkish government estimates were close to 7 million.[62]

The workers responded throughout the 1970s by staging mass strikes and demonstrations, factory occupations, and open confrontation with the police and armed forces. Between 1970 and 1980 there were 1,171 strikes, involving 296,904 workers and 19,520,208 lost workdays—increasing from 72 strikes in 1970 to 227 strikes in 1980, and from 220,189 lost workdays in 1970 to over 5.4 million lost workdays in 1980.[63]

In September 1976 a general strike was called, demanding the elimination of the State Security Courts. In May 1977 40,000 metalworkers belonging to the Metalworkers Union (*Maden-İş*) began a historic strike that lasted eight months and ended in victory. In March 1978 more than two million people took part in a two-hour general strike called by DISK. On May Day 1977, and again in 1978, more than half a million workers marched to Istanbul's May Day Square for the largest May Day rally in the capitalist world, with hundreds of trade unions and national and local organizations participating in these demonstrations.[64] In December 1978 nearly 30,000 people from over 50 different organizations marched against martial law in Izmir. In January 1979 all trade unions affiliated with DISK were joined by tens of thousands of teachers and working people when nearly one million workers stopped work throughout the country to take part in this successfully organized action. The struggle of the working class continued to intensify during the remainder of the decade, as thousands of workers at Maysan, Renault, and other nearby factories in Bursa clashed with military police.[65] Strikes, factory occupations, protests, and demonstrations continued in early 1980, when workers in Izmir occupied the state-owned Taris thread factory for a month. Thousands of troops stormed the plant and broke up the occupation. A few days later, a two-day strike by 50,000 workers was called to protest the brutal action by the army.

The economic and social crises of the late 1970s accelerated the working-class and people's struggle by the end of the decade. Alarmed by the growing workers' movement and the maturing revolutionary situation, the Turkish capitalists once again turned to the military for a way out of the crisis and to avert a possible civil war. Thus, in September 1980, a third military coup, led by pro-NATO generals, imposed yet another military dictatorship.[66]

The leaders of the coup dissolved the National Assembly and declared martial law in all 67 provinces. All democratic rights were abolished, as people were searched at gunpoint in buses, at public gatherings, in the streets. Homes were entered without search warrants and family members taken away in army trucks. Those resisting arrest were taken to torture chambers and severely punished. Imprisonment, torture, and summary executions became the order of the day.

In the decade since the last coup, Turkey has continued to fulfill its neocolonial functions as a reliable NATO ally of the United States. Turgut Özal, a former official of the World Bank and the head of the reactionary Motherland Party, is the current prime minister.

As the economic crisis worsens and popular resistance builds against the repressive puppet regime, it is only a matter of time until all the laboring masses of Turkey mobilize and rise up to take power through a popular social revolution now in the making.

CHAPTER 8

THE ROLE OF THE STATE IN DEVELOPMENT IN ASIA: THE EXPERIENCE OF INDIA

Vast areas of Asia were colonized by Western powers until the middle of the twentieth century. British and European imperialism plundered these regions at the height of their empires. Through their presence in the area, they effected major changes in the social and economic structures of the societies of Asia they came to dominate.

Feudal relations of production were introduced in Spain's Asian colony, the Philippines; the slave mode was introduced and despotic rule was reinforced in Java and other parts of colonial Indonesia by the Dutch; and capitalism made headway in British India and British-controlled parts of Southeast Asia. Although not formally colonized, China, too, came under the influence and control of the Western powers, as traditional forms of exploitation were reinforced by the link to Europe and other centers of Western imperialism.

Before the arrival of colonial and imperial powers, many Asian societies evolved within the framework of an Oriental despotic state where the Asiatic mode of production was dominant. With the expansion of Europe to remote corners of Asia, these societies came into contact with and were transformed by different colonizers. Thus, the results in the British colonies were different from those in colonies held by Spain, Holland, France, or other colonial powers. While today the remnants of semifeudal relations are the product of an earlier phase of colonial transformation, capitalism and capitalist relations were introduced in later periods of imperial expansion in Asia.

This chapter provides an analysis of the development process in Asia's largest and most populated capitalist state, India. Following a brief outline of the mode of production and social formation in India in the precolonial period and during British rule, we examine the political economy of development in modern India since independence and draw some conclusions on the unfolding social, economic, and political contradictions that are setting the stage for a major social transformation in that country that is to come in the period ahead.

HISTORICAL BACKGROUND

Before the arrival of the British, land in India did not belong to any private landlord; the state was the supreme owner of the soil. The central authority, the king, delegated to some persons the right of *zamin*, or the right to collect revenues for the state. The *zamindars* were intermediaries between the communal villages and the state, and had no rights over the land. In return for their function as tax collectors, the *zamindars* were given a share of the taxes they collected. The absence of proprietary rights in land thus hindered the accumulation of wealth and the development of social classes on the basis of ownership of the means of production.[1] From the late sixteenth century onward, however, the *zamindars* had the right to sell their *zamindari* with the approval of the state, but were unable to acquire proprietary rights over the land.[2] Such prescriptions for the mode of surplus extraction made the nobility in pre-British India a class dependent on the state.[3]

During the eighteenth century large portions of India came under the control of France and Britain. By the 1740s the French had gained access to a number of key port cities of India, including Mahe on the western coast, Pontichery, Karikal, and Madras, as well as cities around Calcutta on the eastern coast. The acquisition of these territories facilitated the expansion of French trade and economic influence in the region for nearly a century.[4]

Following Britain's political control of India in the latter part of the eighteenth century, the *zamindars* emerged as an independent class with full rights in the ownership of land. In some parts of India, such as Bengal, the British decreed that the *zamindars* were to be considered landlords, thus creating a class of large landowners with inheritable ownership rights in the land. Elsewhere in India (e.g., in the south), the British considered the peasants to have ownership rights in the land and collected taxes from them directly. As a result, this section of the country saw the development of the small landholding.

During the course of the nineteenth century, market forces led to an increasing concentration of wealth and gave rise to a large landowning class on the one hand, and renters, sharecroppers, rural laborers, or urban proletarians on the other. British entry into India accelerated the activities of merchants, as well; they were to become the intermediaries through whom the British would control the local economy. Engaged in import-export trade and incorporated into the world capitalist system, these merchants became the equivalent of the comprador bourgeoisie. Through both the landlords and the compradors, who together constituted the local upper classes (tied to a weakened central state), the British colonialists were able to preserve the existing order and protect and advance their interests.[5]

While the domination of a class of landlords in the countryside ensured the development of feudal or semifeudal relations of production in agriculture in some parts of the country (and the emergence of capitalist relations through wage labor in other parts), the growth of merchants' capital led to the development of an urban commercial economy tied to Britain through international trade.[6] As trade with Britain increased, and the demand for Indian goods grew, local capital expanded into crafts, textiles, and industrial production. This gave rise to a renewed expansion of local manufacturing industry and with it the development of a national industrial bourgeoisie that came to be seen as a competitor of British imperialism. This prompted Britain to take steps to crush Indian industry and turn India into an appendage of Britain's colonial economy.[7] Antagonism between the British and local industrial capital led to the national bourgeois alliance with the peasantry to throw off the British yoke through the independence movement.[8] Much as in North America, but unlike the situation in Latin America, the national bourgeois forces were able to consolidate power and capture the leadership of the movement in a victory over the British. By the late 1940s they installed a state committed to the development of local capitalism in India following independence. Given the relatively weak position of the national bourgeoisie, the victorious national forces were able to utilize the powers of the state and establish a state capitalist regime to assist the accumulation of capital by the Indian bourgeoisie.[9]

THE POSTINDEPENDENCE DEVELOPMENT OF INDIA

In the period following independence in 1947, the state played an important role in accelerating the development of capitalism in India.

This is because the Indian bourgeoisie was too weak to initiate a large-scale industrialization process on its own; it needed protection and aid from the state to expand production and thereby the accumulation of capital.

The Role of the State in the Industrialization Process

Pointing out that "The state has played a crucial role in India's industrial development," Paresh Chattopadhyay states that "The Indian bourgeoisie who, on the whole, had led the movement for national independence, wanted to carry India along an independent capitalist path."[10] "However," he adds:

> without a strong industrial base, this was out of the question. This bourgeoisie, perhaps the most mature in Asia outside of Japan, was fully aware that the successful implementation of such a strategy could not be the work of individual capitalists in India, given the enormous backwardness of the state of capitalism in the country. That is why it envisaged for an independent India with active intervention by the state in the economy in the interests of the *capitalist class as a whole*.[11]

This process was unleashed by the historical transformation of colonial relations with Britain, which led to the formal independence of India. But the nature of postindependence developments in India was the result of the leading role played by the Indian national industrial bourgeoisie in the independence movement itself. Thus, as A. I. Levkovsky points out:

> In India the changes in political life in 1947 were profound and fundamental, though highly specific in class content; political power passed from the hands of foreign monopolists into the hands of the domestic bourgeoisie. . . . Once political power was wrestled from the hands of the British imperialists, national capitalism, whose normal, all-round functioning had been "cramped" and distorted under the colonial yoke, acquired the objective opportunity of "straightening out its shoulders" and gradually altering the socioeconomic structure of society in accordance with its own class interests.[12]

The active enlistment of the state by the Indian capitalist class had begun even before independence in 1947: "During the closing year of the Second World War," writes Anupam Sen, a blueprint for the industrialization of India after the War—known as the Bombay Plan—was drawn up by a few industrialists headed by Tata and Birla, with this purpose in view. The plan called upon the state to play an active role in laying the groundwork for the future industrialization of India.[13]

"The 'Bombay Plan,' also popularly called the 'Tata-Birla Plan'," A. R. Desai explains, "urged that the state should take an active interest in the economic reconstruction of the country":

> The plan categorically stated that the state should evolve and expand the public sector as an important instrument for building the economy that had been smothered by the British rulers, and for leading it to prosperity along a path of capitalist development. The plan not only proposed that government should provide an umbrella under which the Indian capitalist class could undertake development but also urged, since the capitalist class did not have the means to undertake certain vital economic activities itself, the government should undertake these and also provide the infrastructure necessary for industrial development.[14]

Following independence, when the national bourgeoisie took power and established itself as the hegemonic class in charge of the state apparatus, the leading capitalists of the country headed by the Tatas and Birlas began to implement their "Plan" by enlisting the state to carry out their industrialization program. This was done through the promulgation of Five Year Development Plans modeled after that in practice in the Soviet Union. By utilizing a "socialist" mechanism to promote capitalist accumulation via planned industrialization, an otherwise capitalist state was thus able to maintain its legitimacy among the masses who had great expectations from it in the aftermath of their victorious independence struggle. State capitalism in India in the immediate post-independence period thus served a dual function: one of social legitimacy and another of capital accumulation without external dependency. The independent capitalist state thus took a number of measures to facilitate capital accumulation via industrialization geared to the future development and strengthening of the national bourgeoisie which would in time develop its own momentum in the accumulation process. To this end, the state made available to private capital "considerable financial resources through its lending institutions, the most important of them being the Industrial Development Bank of India (IDBI), Indian Finance Corporation (IFC), and the State Finance Corporation (SFC)."[15] Moreover, as M. R. Bhagavan points out,

> the state provided cheap transport, communication and social
> infrastructure, cheap basic materials and power that acted as
> inputs into private industry (e.g., steel, chemicals, electric power),
> imposed tariff barriers and bans against imports, and created pro-
> tected markets for the consumer goods produced by private
> industry.[16]

The state-aided import-substitution industrialization pursued in
India during the first two decades after independence resulted in the
establishment of a strong industrial base—in both the state and private
sectors—and led to a significant rise in material production in different
branches of industry. Industrial production grew at a rapid rate, as did
total productive capital in large-scale industries. The most significant
growth took place in capital goods industries. This growth which continued throughout the 1950s and 1960s, led to a steady increase in the share
of industry in the gross domestic product in subsequent decades, such
that while the agricultural sector declined from 51.2 percent of the GDP in
1950 to 33.2 percent of the GDP in 1985, the industrial sector grew from 21
percent of the GDP to over 36 percent during this same period—thus sur-
passing agricultural production by the mid 1980s (see Table 8.1).

The rapid expansion of the biggest industrial groups—such as
Tata, Birla, Burn, and Sahujain—led to an accelerated concentration and
centralization of capital, bringing about accumulation of wealth in the
hands of Indian capitalists whose assets had steadily grown since the
1950s (see Table 8.2).

Growth of Monopoly

"A particular aspect of the growth of the private sector," Chattopadhyay writes, "has been the flourishing of monopoly capital, confirming
at the same time a basic tendency of capitalist development."[17] Thus, as
the already prosperous capitalist groups expanded their operations in
different sectors of the economy during the past several decades, they
began to acquire controlling interest in a growing number of companies
which gradually became incorporated into their holdings. "The concentration of production and capital," Levkovsky argues, indicates "the
accelerated process whereby the big bourgeoisie is growing stronger
and new monopoly groups are emerging from its ranks."[18]

In the fifties and sixties, India's big bourgeoisie had come of age. It
was a heyday for private capital with the drive for industrializa-

TABLE 8.1
Distribution of GDP, by Sector,[a] 1950-1985
(in percent)

Year	Agriculture[b]	Industry[c]
1950	51.2	21.0
1960	50.9	24.4
1970	49.6	28.0
1980	39.6	32.1
1985	33.2	36.2

Notes:
[a]The two sectors do not add up to 100 percent as other sectors are not included in this table.
[b]Agriculture: includes forestry, hunting and fishing.
[c]Industry: includes manufacturing, mining, construction, utilities, transport, and communications, and excludes wholesale and retail trade, finance, insurance, real estate, and business, community, social and personal services.

Sources: United Nations, *Yearbook of National Accounts Statistics, 1958* (New York: UN), p. 104; *1968*, p. 303; *1985*, p. 597.

TABLE 8.2
Total Assets of the Private Corporate Sector, 1955-1976
(in 100 million rupees)

Year	Private Corporate Sector (PCS)[a]		
	PULC[b]	PRLC[c]	Total
1955-56	186.6	84.3	270.9
1960-61	330.1	110.4	440.5
1965-66	506.1	182.4	688.5
1970-71	817.3	313.6	1130.9
1975-76	1306.7	447.0	1753.6

Notes:
[a]PCS = PULC + PRLC.
[b]PULC = Public Limited Companies.
[c]PRLC = Private Limited Companies.

Source: Ranjit Sau, *India's Economic Development* (New Delhi: Orient Longman, 1981), p. 101.

tion, import substitution, and subsidies for public investment. Capital accumulation went by leaps and bounds; concentration was the order of the day. . . .

By mid-sixties, competition among capitals became fierce. Sick, inefficient production units were quickly jettisoned, and the government policy came in handy.[19]

Referring to developments in the late 1970s and early 1980s, Ranjit Sau points out that:

During this phase of centralization, productive investment is not on the agenda of the big bourgeoisie which is bent on grabbing other capitals. This is one of the causes of the present crisis of Indian economy. The intense conflict among the big business houses, and between the big houses on the one hand and smaller capitals on the other is there for all to see.[20]

Examining this process over the past four decades, Chattopadhyay concludes:

At the end of the fifties the four largest groups of capitalists owned 22% of the capital of all nongovernmental public companies. In the mid sixties the top 75 groups of monopolies, owning less than 6% of the non-governmental, non-financial companies, accounted for 47% of all net assets of the latter. At the end of the sixties, the corresponding share of these groups were 8% and 54% respectively. A study in the late seventies showed that taking only the so-called "medium and large" non-governmental, non-financial companies at work, the top 48 companies constituting only 2% of their total number had a share of 31% in their total paid-up capital and about 29% in their total net assets.[21]

Recent data for the top twenty businesses registered under the Monopolies and Restrictive Trade Practices Act (MRTPA) show that the assets of these companies increased from Rs 2,430.61 crores in 1969 to Rs 4,465.17 crores in 1975.[22] Moreover, the two largest industrial companies of this group of 20 had combined assets of Rs 1,768.49 crores in 1975—an amount equivalent to 40 percent of the total assets of the top 20 industrial companies.[23]

The concentration of economic power in the hands of large monopoly groups has continued to grow in the 1980s. Thus, to take two of the largest monopoly groups, "the assets of the Birlas have increased from 90.5 billion rupees in 1975 to 477.1 billion rupees in 1986-1987, and the corresponding figures for the Tatas were 92.4 billion and 493.9 billion rupees."[24]

The concentration of capital is not confined to production alone, however. The process is especially rapid in banking:

> The power of the upper crust of the Indian bourgeoisie stems not only from the concentration of production and capital in the sphere of industrial production; it is amplified tenfold by the concentration of capital and formation of monopolies in the credit-monetary field and in commerce.
>
> In banking, concentration is proceeding very rapidly, which is hastening the ruin of small firms. . . .
>
> [T]he operations of India's banking system had become a constituent part of the circulation of Indian industrial capital, in other words, that it had come to be based primarily on capitalist production and trade and served them. However, the industrial borrowers had achieved a higher degree of "capitalist maturity" than the commercial borrowers: out of the total bank advances to industry, joint-stock companies accounted for 82.4%; wholesale trade, for only 29.7%.
>
> Bank advances had become a very substantial source of capital for the factory industries. . . .
>
> Especially great was the part played by the banks in financing big new joint-stock companies. . . .
>
> The rising strength of the numerically diminishing group of banks thus enables them to make enormous profits.[25]

The development of private industry in the postindependence period, together with the expansion of state enterprises since the 1950s, accelerated the development of capitalism and capitalist relations in India. Together with the development of industry, finance, and services, capitalist relations also flourished in the agrarian sector.

The Development of Capitalism in Agriculture

The debate on the mode of production in Indian agriculture which began in the late 1960s with Ashok Rudra's article "Big Farmers of Punjab," followed by a series of articles in the pages of *Economic and Political Weekly* (Bombay), continued throughout the 1970s, in which such prominent observers of Indian agriculture as Utsa Patnaik, Daniel Thorner, Paresh Chattopadhyay, Jairus Banaji and others took part.[26] Later, in the 1980s, other observers such as Gail Omvedt, expanded the debate to provide a closer look at the transformation of class relations in Indian agriculture and began to examine the impact of changes in agriculture on the class structure of India as a whole, in order to assess the relationship of agriculture to industry and the effects of this relationship on the development of the productive forces and relations of production—i.e., the development of the mode(s) of production in India in *class* terms.[27]

Without going into the details of the debate itself—which initially focused on the conceptual, theoretical, and methodological issues surrounding the definition of capitalist farming—suffice it to say that there emerged in this debate two opposing views on the nature of the mode of production in Indian agriculture: one that characterized it as capitalist and another as precapitalist or semifeudal. To the extent that such precapitalist relations still played an important role in the agrarian sector, to that extent it would hold back the development of capitalism in the urban industrial sector as well, for the two sectors are interdependent. But, if capitalism and capitalist relations were in full swing in the agrarian sector, then the problems associated with stagnation, poverty, and exploitation cannot be attributed to the persistence of backward feudal or semifeudal practices. If this were the case, the struggle in the countryside would not be one of promoting the spread of capitalism, but its overthrow by the exploited masses.

Whatever the merits of this debate on the identification of the nature of production relations in Indian agriculture and its political implications, one thing that emerged clearly was that the overall development of capitalism in India in the decades following independence was having its impact on the agrarian structure as well, such that despite the continued existence of precapitalist semifeudal relations in some areas of the country, capitalism and capitalist relations were spreading in more and more sections of the country and confronting the power of the landlords in the attempt to transform agrarian relations in a capitalist direction. Thus, despite the persistence of precapitalist relations and practices which held back industrialization and rapid capitalist transformation of the agrarian structure, the trends in Indian agriculture were in the direction of increased movement toward capitalism and capitalist relations. It is for this reason that subsequent studies of Indian agriculture began to focus on the differentiation of the rural social and class structure in an attempt to locate the varied sources of capitalist development that included a spectrum of agrarian practices—from capitalist landlordism to commercial agriculture to small-scale private farming.

The simultaneous persistence of semifeudal relations and the development of capitalist farming confronting the preexisting precapitalist production relations and practices is what Levkovsky had identified a number of years ago as the crisis of Indian agriculture. Writing in the mid-1960s, Levkovsky argues that:

> The peasant masses, supported by all the democratic forces in the country and, first and foremost, the working class, seek to resolve the crisis by the consistent and full abolition of feudal landownership and by providing the peasants with land and other means of production. But such a solution of the agrarian problems comes up against the frenzied opposition of the landlords.
>
> The upper crust of the propertied classes, led by the big bourgeoisie, seeks a way out of the situation by encouraging the development of capitalism in agriculture and, specifically, by fostering capitalist landlordism and a rich-farmer economy.[28]

Thus, as a result,

> The power of feudal and semi-feudal landlord elements in the countryside today, as well as the influence of feudal survivals, have been noticeably weakened, but the fight against them has become more acute. The development of capitalism in agriculture is reflected in greater differentiation of the peasantry according to property and class, in the growth of the rich-farmer stratum, and in the increasing use of capitalist economic methods by landlords.[29]

Pointing out that "elements of capitalist enterprise had been gaining strength in agriculture with every passing year," he goes on to argue that

> the share of farming methods transitional to capitalism had been growing, and there had arisen and were spreading (in the more advanced parts of the country) more or less established forms of rural capitalism (in the Punjab, in the areas of intensive farming in the deltas of the major rivers, etc.). Now, however, all these phenomena had become more pronounced and had produced a new quality: the establishment and consolidation of the capitalist mode of production in rural areas.[30]

"It goes without saying," Levkovsky continues, "that the new system had by no means crowded out other forms of farming yet; it was, in fact, curiously intertwined with them."

Nevertheless, this was already, on the whole, a mature, distinct, and developed (although unevenly) capitalist mode of farming in some areas. As for the agrarian crisis, its gravity has been attenuated for a time by land reforms and the existence of some scope for the development of the newly-established capitalist system. It is, however, bound to become more acute when capitalism in the rural areas assimilates what it has encompassed and when its further development calls for the further curtailment (or overthrow under another type of evolution) of the remaining and still active feudal and merchant-and-usurer survivals and for further inroads upon small-scale peasant commodity production.[31]

While it is generally agreed that capitalism has made great inroads into the agricultural sector over the past several decades, it is this "curiously intertwined" relationship of capitalist and precapitalist elements, as Levkovsky puts it, that has prompted Chattopadhyay and others to argue, as recently as in 1991, that is the prime cause of the slow growth of industry and agriculture:

Obstacles to . . . the low rate of industrial growth . . . [and] a faster development of capitalism . . . arise mainly from the fact that, given the exigencies of class struggles in India, the Indian bourgeoisie is incapable of mounting a determined onslaught on the existing pre-capitalist relations, without which capitalism and hence the "internal market" cannot grow at the desired rate. This is, of course, true of the agricultural sector where a slow rate of growth has been associated with the preservation, to a significant extent, of the pre-capitalist relations of production based on the alliance between the bourgeoisie and pre-capitalist elements.[32]

Anupam Sen reaches a similar conclusion with regard to the low level of development of the productive forces, hence growth, in agriculture, but bases his reasoning on the insufficient development of capitalist relations in the countryside, where despite the expansion of capitalism in some regions of the country, the absence of a profit margin higher than that obtained by semifeudal forms of surplus extraction among the well-to-do landowners has been an important contributing factor in the persistence of precapitalist practices that are holding back the development process. Sen writes:

there is no reason why the rich peasants should invest in capitalist farming if their capitalist profit does not exceed the pre-capitalist ground rent (which varies from 40 to 60 per cent of produce) which can easily be extracted from the sharecroppers or the attached farm servants. A farmer would agree to invest an extra amount of capital only when that would give him an extra amount of profit over and above the pre-capitalist ground rent: a possibility if the productivity of the land can be increased substantially in a sudden leap.[33]

But, despite the "Green Revolution" and the techniques and equipment made available by it, "the small size of the average holding," Sen argues, "makes it very difficult for farmers to employ modern methods of cultivation."[34] "Even the rich peasants in the 25-acre and above size group," he adds,

> seldom own land in a single plot: holdings are fragmented and dispersed throughout the village. On these tiny plots the use of small machinery or scientific cultivation is uneconomic, and the best practicable way to maximize income is to lease holdings to sharecroppers or engage attached farm servants.
>
> It may be pointed out in this connection that what owners extract from attached farm servants is more in the nature of pre-capitalist ground rent than capitalist profit. This is one of the reasons why human labor is disproportionately high compared with mechanized techniques in Indian agriculture.[35]

Thus, in this context, it can be argued, as Sen does quite convincingly, that:

> Landowner profits are derived not as a result of increasing labor productivity from more capital investment, but through the payment of barest reproduction remuneration to farm servants, both in kind and cash, and the forcible appropriation of the major part of the surplus produced by them.[36]

Big landowners, who might otherwise gain from the introduction of technological improvements, may, according to Amit Bhaduri, resist such action on purely social grounds:

> Indeed, in certain circumstances, the semi-feudal landowner . . . may be put off from a big improvement because it makes the kisan [peasant] free from perpetual debt and destroys the political and economic control of the landowner over his kisan, even though on

exclusively economic grounds it may be profitable to him.[37]

Moreover, "It is not at all certain whether even on economic grounds he would gain" Sen adds: "the landowner might decide to invest his capital in usury because here the rate of return may be higher than in agriculture."[38]

To the extent the large landowning class, as well as rich peasants, despite continued capitalist encroachments on them, remain intact and constitute an obstacle to further capitalist development, to that extent the potential growth of capitalist relations in agriculture are arrested or slowed, and this in turn may further reduce the growth of capitalism in general, affecting the growth of a wage-labor working class and its potential to wage a struggle against it. Thus, as Prabhat Patnaik points out:

> Where industrialization occurs within a framework of extreme land concentration, and the consequent dominance of a class of landlords over the social and economic life of the countryside, the meagerness of agricultural growth and the widening class and regional disparities in the countryside, which follow from this dominance, keep the large potential rural market untapped for industry. The domestic market remains confined largely to the urban consumers, who, no matter what their absolute numbers are, constitute a small segment of the population. This form of industrialization has a narrow social base, becomes plagued fairly soon with balance of payments difficulties, has little impact upon unemployment and the sectoral distribution of the work force and is altogether of a fragile character.[39]

"As against this," Patnaik continues, "one can think of an alternative trajectory of growth,"

> a pre-condition for which is an attack on landlordism, where industrialization is based essentially upon the potentially vast rural market that comes into its own as a result of rapid agricultural growth with an even regional spread. Such industrialization is socially more broad-based, is more intensive in its use of local resources, and is hence more effective as an antidote to unemployment and backwardness. . . .
>
> A removal of fetters upon agricultural advance constitutes a pre-condition for the economic advance of our society. If the prospects for capitalist industrialization in economies like ours appears limited, the basic reason for it lies in the inability of the

bourgeoisie to remove these fetters upon the release of productive forces in agriculture.[40]

The extreme level of poverty in the rural areas, where upwards of 50 percent of the population live below the poverty line and another 20 percent just on the verge of it, millions of dispossessed peasant families, together with millions of poor agricultural workers throughout the country, have become part of a wage-earning work force in urban industrial areas, thus contributing to the growth and expansion of the working class.

Growth of Wage Labor

The number of wage earners in India doubled between 1951 and 1971—reaching more than 30 million—and kept growing during the 1970s and 1980s, to over 45 million workers by the mid-1980s.[41] The number of workers in industry grew from 5.9 million in 1951 to 10.8 million in 1961 to nearly 14 million in 1971 to over 21 million in 1981—representing 50 percent of all wage earners in India (see Table 8.3). By the late 1980s the number of workers in industry reached 27 million, while wage earners as a whole numbered over 55 million. Within the industrial sector itself, in manufacturing and transport (sectors that are the most dynamic and contain the largest number of workers), whereas the number of wage earners totaled 12.4 million and 4.4 million, respectively, in 1981 (see Table 8.4), by 1989 the number of workers in these sectors rose to 17 million and 6 million respectively. Moreover, workers in the manufacturing sector, now representing over 30 percent of all wage earners in India, reached and surpassed the level prevalent in the advanced capitalist countries.[42]

With the growth of the industrial working class, conflict between labor and capital intensified. The capitalist assault on workers' wages and democratic rights met stiff resistance from organized labor and the trade union movement and led to the radicalization of large segments of the working class, whose demands became increasingly political. Threatened with these developments and fearful of a general social explosion based on a revolutionary alliance of workers and peasants, the state became more repressive; it also opened its doors to transnational monopolies, thus seeking refuge in imperialism.

From State Capitalism to Neocolonialism

Referring to the role of foreign capital in India during the two decades following independence, Levkovsky writes:

TABLE 8.3
Wage Earners,[a] by Sector, 1951-1981
(in number and percent)

Year	Total	Agriculture[b]		Industry		Services		Others	
		N	Percentage[c]	N	Percentage[c]	N	Percentage[c]	N	Percentage[c]
1951	15,859,211	2,316,497[d]	(14.6)	5,929,280	(37.4)	7,613,434	(48.0)	—	—
1961	24,060,299	2,158,995	(9.0)	10,768,563	(44.7)	10,765,402	(44.7)	367,339	(1.5)
1971	30,776,029	2,062,743	(6.7)	13,850,867	(45.0)	14,862,419	(48.3)	—	—
1981	42,465,205	2,187,891	(5.2)	21,157,399	(49.8)	19,119,915	(45.0)	—	—

Notes:
[a]Includes salaried employees.
[b]Includes livestock, forestry, fishing, and hunting.
[c]Percent of all wage earners.

Source: International Labour Organization, *Year Book of Labour Statistics, 1955* (Geneva: ILO), pp. 20-21; *1969,* pp. 92-93; *1979,* pp. 50-51; *1988,* p. 90.

TABLE 8.4

Wage Earners[a] in Industry, by Sector, 1951-1981

(in number and percent)

Sector	1951		1961		1971		1981	
	N	Percentage[b]	N	Percentage[b]	N	Percentage[b]	N	Percentage[b]
Mining	445,133	(2.8)	731,442	(3.0)	789,255	(2.6)	1,132,379	(2.7)
Manufacturing	3,479,991	(22.0)	6,331,397	(26.3)	8,052,587	(26.2)	12,441,447	(29.3)
Construction	434,055	(2.7)	1,070,870	(4.5)	1,229,123	(4.0)	2,257,633	(5.3)
Utilities	279,148	(1.8)	490,684	(2.0)	518,996	(1.7)	974,397	(2.3)
Transport[c]	1,290,973	(8.1)	2,144,170	(8.9)	3,260,906	(10.6)	4,351,543	(10.2)

Notes:

[a]Includes salaried employees.

[b]Percent of all wage earners.

[c]Includes storage and communications.

Sources: International Labour Organization, Year Book of Labour Statistics, 1955 (Geneva: ILO), pp. 20-21; 1969, pp. 92-93; 1979, pp. 50-51; 1988, p. 90.

neither the absolute nor the relative size of foreign investments gives a correct picture of the influence of the foreign monopolies. This influence is actually much greater, since these monopolies operate in key branches of the economy, reflect a high degree of concentration of production and capital, control considerable amounts of Indian capital, possess enormous connections, and have at their disposal the latest technical inventions and engineering personnel.

Nor should it be forgotten that in recent years the foreign monopolies, which have partly reorganized their mode of operation and adapted themselves to the new situation, have been extending their positions at a rapid pace. A substantial part of the development of capitalism in depth in India is represented by them or connected with their activities.[43]

Although British investments in the late 1950s accounted for the bulk of total foreign investments in India during this period, U.S. corporate expansion into the Indian economy posed a serious challenge to British capital even at that time:

American businessmen are both the chief rivals and the allies of the British in India at the same time. The curve of their investments is a rather steeply ascending one, and there are practically no removals of capital. A most important part in extending the influence of the American monopolies in India is played by the state-monopoly measures of the U.S. government (nor should it be forgotten that the International Bank for Reconstruction and Development grants its loans in the interests of American monopoly capital). As a result, not only the rate of increase of American investments, but also their absolute size have, since 1957, been greater than corresponding British figures.[44]

Over the years the U.S. monopolies gradually expanded their operations in India and emerged as a powerful force with the promotion of the "Green Revolution" in the 1960s. Thus, while the British share in total foreign investment in the private sector was roughly 80 percent in 1948, it fell to 48 percent by the mid-1960s; in contrast, the U.S. share in total private foreign investment increased from 4 percent in 1949 to 25 percent by the mid 1960s.[45]

During the 1960s and 1970s U.S. capital made further inroads into the Indian economy—especially in manufacturing, transport, machinery

imports, trade, and banking, as well as in other branches of the economy, including oil refining to process crude oil shipped from the U.S.-
controlled oilfields in the Middle East.

In a series of studies of the Thanjavur District in the State of Tamil
Nadu, in southeast India, Kathleen Gough has found that:

> The imperial bourgeoisie and the Indian monopoly bourgeoisie
> have become more intertwined through joint ventures since Inde-
> pendence. Both have increased their hold on Thanjavur's econ-
> omy, although few of them live there. Largely through intergov-
> ernmental and World Bank programmes, the transnational
> corporations and their Indian subsidiaries have been active
> through further investment in semiprocessing industries, banking,
> trade, transport, and the importation of agricultural machinery
> and inputs. . . .
>
> [T]he medium and small bourgeoisies, like the big bour-
> geoisie, became more closely tied to imperial capital through loans
> and subsidies or through serving as agents for foreign, or mixed
> Indian and foreign, corporations. But while the medium bour-
> geoisie tended to profit from its links to foreign capital, the small
> bourgeoisie often did not. At least partly as a result, the percentage
> of the small bourgeoisie in the total population declined.[46]

Observing the increasing penetration of foreign capital into the
Indian economy and, as a result, the monopolization of its various
branches by foreign corporations, Ranjit Sau writes:

> foreign capital has captured an increasing part of the Indian corpo-
> rate sector. It appears that the Indian bourgeoisie, after surrender-
> ing without a fight an ever growing portion of the corporate sector
> to foreign capital, is taking refuge in the safety of commercial and
> mercantile operations in the form of registered firms. The end
> result is, of course, centralization of capital in fewer hands.[47]

This trend which began to unfold with full speed in the 1960s, continued during the 1970s and 1980s, and today the U.S. transnational
monopolies, along with their Indian capitalist partners, have a dominant position and control the major branches of the Indian economy.

A move from a state-capitalist to a neocolonial comprador capitalist path tied to foreign capital is the typical outcome of a state-capitalist
formation developing within the framework of the world capitalist sys-

tem. India, like many other state-capitalist regimes in the Third World, has not been able to escape from this general rule of capitalist development in the age of imperialism. Its development within the context of the world economy has resulted in massive economic dislocations and crises over the past decade and has further consolidated the grip of collaborationist forces on the state in more fully integrating India into the world capitalist system. This, in turn, has galvanized popular opposition forces in their struggle against the capitalist state and has given new impetus to their efforts to transform Indian society.

CHAPTER 9

THE STATE AND DEVELOPMENT IN
AFRICA: FOCUS ON TANZANIA

To gain greater insight into the process of development and the role of the state in Africa, we turn to the experience of Tanzania during the first two decades following its independence in 1961—in particular, from the Arusha Declaration of 1967, which marked a turning point in Tanzanian politics, to the mid-1970s, when this phase of development came to an end. After a brief outline of the development process in postcolonial Africa in general, we will focus on the dynamics and contradictions of the Tanzanian experiment in national economic development.

THE POSTCOLONIAL EXPERIENCE IN AFRICA

Until the middle of the twentieth century, when most African states won their formal independence, the local African economies were a direct appendage of the colonial center, which controlled the development process in the colonies. The different forms of exploitation and the different class structures that developed in Africa during the colonial era can thus be explained in terms of the dominant mode of production in Europe and its interaction with the prevailing modes of production in the colonies. In this sense, while the precapitalist colonialism of Spain in Latin America and elsewhere produced a legacy of feudalism in the Spanish colonies, the capitalist imperialism of a more developed industrial Europe at a later period produced a qualitatively different result in Africa, where capitalist relations of production began to take root in mining and other branches of industry.[1] The pattern of development that became prevalent in colonial Africa thus evolved according to the dictates of capital accumulation by the colonial empires, resulting in uneven development between the imperial center and the colonies, and also within the colonies. In general, most African colonies specialized in one or a few raw materials for export and depended on the importation from the imperial center of finished manufactured goods.

This classic colonial relationship prevailed in a number of African countries after the granting of formal independence, and led to the restructuring of social-economic relations on a neocolonial basis—that is, the continuation of colonial relations through the intermediary of a local ruling class dependent on and aided by imperialism. This has been the case in various parts of the continent, from Kenya and Uganda in the east to Nigeria and the Ivory Coast in the west, to Zaire, and other countries elsewhere in Africa.[2] As in the colonial period, the main characteristic of these neocolonial states is their heavy dependence on the export of raw materials to advanced capitalist countries and the importation of finished manufactured goods from them.

Elsewhere in Africa, nationalist forces have taken the initiative to lead the newly independent states along a less dependent path. Utilizing the military and state bureaucracy as supportive institutions to carry out their development programs, the petty-bourgeois leaders in these countries have opted for a state-capitalist path that has corresponded well with their class vision of society and social-economic development.

THE POSTCOLONIAL STATE IN TANZANIA

Tanzania gained its independence from British rule in 1961. In a manner similar to that in India, the newly independent state inherited an established colonial bureaucratic structure that had a great impact on the development process in postindependence Tanzania.[3]

From the very beginning the Tanzanian state has played a central role in the economy. Its ownership and control of some of the major industries, its lenient attitude toward the remnants of petty-capitalist agriculture, and its promotion of village collectivism through *ujamaa* agriculture,[4] effected a unique process of "self-reliant" development that is sometimes called "African socialism."[5]

The proclamation of the Arusha Declaration in 1967 is generally seen as a turning point in Tanzania's postindependence political economy. There is, however, considerable disagreement between various observers of the Tanzanian experience as to the real nature and meaning of the process that began to unfold following the Arusha Declaration. On the face of it, the Declaration made explicit the official ideological position of the ruling Tanganyika African National Union (TANU): "the policy of TANU is to build a socialist state." President Julius Nyerere was equally clear on this point, when he proclaimed:

> The Arusha Declaration marked a turning point in Tanzanian politics. The ideology of the country was made explicit by it; also the introduction of "leadership qualifications," and the measures for public ownership, began a new series of deliberately socialist policy objectives.[6]

Sweeping statements of broad ideological principles set forth in the TANU constitution were reaffirmed by the Arusha Declaration with regard to the role and aims of the state:

> it is the responsibility of the state to intervene actively in the economic life of the nation so as to ensure the well-being of all citizens, and so as to prevent the exploitation of one person by another or one group by another, and so as to prevent the accumulation of wealth to an extent which is inconsistent with the existence of a classless society.[7]

These broader pronouncements were accompanied by large-scale nationalization of corporations and banks, including insurance, commercial firms involved in import-export trade, and various businesses in other branches of the economy. Added to this was the concept of "self reliance," primarily directed at the rural agricultural sector through the introduction of *ujamaa vijijini* or "socialism in villages," as it was conceived officially.

While some observers have taken these at face value, based on official declarations of government intent, others have argued that they represent the social project of an ascendant class of intermediate state functionaries who have adopted such socialist rhetoric to legitimize their rule over society. Thus, on the one hand, authors such as Idrian Resnick accept uncritically the position that Tanzania in the post-Arusha period was developing as a "socialist" society and speak of "the transition to socialism along the lines chosen by Tanzania" as one characterized by "impressive strides made toward socialism."[8] "Tanzania's revolution," Resnick writes, "is about liberty, human dignity, collective participation and control, the liberation of southern Africa, socialism, economic development, and political independence."[9] He goes on to argue that:

> The complex framework of Tanzania's socialist strategy thus involved building socialism without a leftwing vanguard ... taking control over the means of production, and reducing inequalities in income and wealth within the broad confines of what appeared to be consistent with material development, and melding the power of those who controlled the state and the party with evolving participation by peasants and workers.[10]

Such an approach, according to A. M. Babu, "is obviously the result of a profound misunderstanding, to say the least, of what socialism is about."[11] Issa Shivji, in a similar critique, goes on to point out the emergence of a "new ruling class" of the "state bourgeoisie" which entered center stage with the implementation of the Arusha Declaration:

> The high point in the emergence of the state bourgeoisie was the Arusha Declaration of 1967 which nationalized important means of production and declared *Ujamaa*, a variant of petty bourgeois socialism, the official ideology of the state. The nationalizations also expressed the end of the hegemony of British capital and the multilateralization of relations with imperialism. The organizational hegemony which the emergent state bourgeoisie had begun to establish with the banning of the trade union movement in 1964, the formation of the new army in the same year after the mutiny and the establishment of a one-party state a year later, now received a further fillip with the consolidation of its ideological hegemony through the Arusha Declaration.
> Although petty bourgeois in its character, *Ujamaa* objectively served the interests of the state bourgeoisie. For the next ten years the organizational and ideological hegemony of the state bourgeoisie reigned supreme while its relative autonomy from imperialism was at its greatest.[12]

Thus, with its origins in the petty bourgeoisie, the new class of state bureaucrats who came to control the state apparatus during the post-Arusha period to the mid-1970s can be said to have reigned over what can best be described as a state capitalist society. As we shall see later, Shivji goes on to point out that, in time, this state bourgeoisie became transformed into a comprador capitalist class and in the post 1976 period became integrated into the world economy, thus transforming Tanzania itself into a neocolonial society.[13]

Although the characterization of Tanzania as state capitalist during the period 1967-76 and neocolonial in the post-1976 period would be an accurate one, as against a wholesale acceptance of the official ideology and state policy claiming affinity to "socialism," it would be instructive to critically examine the concept *ujamaa* agriculture, based on "self reliance," and developments in the industrial sector, with the problems inherited from the colonial period that continued to affect Tanzanian society in the post-independence period.

Ujamaa Agriculture

Focusing on the agrarian sector, after the proclamation of the Arusha Declaration in 1967 the state announced a program for the voluntary collectivization of agriculture through the setting up of *ujamaa* villages throughout the countryside that were to be the basis of Tanzanian socialism. According to David Vale, *ujamaa* was "intended to be gradual, incremental progression toward communal ownership and deployment of productive resources."[14] Moreover, the *ujamaa* approach stipulated that

> decisions on village resource allocation are to be taken through democratic procedures. . . . Ultimately, access to goods, services, and cash income will either be equal (for collective services such as health care) or according to work performed (in the case of money income and private consumer goods such as foodstuffs).[15]

Two important elements in Nyerere's conception of *ujamaa* agriculture were its "gradualism" and its reliance on "local initiative."[16] "The gradualist approach" arose "from both a recognition of peasants' wariness about an immediate full commitment to communal life and the state's limited capability to provide *wajamaa* [village members] with physical infrastructures, services, and directly productive capital."[17] Thus, in planning, and especially in the mobilization of productive resources, it was seen as essential to promote local initiative and self-reliance.

However, since its inception in 1967 *ujamaa*-based collective agriculture has encountered a number of difficulties: "These stemmed in part from the limited organizational and implementational capacities of the Government and the ruling TANU Party. . . . [They] also stemmed from the failure of the *ujamaa* village concept to attract the majority of rural Tanzanians."[18] Moreover, there were further obstacles to the development of Tanzanian agriculture and the success of *ujamaa* as a form of social organization. These were primarily based on the attitudes of the rural masses toward collectivization—attitudes that were a direct consequence of the material (and ideological) condition of the rural masses formed during the colonial period. The lack of enthusiasm among most Tanzanian peasants toward collective initiative can thus be explained by colonial, individualistic, ideological molding. It can also be ascribed to the missing revolutionary element in the transition from colonial rule to independence, which precluded the development of the revolutionary mass political consciousness that we have seen develop during the course of national liberation struggles elsewhere in the Third World (such as in China, Vietnam, Cuba, Nicaragua, Zimbabwe, Angola, Mozambique, and South Africa, among others).

Another threat to the collectivization of the agricultural sector during this period was the petty-capitalist variant of private commercial farming. In this scheme, Vale explains,

> enterprising Africans use the surplus from cash crop sales to acquire land in addition to their patrimony and begin to use wage labor for cultivation tasks. . . . The returns to land, capital, and entrepreneurship accrue to the owner, while his employees are reduced to selling their labor power, with no share in the surplus value they generate.
>
> As cash crop production expands and as population density increases, making arable land relatively scarcer, the economic power of the landowner class increases and that of landless or land-poor laborers declines. The danger is that this cumulative tendency might ultimately develop to the point where the predominance of independent smallholders gives way to a polarized rural society of landlords and the landless.[19]

Developments in the Industrial Sector

In the industrial sector, a large number of nationalizations were carried out immediately following the Arusha Declaration, published on February 5, 1967. "The next day," Andrew Coulson writes,

> Nyerere announced that all the commercial banks in the country would be nationalized. Within the next week eight firms involved in grain milling (seven Asian-owned, one a branch of a large Nairobi company) were also nationalized, as were the six largest foreign-owned import-export houses. All insurance business was

confined to the state-owned National Insurance Corporation, and the government announced that it would buy controlling interests in seven subsidiaries of multinational corporations: two brewery companies, British-American Tobacco, Bata Shoe Company, Tanganyika Metal Box, Tanganyika Extract (a subsidiary of Mitchell Cotts involved in the refining and export of pyrethrum), and Tanganyika Portland Cement. It also promised to take a controlling interest in the sisal industry, although exactly how this was to be done had not been worked out. In all these cases existing commitments would be honored and the government would pay "full and fair compensation for the assets acquired."[20]

Moreover, "In nationalizing the banks and milling companies," Coulson continues, "the state took 100 percent of the assets, while in the case of the manufacturing companies it asked for majority control."[21] Furthermore:

> It took up its option to purchase 50 percent of the shares in the oil refinery, and in early 1970 the President announced that by the end of that year all importing and exporting would be handled by the state. . . . Many other nationalizations and share purchases took place on a smaller or less publicized scale. . . . The main distributors of petrol (Esso, Shell, Agip, and Caltex) offered to sell a controlling interest in their local companies to the government . . . [but] the government decided to purchase shares in only two of the four—Agip and Shell. . . . In less than ten years from the Arusha Declaration, the state had taken a controlling interest in virtually all productive institutions that could easily be nationalized.[22]

Despite these nationalizations, however, the colonial legacy continued to impede (and the government failed to initiate) the development of a new, independent production and management process that would end neocolonial bondage to imperialism and the transnationals.[23] Thus,

> nationalized industries continued to be run by the former investing monopolies on the basis of management agreements. These nationalization measures did not in any way affect private property relations in the country, and, as long as the characteristic neocolonial export-import orientation continued, there was no change in the production pattern. All the nationalized industries were by

law to continue to operate on the "best commercial principles." Through the good offices of the World Bank, the IMF, GATT and other international institutions, the imperialist monopolies continued to oversee and supervise the economy.[24]

As a result, as M. Bhagavan has pointed out, "the Tanzanian government owns 51 percent or more of shares in the industries in which [international] monopolies participate, yet it leaves the entire running of these industries in their hands, letting them fill all the important managerial and technical jobs."[25] "This arrangement may benefit the government temporarily," Bhagavan wrote in 1972, "but in the long run doesn't this mean that the economy and hence the politics of the country will be determined by these capitalist monopolies?"[26] Indeed this is precisely what happened from the mid-1970s on.

According to a local observer at the time, "This awareness, though not widespread, is growing in certain circles . . . [but] some of the top bureaucrats are afraid of discussing this fully, and some don't even understand the implications."[27]

> No thinking in depth has been done [on the part of the authorities] about whether we should invest in heavy or light industries. They think that economic development consists in running the institutions taken over from the colonialists in the same capitalistic manner as before independence. In the agricultural sector, for example, money is invested largely in producing crops that can be exported to markets abroad. It is not seriously realized that for the development of the country the internal markets have to be developed, then an integrated economy involving both agriculture and industry has to be created. It is believed that development is assured if the economy is left in the hands of the technical experts, only making sure that they work efficiently. There is a mystique surrounding the work of these foreign and local experts who are employed by the parastatal organizations like the NDC and the STC, and it is therefore considered unnecessary to have political commissars examining their work.[28]

Obstacles to the economic development of Tanzania in this context lie for the most part in the superstructure of planning and implementing agencies of the state, which has heavily relied on the continuation of past colonial practices. As some faculty members at the University College in Dar es Salaam have pointed out, the training programs of managers and technicians of state organizations like NDC and STC are strongly tied to metropolitan economic institutions and ideology:

> The management and technical training programs of the NDC are
> carried out by Arthur D. Little, Inc., which is an American man-
> agement consultancy firm. . . .
>   The National Insurance and National Banking Corporations
> are together starting an institute to train people in banking and
> commerce. . . . Most of the subjects to be taught will inculcate typ-
> ical bourgeois knowledge. The training relies heavily on British
> concepts and British literature.[29]

The problems encountered in industry and management were
compounded by those of the bureaucracy in general, as well as those
associated with rural collectivism *(ujamaa)* and the agricultural sector in
general. Together, these problems slowed down and in many ways
reversed the policies advanced by the Arusha Declaration in the late
1960s.[30]

Which Way Out of the Crisis?

Faced with these problems, Tanzania during the 1970s found itself with
two distinct alternatives: either to press forward the process of development toward the overall consolidation of *ujamaa* socialism, or remain
indifferent, drawing the nation along the current path into economic
and political crisis that would lead to the restoration of neocolonial
bonds with imperialism and transnational capital. Developments in
Tanzania since the mid-1970s indicate that the Tanzanian state has,
through the logic of its own evolution along the bureaucratic state-capitalist path, become integrated into the world economy and gradually
transformed into a neocolonial state.[31]

The experience of other African countries on the state-capitalist
path (Algeria, Ghana, Zambia, and Somalia) has shown similar results:
independent capitalist development through state aid, under the leadership of a petty-bourgeois technocratic elite, cannot succeed as long as it
remains firmly within the boundaries of the world capitalist system. On
the other hand, other African countries, like Angola, Mozambique, and
Zimbabwe, in which workers and peasants have played an active role in
the struggle for liberation against colonialism and imperialism, have
made strides toward genuine economic and political independence,
accompanied by deep social transformations. With political power in
the hands of workers, peasants, and intellectuals committed to advancing the interests of the masses, these countries have progressed in many

facets of social-economic life, despite the enormous international (imperialist) and regional South African (colonial/racist) encroachments into
their territories.

Whether Tanzania will be able to overcome its problems and
move forward in a progressive direction depends in large measure on
the relative strengths or weaknesses of the different class forces struggling in the context of the present global political-economic situation.

MILITARY RULE AND THE POLITICS OF DEVELOPMENT IN LATIN AMERICA: THE CASE OF PERU

In Latin America the military has for decades played a central role in setting the parameters of national politics and international relations with dominant imperial centers. Often, the military has played a violently reactionary role—as in Brazil, Chile, Argentina, Bolivia, Guatemala, El Salvador, and many other countries of South and Central America—brutally suppressing the people under repressive dictatorships. Such has been the case in countries in the grip of imperialism, where military rule has facilitated neocolonial relations with the imperial center to expand the interests of the transnational monopolies in these countries.

Yet there have been instances when a rival nationalist faction within the military has made a successful bid for political power and captured the reigns of the state, imposing a regime decidedly contrary to the interests of the traditionally dominant, neocolonial class forces tied to imperialism. Peru during the Velasco regime, from 1968 to 75, is a case where military intervention in Latin America has played a role in national politics and economic development entirely different from those seen elsewhere in the region. Before we examine in detail the nature and dynamics of national development in Peru during this period, however, we begin by placing this development in the broader historical context of the Latin American experience, and of the prevailing political and economic realities that gave rise to it.

HISTORICAL BACKGROUND

The outbreak of major global crises during the first half of the twentieth century brought about important changes in the external relations and internal structures of the majority of Latin American states. The disruption of world trade during World War I was later intensified by the Great Depression and by World War II. The decline in foreign trade and foreign capital substantially weakened Latin America's economic ties with the colonial and imperial centers. These changes in the structure of the world economy created economic conditions and led to political changes in Latin America that were to begin the region's strongest nationalist response and largest independent industrialization drive since the early nineteenth century.[1]

These developments subsequently opened for the Latin American national industrial bourgeoisie a period of import-substituting industrialization directed toward the diversification of production in manufactures. International crises of the early twentieth century thus freed Latin America from outright subordination to imperial centers and accelerated its growth toward independent capitalist development. During this period, the state came under the control of the national bourgeoisie, whose interests dictated the development of a strong capitalist state.

The ascendancy of the United States in the Western hemisphere after World War II—a result of Britain's declining economic power and near defeat during the war—effected the interimperialist transfer of control over Latin America from Britain to the United States.[2] U.S. economic expansion to Latin America accelerated during the 1950s as the United States came to rely increasingly on strategic raw materials from abroad. The need for metals and minerals brought about a rapid expansion of U.S. investment in Latin America in subsequent decades.[3]

While extractive industries (e.g., petroleum and mining) continued during the 1950s and 1960s to constitute an important part of U.S. investment in Latin America, by the mid-1960s the pattern of U.S. economic penetration in the hemisphere had taken on new forms. From this point onward, U.S.-based transnational corporations began to penetrate the national industries of Latin America and control the manufacturing sector developed by the local industrial bourgeoisie.[4] As a result, the independent industrialization process initiated in the 1930s by the national bourgeoisie in the more advanced countries of the region was gradually transformed, such that their economies now became an appendage of the world capitalist system dominated by the U.S. transnational monopolies.

Moving them in the direction of export-oriented economies as they fulfilled their role in the new international division of labor, the economic changes effected by this new relationship also required the introduction of political changes. Repressive military rule was imposed to stabilize the new social order, and the "democratic" capitalist state of an earlier period—in Brazil, Argentina, Chile, Peru, and elsewhere—gave way to the authoritarian and repressive neocolonial state followed by a transition to civilian rule orchestrated by the military. Capitalist development in Latin America in the postwar period thus brought about a transformation in the balance of class forces and transferred state power into the hands of comprador elements tied to the transnationals and the U.S. imperial state.

It is in reaction to the subordination of Latin American states by the transnational monopolies, especially those of the United States, that a number of countries in the region—among them Peru—embarked on an independent, nationalist development path, challenging the U.S.'s traditional hegemony over these countries.

MILITARY RULE AND THE ROLE OF THE STATE IN DEVELOPMENT IN PERU, 1968-75

In October 1968, after decades of compliance with foreign capital that had reduced Peru to a mere satellite of the U.S.-dominated world economy, a group of army officers led by General Juan Velasco Alvarado carried out a military coup that was characterized by the new government as the "Peruvian Revolution."[5]

The intentions of the new regime were spelled out in documents prepared by the junta itself for international public relations purposes. In one such document the junta states in quite unambiguous terms that "it is necessary to point out the range and scope of . . . the Peruvian Revolution, both in order to understand its true significance and also to avoid any possible confusion."[6] Quoting excerpts from the "Manifesto of the Revolutionary Government," the document states:

> The Revolutionary Government declares its observance of the international treaties of which Peru is a part, its resolution to remain faithful to the principles of the Christian and Western tradition and its determination to encourage all foreign investments which are willing to abide by the laws and interests of Peru.[7]

However, in late 1968, a controversy developed around the government's decision to nationalize the International Petroleum Company (IPC), a subsidiary of Standard Oil of New Jersey. To some, this action seemed to place the junta on a collision course with the transnationals, making it a challenge to imperialism. The demand for compensation of IPC by the United States did, in fact, bring the junta into direct conflict with the U.S.

> A U.S.-Peruvian confrontation developed over the threatened implementation of the Hickenlooper Amendment, under the terms of which all U.S. government economic aid to Peru . . . would be cut off if IPC was not compensated. Additional pressure existed in the threat to cancel Peru's sugar quota, a move which would have serious repercussions on the country's economy.[8]

These pressures, coupled with General Valdivia's declaration that "the Peruvian government had been threatened by the International Monetary Fund with cancellation of credits amounting to $75 million if Peru did not restore the property of IPC,"[9] led to a tense situation that put the nationalist project into jeopardy.

To calm the fears of foreign investors and to reassure them of the junta's favorable stance toward foreign capital, General Velasco stated in his February 1969 presidential address that "the case of the International Petroleum Company is unique, it is a singular case" and went on to declare: "Wherefore the Revolutionary Government declares before the world that any foreign investor need not entertain the smallest concern."[10] Going a step further, he tried to reassure the world of the junta's position regarding foreign capital, and private investment in general, by placing full-page ads in *The New York Times*, stressing the government's commitment to the "free enterprise system."[11]

Moreover, in a statement delivered at the annual meeting of the International Monetary Fund and the World Bank, the Peruvian minister of economics and finance insisted that the junta's monetary and fiscal measures were aimed at gaining the confidence of foreign investors, and that the projected structural reforms of the regime would offer them even greater possibilities. Maintaining that domestic efforts are insufficient to meet Peru's needs for investment, the minister declared, "we want to make it clear to all the developed countries of the world that the doors of our country are open to foreign investment, with no discrimination whatsoever."[12]

Finally, in an official document titled *Petroleum in Peru*, published by the junta in 1969, the government assured foreign capital that it had no intention of large-scale nationalization of transnational corporate operations and went out of its way to dispel any such fears:

> Many petroleum enterprises operate in Peru and have no problem whatsoever with the state. Among these are important companies such as Gulf Oil, Mobil Oil, Texas Petroleum, Cerro de Pasco, Belco Petroleum, Occidental Petroleum, Chevron and several more. . . . They are aware that no threat exists of massive expropriation, because the Government of Peru understands that foreign capital is a vital instrument of economic and social progress. And it guarantees those investments, as well as any others that wish to be made under similar conditions.
>
> In the mining field, Peru also offers special conditions. Companies such as Southern Peru, a subsidiary of the American Smelting Company, Cerro de Pasco Corporation and Northern Peru have made, and shall continue to make, large investments under full guarantees of stability.
>
> Commercially speaking, giants such as Sears Roebuck lend valuable service to the country and deserve public confidence due to their policy of supporting national industry. In the manufacturing field, General Motors, Ford, Fiat, Volkswagen, Mercedes Benz, and many others, also operate without a cordial relationship deteriorating.[13]

Such pronouncements by the junta with regard to foreign capital led some critics to argue that the Velasco regime represented a new form of neocolonial relations with imperialism, and that the coup of October 1968, a response to the growing peasant revolts of the 1960s, was carried out to neutralize the mobilization of revolutionary forces, thus preventing the possibility of civil war leading to revolutionary change in favor of the laboring masses. The primarily middle class-supported military coup was thus intended precisely to prevent a mass-based social revolution.[14]

Others argued that with the coming to power of the new political forces in the aftermath of the coup, the traditional alliance of the landed oligarchy with foreign capital, lodged primarily in raw materials and extractive industries, gave way to a new alliance of local industrialists with the transnational monopolies in manufacturing industry; the state thereby came in as part of a new tripartite arrangement, negotiating the nature and terms of its ties with imperialism.

Julio Cotler, who agrees with this view, asserts that the military government that came to power in 1968 has brought profound transformations in the economic, political and social life of Peru. Perhaps the central feature of these transformations has been the elimination of what had been in the twentieth century the most important center of economic and political power in Peruvian society—the export oligarchy and the foreign economic interests with which this sector of the oligarchy had been closely associated. In place of this dependent-oligarchic mode of economic organization, the military government is moving toward the full development of modern capitalism in Peru.[15]

Although Cotler considers "the antioligarchic and nationalistic revolutions in Latin America [like Peru's in 1968] as, in a sense, equivalent to the bourgeois revolutions of Europe"[16] (though carried out by the military and not the bourgeoisie itself), he goes on to point out that this change in the severance of ties between the "export oligarchy" and foreign capital linked to it does not represent a break with imperialism, for the new alignment of forces led by the military continue the presence of and relations with imperialism, albeit through a new arrangement that permits the state to participate in local capital accumulation:

> The elimination of the oligarchic-dependent structure goes hand in hand with expanding and strengthening the state, which . . . has acquired an unprecedented capacity to accumulate capital and reach new agreements with international capitalism (in the form of multinational corporations), agreements which form the basis for the joint economic exploitation of the country.[17]

Going a step farther, Anibal Quijano argued at the time that the state's new role in capital accumulation was geared to effecting this change in favor of the local, dependent bourgeoisie,

> both through creating and developing a state economic-administrative apparatus that will serve as an infrastructure for the development of capitalist accumulation in the country, and through putting legal limits on the margins within which the imperialist bourgeoisie can continue to operate here—i.e., by strengthening the position and power of Peru's dependent bourgeoisie so as to enable it to obtain a larger share of the benefits of the accumulation process without its having to break off its fundamental alliance with the imperialist bourgeoisie. As a matter of fact, this is precisely what the present military regime is attempting to do.[18]

This line of argument is also supported by Elizabeth Dore and John Weeks, whose analysis of these developments is based on the changes in the mode of accumulation in Peru during the early to mid-1960s away from agro-mineral and extractive industries and toward manufacturing and other industrial activities.[19]

The expansion of foreign manufacturing investment in Peru during this period, Dore and Weeks argue, effected a shift in favor of industrial production wherein the role of local industrial capital likewise expanded beyond its earlier subordinate position in the economy.[20] But this economic expansion did not translate into political power, as the state continued to be controlled by elements tied to the agro-mineral landed oligarchy. The economically strong but politically impotent position of the national industrial bourgeoisie, therefore, is what prompted it to take political action and capture state power in the military coup of October 1968. Thus, "we interpret the coup of 1968," Dore and Weeks write, "as engineered by the national industrial bourgeoisie, whose power was on the rise, but whose successful advance was blocked by the rule of the grand bourgeoisie [i.e., the landed oligarchy]."[21]

Dore and Weeks conclude that in Peru "the form and role of the state is dictated by the terms of the new alliance between the national industrial bourgeoisie and imperial capital."[22] However, in a step beyond Quijano and Cotler's view that the military aided the national bourgeoisie in fulfilling its "historic mission" of capital accumulation and capitalist development, Dore and Weeks contend that "the coup of 1968 established the dictatorship of the national industrial bourgeoisie."[23]

A similar position, taken by William Bollinger, also argues in favor of characterizing the coup of 1968 as a culmination of the "bourgeois revolution" in Peru.[24] Bollinger writes:

> The central thesis [of this article] is that there has indeed been a bourgeois revolution in Peru, that the Peruvian bourgeoisie has thus fulfilled its historical destiny, . . . and that the military regime which came to power in 1968 is the culmination of this 200-year struggle.[25]

"The military's ideology and program," Bollinger continues, "are unmistakenly those of . . . Peru's national industrial bourgeoisie."[26]

These interpretations of the Peruvian state under the Velasco regime contrast with those put forward by E. V. K. Fitzgerald and David Slater. Though differing in their focus of analysis and interpretation of the Peruvian experience, these authors provide us with an alternative explanation of the nature of the military government in Peru during this period.

Fitzgerald argues:

> Although it is true the arrangement of a new alliance between the industrialists and multinationals in place of the traditional one between the 'oligarchy' and the multinationals . . . might turn out to be the long-run consequence, it grossly underestimates the initial autonomy of the state in the 1968-75 period, almost totally ignores the evident conflict between domestic capital and the state, and plays down the weakening hold of foreign enterprise.[27]

"Although multinationals did not 'lose out' completely in the end," he adds, "they certainly would have preferred Bellaunde or Prado to Velasco."[28]

What was unique about Velasco? Let us take a closer look at the arguments presented by Fitzgerald and Slater, for we believe their analyses of the nature and role of the military in Peru during this period come closer than those provided by the authors discussed earlier to the reality of the situation.

"The main thrust of the economic strategy of the Velasco regime," according to Fitzgerald, "was based upon the expansion in breadth and depth of public enterprise activity so as to take up the task in which the domestic capitalists were held to have failed."[29] In line with this objective,

> The state was to be the center of accumulation in the economy, constructing a new state enterprise sector on the basis of the nationalized export sector, heavy industry, banking, transportation networks and infrastructure coordinated through a national planning system. The new cooperative sector, based on the land reform . . . and the establishment of new *propiedad social* ('social property') firms in the light manufacturing and service sectors, would be coordinated through central state-controlled boards responsible for finance and marketing. The manufacturing sector was to be the spearhead of the industrialization drive, but it was nonetheless to be left to the private domestic industrialists who would be supported by guaranteed markets, import protection, subsidized inputs, cheap credit and fiscal incentives.[30]

"This model," Fitzgerald concludes, "emerged gradually over the 1969-

75 period although the main outlines were clear as early as 1970."[31]

> It amounted to state capitalism as a distinct variant on the capital-
> ist mode of production: the coordination of state enterprise, coop-
> eratives and large private firms from the center, maintaining wage
> relations at the enterprise level but centralizing the accumulation
> of capital and production decisions—an image of socio-economic
> organization naturally preferred by the military.[32]

Slater concurs with this view of the state-capitalist model: in the
"Velasco period, the military introduced a wide series of structural
reforms and launched an ambitious programme of modernization and
state capitalist development."[33] Slater's characterization of the regime as
"state-capitalist" rests on his argument that

> the military, once it assumed state power, attempted to generate the
> necessary conditions for a new phase of capital accumulation. . . .
> The reforms that were introduced, rather than heralding a rupture
> from policies of capitalist development, were aimed at modernizing
> and reorganizing the inherited structure of production.[34]

At the center of the structural reforms introduced by the Velasco
regime was the Agrarian Reform Law of 1969. This law helped transform the agrarian social structure: it "provided for the expropriation
and conversion into co-operative organizations of the coastal export
plantations and the Sierra *haciendas*."[35] Thus,

> An essential objective of the reform measures was the reorganiza-
> tion of production in the agricultural sector, and especially in the
> coastal export-oriented estates; hence, through rationalization and
> increased efficiency it was hoped that greater success on world
> markets would ensure the acquisition of a continuing source of
> foreign exchange. . . .
> Perhaps most crucially of all, since the Agrarian Reform Law
> provided for the expropriation of the means of production hitherto
> owned and controlled by the oligarchic bourgeoisie, the new law, as
> a political and economic measure, was designed to destroy the
> power of this particular social class, and that is exactly what it did.[36]

As a result, class relations in the rural sector were fundamentally
changed such that more and more peasants and agricultural workers
came under the direct control and supervision of the state.

SOME CONTRADICTIONS OF THE
STATE-CAPITALIST REGIME IN PERU

The growing contradictions of state capitalism in Peru under the Velasco regime began by the early 1970s to affect broad segments of the laboring masses unfavorably; the internal and external constraints placed on the regime put the squeeze on the living standards of an increasing number of workers and peasants. As early as 1970 Quijano was able to conclude:

> the workers have continued to pay the heaviest price for the process now under way: unemployment has not diminished, the cost of living has risen so high that Lima is now the most expensive city in Latin America, there has been no compensation either in the form of steady work or raises in wages, and all of this has been aggravated by certain hints that the repression of worker and peasant movements that are pressing their demands will be stepped up.[37]

As the initial popular support for the government began to diminish, the regime resorted to coercive methods to control the population in order to prevent or limit the development of radicalism and class consciousness among the masses. The agrarian reform law, for example, was used as a mechanism to achieve such control in rural areas. "By replacing private landowners with state functionaries and establishing peasant cooperatives," Slater writes, "the land reform was an instrument with which the military hoped to limit the development of radical forms of consciousness in the countryside."[38] Those who did not comply with the state's dictates were dealt with harshly.[39]

Despite efforts to maintain such control, however, "the military's corporatist ideology did not quell the development of more radical forms of consciousness within the dominated classes."[40] This was as true in urban areas as it was in the countryside, where the workers began to assert themselves more and more. "As the parastatal sector expanded, the class struggle would inevitably be 'internalized' within the state as workers came into direct conflict with the government."[41] This led to increased strike activity in all major branches of industry, bringing to a halt the operations of dozens of industrial enterprises throughout the state-capitalist period: "the annual average of days lost through strike action rose from about one million in 1969-73 to over three million in 1974 and 1975."[42]

With increasing pressure from the masses on the one hand and local and foreign capital supported by reactionary forces within the regime on the other, the effectiveness of the government's hold on power was weakened. As a result, the regime's developmental policies during its seven-year tenure in office evolved from an initial "populist" and "nationalist" posture to a conservative, reactionary one on matters of foreign and domestic policy, especially in maintaining order. While pressure by openly pro-imperialist forces within the regime played an important role in pressing for the adoption of conservative policies, external pressure—primarily from the United States—became a key determinant in redirecting the already limited measures of the state.[43] This, in turn, provided an opening to the anti-Velasco forces who finally moved in and seized the reigns of state power, thus ending seven years of nationalist, state-capitalist rule in Peru.

POLITICAL DEVELOPMENTS AFTER 1975

Political developments from the mid-1970s on played a major role in moving the country toward the reestablishment of neocolonial relations with the United States and its transnational monopolies, which were fully restored following the 1975 rightist takeover led by General Francisco Morales Bermudes.

A 1976 report on the internal political composition of the new ruling junta stated that in the year following the ouster of President Velasco Alvarado "reform-minded ministers have been purged and replaced by rightists":

> The latest government shakeup occurred July 17 [1976] when President Morales Bermudez appointed an extreme anti-communist, Gen. Guillermo Arbulo Galliani, as prime minister. Three other progressive ministers were also replaced by rightists at the same time.
>
> The ousted prime minister, Gen. Jorge Fernandez Maldonado, had also served as war minister and head of the army. He headed the ministry of mines under ex-President Velasco Alvarado and was considered one of the principal architects of the program of nationalizing U.S. and other foreign mining and petroleum interests.[44]

"The latest purge of reformers," the report continues, "occurred after the adoption of an austerity program at the end of June [1976], the imposition of a state of emergency, a series of strikes and other manifestations of popular unrest, and an abortive attempt at a military coup by an extreme rightist general on July 10 [1976]."[45] A follow-up report on subsequent political changes in Peru states that"moderately conservative" President Francisco Morales Bermudez "has been warned by rightist elements to go along with a shift to the right or be confronted with an attempt to oust him."[46]

Clearly, such changes were welcomed and encouraged by the U.S. and the transnationals. In early 1976

> the U.S. resumed arms sales to Lima after a long period of refusing to sell arms to a government that was deemed too radical by the State Department. During the last week in July, it was reported that the U.S. banking consortium was satisfied with the austerity measures and was expected to advance the Peruvian government $150 million. The banks in the consortium are Citibank, Bank of America, Morgan Guaranty Trust, Manufacturers Hanover, Chase Manhattan and Wells Fargo.[47]

By late 1976 the rightist move in Peru had gone so far as to participate in the formation of a "triple alliance" with the fascist military rulers in Chile and Argentina: "According to Chilean dictator Augusto Pinochet," read one report at the time, "negotiations are under way for having a summit meeting of the Argentine, Chilean and Peruvian presidents before the end of the year."[48]

The consolidation of the reactionary forces within the new junta and its consistent steps toward the reestablishment of neocolonial political-economic links with the United States thus exacted the heaviest price from the working class and the peasantry. The motto under which the earlier junta ruled—what it called "national progress"—was, of course, a cover to legitimize repression—of workers, peasants, progressive students and intellectuals, and other revolutionary and progressive forces demanding a profound social transformation of Peruvian society. But the openly reactionary junta led by General Morales—which set the stage for the neocolonial regimes that have ruled Peru to this day—could easily dispense with the slogans of the earlier years: the ruling circles in Peru now realize that in the age of imperialism, with a world political economy dominated by the transnationals and the imperial state, no exploiting class can expect to remain in power except through a total surrender to imperialism.

CONCLUSION: THE PROSPECTS FOR
CHANGE IN THE THIRD WORLD

What, then, can we conclude from our analysis of development theory and the development experience in the Third World? What conclusions can we draw from our political-economic analysis of the global development process in the world-historical context? What are the implications of such analysis in assessing the prospects for change in the Third World in the years to come? Some tentative answers to these critical questions may emerge from the following brief observations.

First, with respect to development theory, it is quite clear that a major shift of paradigmatic proportions has occurred during the course of the past three decades. This shift has corresponded to changes in the global political economy, especially in relation to its impact on the Third World. Thus, just as the programs and prescriptions of modernization theory and developmentalism were proposed within the context of the postwar expansion of U.S. imperialism, when the U.S. pushed to establish a neocolonial foothold in the Third World, the critique of developmentalism and the emergence of an alternative, anti-imperialist reformulation of development theory corresponded to the deteriorating political-economic conditions in the Third World during the 1960s and early 1970s.[1]

This was also a period of increased popular insurgencies and movements of national liberation around the world. From southeast Asia—where "development specialists" on the Pentagon and CIA payrolls were mapping out counterinsurgency strategies for the imperial state—to Latin America—where these very same "specialists" were busy devising pseudo-land reform programs to prevent the spread of the guerrilla movement and communist influence among the peasants and thus the emergence of "another Cuba" in the hemisphere—to Africa, particularly in Algeria, Ghana, Tanzania, and other states that had just won formal independence, imperial capital and its political-military arm, the imperial state, came to be identified as the enemy of the laboring masses throughout the Third World. Moreover, it is precisely during this period of worldwide rebellion and revolution across the Third World, which saw the postcolonial or postnationalist collaboration of local ruling classes (landlords and compradors) as allies of imperialism, that the theory of dependence and underdevelopment was forged.

The paradigmatic shift from developmentalism to dependency theory thus took palace at a time when mainstream theories of modernization and development economics could no longer explain the crisis of development in the Third World, and when the structuralist "remedies" applied in various U.N.-sponsored initiatives were officially declared failures.[2] Dependency theory emerged and took center stage in response to "the ideology of developmentalism" and the failed reformism of the U.N. Economic Commission for Latin America.[3]

Still, as was pointed out in chapter 3, new Third World perspectives on development advanced by dependency theory and its numerous variants—those formulated by Frank, Amin, Wallerstein, and others—were short-lived. By the mid-1970s these theorists, and their positions, had come under increasing criticism for failing to examine the class nature of development and exploitation, and thus for being unable to develop a class-based strategy to overcome "underdevelopment." They were torn by the plight of the "wretched of the earth" and moved by the courage and heroism of dedicated revolutionaries, like Che Guevara, fighting to overthrow imperialism and neocolonialism through guerrilla warfare (at the time a prominent strategy of anti-imperialist struggle); yet they were attacked for failing to provide a class analysis of the prevailing social order based on relations of production; for avoiding a discussion of class struggle and ignoring the centrality of the working class in the revolutionary process; and, as a result, for failing to put forth a strategy specifying the type of society and the system that would replace not just imperialism and neocolonialism, but capitalism itself.[4]

Thus emerged Marxist theory and its variants—from classical Marxism to a variety of postdependency "neo-Marxist" positions—to take a prominent place in critical development studies during the late 1970s and throughout the 1980s.[5] Although not fully able to replace the entrenched positions of mainstream development theorists and their dependency and world system critics, which still play a prominent role in development studies and have in fact become part of the mainstream development problematic, the emergence and rapid expansion of Marxist theory among a growing number of critical scholars in the late 1980s signaled the beginning of another paradigmatic shift—away from the dependency theory and toward Marxism.[6]

This brings us to the question, discussed in the second and third parts of this book, of paths of development in the Third World. We have argued that capitalist development through export-oriented industrialization has, on the one hand, effected a shift in investment in favor of the manufacturing sector and thereby contributed to the growth in size of the working class in a small number of neocolonial states in the Third World. On the other hand, the contradictions embedded in this mode of growth and development, which is geared to the maximization of profits of the transnational monopolies and their local collaborating class agents (who are protected by the increasingly authoritarian, imperialist-backed neocolonial state), have made these countries unstable and generated a crisis of legitimacy; an increasingly militant working class (as in South Korea, Brazil, Mexico, and elsewhere) is posing an ever-greater challenge to the rule of the neocolonial state.[7]

In addition to its principal class contradictions based on the conflict between labor and local/transnational capital and a host of adverse consequences for workers—such as long working hours at below subsistence wages, high industrial accident rates, and relative impoverishment[8]—the export-oriented mode now faces a number of other serious problems that will have a great impact on the pace of development in countries that have opted for this path of capitalist industrialization.[9]

In the 1990s these countries can expect to face grave and intensifying problems: First, there is the loss of access to markets in the advanced capitalist countries, as the global rivalry between the major capitalist powers—Europe, Japan, and the United States—leads to the adoption of protectionist measures that will also limit the entry of imports from the export-oriented zones; while the current global recession, which threatens to turn into a bona fide depression, will further exacerbate the problem of access to markets in the advanced capitalist countries.

Second, while wages in Brazil, Mexico, South Korea, Taiwan, Hong Kong, and other export-oriented capitalist countries are very low, they are even lower in Thailand, Indonesia, Malaysia, the Philippines, El Salvador, the Dominican Republic, and elsewhere. With the entry of

China and Eastern Europe into the world economy, through joint ventures and other export-oriented production schemes, foreign investment from the U.S., Japan, and Western Europe will increasingly move into these countries to take advantage of labor costs and investment opportunities much more favorable to the transnational monopolies than those heretofore offered by the above-listed industrializing countries.

Third, and finally, even if this diversion of foreign investment to other countries and the loss of access to the markets of the advanced capitalist countries do not totally bring down the export-oriented model, four other factors closely related to the logic of capital accumulation under capitalism will inevitably halt the export-based industrialization process pursued in these countries: (1) the limited size of the internal, domestic market; (2) the disastrous effects of a drawn-out global recession or depression, from which these countries, being a part of the capitalist world economy, will not be spared; (3) the growing class struggle between labor and capital over wages and profits and its adverse effects on increased capital accumulation, which will drive the local capitalists themselves to move to cheap labor areas elsewhere,[10] as have others in Europe, Japan, the U.S., and other advanced capitalist countries; and (4) the intensified class struggles to end the exploitation of labor may in the end lead to the overthrow of these regimes by the working class.

The economic consequences of a combination of the first three of these problems/eventualities on the countries involved would be as devastating as they are self-evident—manifesting themselves in high unemployment rates, reduced purchasing power, a declining economy, growing trade and budget deficits, increasing debt and debt-servicing, and a big drop in the standard of living.

In other Third World neocolonial countries serving imperialism's agro-mineral and raw material interests, such as Zaire, Indonesia, Bolivia, Guatemala, and other countries of Central America and the Caribbean, the situation is even worse, with hunger, malnutrition, and poverty rampant. Facing the appalling conditions of life under neocolonial exploitation and repression in both export-oriented industrializing and agro-mineral, raw material-exporting countries, workers, peasants, and other laboring people have been struggling to change these societies through a variety of means, including revolution.

In some countries, elements from among the so-called "middle classes"—such as nationalist junior army officers—have been successful in taking advantage of mass discontent and mobilizing the masses through nationalist rhetoric; they have captured the leadership of the national liberation movement in order to prevent a socialist revolution.

With the successful overthrow of the existing neocolonial regimes in some Third World countries, the petty-bourgeois forces leading these movements have set up state-capitalist regimes in their place, proclaiming to have instituted a people's government that will guide the entire nation to prosperity through independent national development. As our case studies have shown, however, these states have in fact promoted capitalist development based on the exploitation of the laboring masses for the profits of a new class of bureaucratic capitalist rulers. Often resembling fascism in their nationalist authoritarian rule, these states have been especially harsh in crushing the labor movement in the name of national unity and national security against foreign states and what they term "foreign ideologies."[11]

Our case studies of regimes that have in the past opted for the state-capitalist path—Turkey, India, Tanzania, and Peru—show that the forces in power, faced with immense internal and external contradictions, have, with a few exceptions elsewhere in the Third World, been unable to sustain their hold on the state apparatus for any extended periods of time; they have either eventually caved in to neocolonial class forces (as in Peru) or been overthrown by the U.S. imperial state from the outside (as in Iran, Guatemala, Brazil, the Dominican Republic, Grenada, and Panama, and as attempted in Libya and Iraq more recently).

In the cases where some state-capitalist regimes have been able to remain in power, the logic of development along the state-capitalist path has, as in Turkey, Mexico, Egypt, and India, led to the development and expansion of capitalism, such that a previously petty bourgeois-controlled state under the rule of middle-level bureaucrats in charge of much of the wealth through public ownership, has come to enrich itself and thus enrich the state functionaries who have later themselves become capitalists. It is in this way, and through a gradual opening to imperial capital, with which they increasingly come to share the national wealth and profits, that the previously bureaucratic petty-bourgeois stratum gradually takes the place of compradors as a fully-developed, neocolonial capitalist class. Thus we find in Turkey the nationalist, state-capitalist regime of Atatürk giving way to the neocolonial regime of Bayar and Menderes, and later Demirel, Özal, and the pro-NATO generals; in Egypt the nationalist, state-capitalist regime of Nasser giving way to the neocolonial regime of Sadat, and later Mubarak.[12]

On the other hand, state-capitalist regimes that have resisted imperialism and defeated internal neocolonial forces and have not evolved in an externally-oriented, neocolonial direction in capital accumulation, but instead have built up an internally-based, national capitalist class, find themselves confronting the logic of capitalist development, the internal contradictions of which are both systemic and inherent to this mode: the growth and development of a working class that is exploited, which in time becomes a revolutionary force setting the stage for intensified class struggles, rebellions, and, ultimately, socialist revolution.[13]

We have argued in this book that in the absence of mass-based popular revolutions in the Third World that place countries on a socialist path, the logic of the capitalist world economy, which leads to the establishment of either neocolonialism or, in response to it, state capitalism, holds no promise of development that would benefit the great majority of the working people throughout the Third World. It is becoming increasingly clear that only through a genuine workers' movement, committed to a thorough social transformation of the inherited capitalist order and the development of popular democratic institutions that ensure the full participation of the laboring masses in the political process, as in the sphere of production and life in general, can an egalitarian society that benefits the masses be built in the Third World.

The problems of development in the Third World are complex and difficult to resolve. No amount of abstract theoretical pronouncements on the remapping of the development project through socialist restructuring of society on an egalitarian basis will guarantee concrete results. Only sustained and cooperative hard work that involves the masses of the laboring population on a grand scale can achieve such a goal.

In this period of social and political turmoil and transformation throughout the world, the building of socialism in Third World countries that have opted for this path will become more and more difficult. In this context, the changes taking place in Eastern Europe and the Soviet Union in the late 1980s and early 1990s, ushered in by the Gorbachev reforms of *perestroika* and *glasnost*, have enormous political implications for the Third World. These internal changes represent a major shift in power relations, which naturally manifest themselves in foreign relations with other states.

Historically, the Soviet Union and, to a lesser extent, the Eastern European states allied with it have played an important role in aiding Third World states in their struggle against imperialism.[14] This has taken the form of aid to rebel forces in various neocolonial societies struggling to overthrow these regimes. Aid to the ANC in South Africa through Zambian channels and to the MPLA in Angola during the anticolonial struggle are two examples of the limited support the Soviet

Union has provided to Third World liberation movements in the past.

In countries where a national, state-capitalist regime has ruled, as in Iraq, Syria, Libya, Algeria, Zambia, Ethiopia, Egypt under Nasser, and India at an earlier period, the Soviet Union and the East European states have provided aid and protection for these states in their struggle against imperialism, ranging from low-interest loans to outright grants, including military aid and weapons systems, in an effort to win them as allies, thus tipping the global balance of forces in favor of the Soviet Union and against Western imperialism.

Finally, Soviet and East European aid to socialist countries, such as Cuba and Vietnam, has been substantial in many spheres of material life: subsidization in the form of raw material supplies, machinery, transport, bilateral and multilateral trade, loans, as well as military supplies to defend them against external aggression. Trade agreements, military pacts, and mutual assistance treaties by the Soviet Union in many fields have thus provided a protective shield to young socialist states struggling to develop along the socialist path.[15]

What the future holds for national liberation movements in neo-colonial states, relations with state-capitalist regimes, and aid and protection to socialist states in the absence of such aid from Eastern Europe and the Soviet Union in the years ahead, is less than clear, while a full assessment of the dramatic events of the past few years will have to wait until more evidence is in. If current trends continue—though they may well be reversed in the Soviet Union and in some Eastern European states, such as Romania, Bulgaria, and Poland—the changes now taking place would have very serious adverse consequences on developments in the Third World. This does not, of course, necessarily signify an end to struggles waged by national liberation movements, or that state-capitalist regimes would be overthrown through imperialist intervention or be transformed into neocolonial ones through the expansion of the power of local comprador capitalists, or that socialist states traditionally dependent on the Soviet Union would become increasingly unstable as they face growing hardships. Nevertheless, all of these are, of course, real possibilities.

It is clear, however, that in the absence of much-needed aid from the Soviet Union and other Eastern European countries, with increasing superpower cooperation in post-cold war international diplomacy and ultimately in other fields as well, and with the decline of the United States as a global superpower relative to its capitalist rivals Europe and Japan in the political as well as economic field, *there exists a growing danger of renewed and more frequent imperialist intervention in the Third World by the United States*—as has occurred in Central America and the Middle

East—in order to safeguard long-established, global geopolitical boundaries, as well as access to foreign markets, sources of cheap labor, and
control over raw materials and other vital resources, such as oil.[16] The
dangers associated with the resurgence of U.S. imperialism, in this
period of decline and disintegration of the U.S. empire, may have a
grave impact on the process of change and development in the Third
World.

In the light of these complicated developments in the global political situation, there will emerge a growing need for cooperation
between indigenous liberation movements, which will have to rely on
their own strengths to wage battle against imperialism and the neocolonial state; so, too, Third World socialist states will find it ever more crucial to cooperate in sharing their resources to promote a development
process aimed at meeting the growing material and cultural needs of
their people. For these goals, and for the promise of a just and egalitarian social order on a global scale, we remain optimistic in our assessment of the prospects for change in the Third World.

ON THE NECESSITY OF A CLASS ANALYSIS APPROACH IN DEVELOPMENT STUDIES

Most Western observers of the Third World, including, until recently, mainstream social scientists, have utilized institutional, national, cultural, and other approaches in studying development in the Third World.

Mainstream economists have often focused on macroeconomic institutional processes such as imports, exports, balance of trade and payments, GNP, growth of output, manufacturing, level of industrialization, and other indicators of economic performance, without any serious regard to social classes. In their preoccupation to record national accounts statistics, the question of which classes benefit and which classes lose is lost sight of. What is the relationship of social classes to the state and to power relations in society? What is the nature of struggles between different class forces vis-à-vis the state? Questions like these are viewed by mainstream economists as either irrelevant or unimportant. Neither are other mainstream social scientists, such as anthropologists, sociologists, historians, and political scientists, exempt from this apparent neglect of class analysis.

Sociologists and anthropologists have often focused on cultural and societal phenomena in terms of values, beliefs, religion, nationalism, and other social and superstructural institutional forms to explain social life in divergent states in the Third World. Political scientists have almost exclusively been preoccupied with forms of the state and bureaucracy, the role of the army, political factionalism as a result of superpower rivalry, and, more recently, forms of terrorism, including state terrorism, to explain the nature of states and their political orientation. Finally, historians have contributed not much more than a chronicle of events, given their primary focus on the history of nation-states as such; they have limited their studies to particular regimes and leaders, not classes and class struggles.

Such approaches have contributed little to our understanding of the real forces at work in conflicts and crises affecting many countries in the Third World. For example, while abstract institutional analyses of trade patterns, import-export structure, indebtedness to Western banks, balance of payments crises, and other such aggregate data, help us catalog the economic performance of states and their positions relative to others on some specific variables, they do not in fact tell us much about the nature of the political crises, the balance of class forces, national and international alliances, social/political movements, and other forces at work in shaping the societal landscape throughout the Third World—forces based ultimately on the nature of social classes and class struggles.

To provide answers to these and other related questions now confronting the Third World, we have argued here for the necessity of a class analysis approach based on relations of production and their attendant superstructure, expressed first and foremost by the state. Thus, as class relations, class struggles, and the role of the state are crucial elements in the study of power and power struggles in society, the study of Third World societies—especially at this critical juncture of crises and conflicts—require such informed scientific analysis.

We have argued throughout this book that abstract notions of modernization; development or underdevelopment; colonialism and imperialism; conflicts between nation-states and between states and national movements; and other such phenomena that have affected the world historical process, cannot be fully understood without the analysis of their class character as they unfold in historically specific social formations dominated by a particular mode of production. It is in this context that we can raise such questions as: Which classes benefit from the development process evolving in a particular direction? How is the nature of the development path pursued affected by the class character of the state? What are the particular class forces that initiate and/or take part in the development process, and what are the results of that process in terms of which classes benefit and which classes lose? What are the class-driven dynamics of colonial and imperialist expansion throughout the world over centuries? How have these changed in accordance with historical changes in the class structure of the colonial and imperial centers? What, in class terms, has been the impact of the interaction of these colonial centers with the colonies, and which classes or groups have benefited or suffered from such interaction, in both the colonial/imperial centers and the colonies and neocolonies? Finally, what is the class content of relations between different states? What is the nature of the class forces in control of the state apparatus in the dominant, imperialist states? What is their class-motivated position toward national liberation movements led by classes (or an alliance of classes) whose interests are antagonistic to and in fact threaten the interests of the dominant classes within the dominant imperial states and in the neocolonies intent on crushing such movements?

The avoidance of careful discussion of questions like these by most development theorists and area specialists seriously hampers our understanding of the nature and contradictions of the development process, and greatly distorts the history of social development and societal transformations now underway throughout the Third World. It is in response to such neglect and the absence of a class analysis rooted in relations of exploitation and struggles over state power that we have undertaken the writing of this book.

In this spirit, we have presented a critical examination of mainstream and radical theories of development in the Third World and provided an alternative conceptualization of the development process through the utilization of the historical-materialist approach. This approach was then applied to explain the historical and contemporary structures of development in different regions and states of the Third World. It is within this framework of the study of the internal class structure of Third World states that we have examined the nature and impact of relations with colonial and imperialist states and assessed the net effect of these relations on the prospects for change and development in the Third World.

An application of a historically grounded, materialist analysis of classes and class struggles in the Third World to the study of the development process is essential for a clear and correct understanding of the forces at work in the global political economy and the impact of these forces on the future course of development in the Third World. As the process of change and social transformation is unfolding with exceptional speed in this final decade of the twentieth century, it becomes all the more important to delineate with greater clarity the social forces behind these changes.

Proponents of development theory now face a new challenge: they can either cling to old, worn-out analyses and remedies of mid-century developmentalism, which is now thoroughly discredited in the minds of intellectuals and the masses the world over, and adopt a so-called "enlightened" liberal reformulation of the dependency problematic for intellectual consumption around the North-South debate; or, as we have suggested, they can help clear the way for the paradigmatic consolidation of class theory informed by the materialist conception of history.

With conflicts and struggles growing throughout the Third World, and the actions of the state assuming a visibly class character, it is becoming clear that if development theory is to become a viable intellectual tool to explain these changes convincingly, it, too, must move forward to adopt a class analysis approach to development that is both concrete and historically specific. The approach best suited to this task is historical materialism.

NOTES

CHAPTER 1

1. We use the term "Third World" advisedly throughout this book, as it has now become part of the terminology of critical development studies. Thus, following James Petras, *Class, State and Power in the Third World* (Montclair, NJ: Allanheld, Osmun; London: Zed Press, 1981), we use the concept "Third World" to signify as a group the less-developed countries of Asia, Africa, Latin America, and the Middle East that are part of the world capitalist system. These countries are variably referred to in the development literature as the "developing" or "underdeveloped" countries of the "periphery." We have deliberately avoided the usage of these latter concepts/terms to distinguish our approach from that of modernization theory on the one hand and the dependency and world system theories on the other. Preferring instead the terminology of historical materialism, we have opted, following Albert Szymanski, *The Logic of Imperialism* (New York: Praeger, 1981), for the more neutral term "less-developed" countries when referring to the countries making up the Third World.

Although these concepts have now become part of the language and conceptual framework of critical development studies, we agree with Harry Magdoff and Paul Sweezy that the expression "Third World," as it was first used in the 1960s, did more to obscure than to clarify the problems of less-developed societies across the globe. This concept, "in its original usage," Magdoff and Sweezy argue, "was intended to conjure up a picture of a group of countries choosing their own road to economic and social development and standing between the advanced capitalist world on the one hand and the Communist world on the other." Clarifying this original (mis)conception of the term, they state that "the countries in question are really the oppressed and exploited majority of the global capitalist system . . . [and] it is more and more taken for granted that 'Third World' is merely a convenient short-hand designation for that large and in many ways diverse collection of colonies, semi-colonies, and neo-colonies which form the base of the global capitalist pyramid." See Harry Magdoff and Paul M. Sweezy, "Notes on the Multinational Corporation" in K. T. Fann and Donald C. Hodges (eds.), *Readings in U.S. Imperialism* (Boston: Porter Sargent Publisher, 1971), p. 94.

2. For recent discussion and reevaluation of mainstream theories of development and modernization, see Magnus Blomstrom and Bjorn Hettne, *Development Theory in Transition* (London: Zed Books, 1984); Andrew Webster, *Introduction to the Sociology of Development*, 2nd ed. (Atlantic Highlands, NJ: Humanities Press International, 1990), Chapter 3; and S. C. Dube, *Modernization and Development: The Search for Alternative Paradigms* (Tokyo: The United Nations University; London: Zed Books, 1988).

3. Manning Nash, "Approaches to the Study of Economic Growth," *Journal of Social Issues*, vol. 19, no. 1 (1963), p. 3.

4. *Ibid.*, pp. 3-4.

5. Charles P. Kindleberger, *Economic Development* (New York: McGraw-Hill Book Co., 1965).

6. "Modernization," in mainstream developmentalist literature, is generally equated with capitalist development.

7. Talcott Parsons, *The Social System* (New York: The Free Press, 1951), pp. 58-67, 101-112.

8. *Ibid.*

9. Bert F. Hoselitz, *Sociological Factors in Economic Development* (New York: The Free Press, 1960).

10. *Ibid.*

11. *Ibid.*

12. Nash, "Approaches to the Study of Economic Growth."

13. W. W. Rostow, *The Stages of Economic Growth: A Non-Communist Manifesto* (New York: Cambridge University Press, 1960).

14. *Ibid.*, pp. 4-10.

15. Keith Griffin, "Underdevelopment in History," in Charles K. Wilber, ed., *The Political Economy of Development and Underdevelopment* (New York: Random House, 1973), p. 69.

16. *Ibid.*

17. James Petras, "U.S.-Latin American Studies: A Critical Assessment," *Science and Society*, vol. 32, no. 2 (Spring 1968), p. 158.

18. Paul Baran and E. J. Hobsbawm, "The Stages of Economic Growth: A Review" in Charles K. Wilber, ed., *The Political Economy of Development and Underdevelopment*, p. 47.

19. *Ibid.*, p. 48.

20. Frank, "Sociology of Development," p. 355.

21. *Ibid.* According to Dale Johnson, "Rostow, who began applying his theories to U.S. foreign policy during the Kennedy administration, became special assistant on national security affairs in the Johnson administration and a chief architect of United States policy in Vietnam." Johnson, *The Sociology of Change and Reaction in Latin America*, p. 22. This is confirmed by a profile in *The New York Times*, April 13, 1967: "Mr. Rostow is an architect of the United States policy in Vietnam, and proud of it."

22. Petras, "U.S.-Latin American Studies," p. 161.

23. *Ibid.*

24. Johnson, *The Sociology of Change and Reaction in Latin America*, p. 24.

25. *Ibid.*

26. David McClelland, "The Achievement Motive in Economic Growth," in Bert F. Hoselitz and Wilbert E. Moore, eds., *Industrialization and Society* (Paris: UNESCO, 1963), p. 76.

27. Frank, "Sociology of Development," p. 385.

28. McClelland, quoted in Frank, "Sociology of Development," p. 385.

29. See David McClelland, *The Achieving Society* (New York: Van Nostrand, 1961).

30. Arthur W. Lewis, *The Theory of Economic Growth* (Homewood, IL: Richard D. Irwin, Inc., 1955), p. 14.

31. McClelland, quoted in Henry Bernstein, "Modernization Theory and the Sociological Study of Development," *Journal of Development Studies*, vol. 7, no. 2 (1971), p. 149.

32. Lewis, *The Theory of Economic Growth*, p. 9.

33. *Ibid.*

34. *Ibid.*

35. *Ibid.*, pp. 9-10.

36. *Ibid.*, p. 10.

37. *Ibid.*, p. 366.

38. *Ibid.*, p. 370.

39. *Ibid.*, p. 371.

40. Art Gallaher, Jr. "Developmental Change and the Social Sciences," in Art Gallaher, Jr., ed., *Perspectives in Developmental Change* (Lexington, KY: University of Kentucky Press, 1968), p. 3.

41. John A. Hobson, *Imperialism: A Study* (Ann Arbor: University of Michigan Press, 1965), pp. 221-222.

42. Rich, quoted in Griffin, "Underdevelopment in History," p. 69.

43. *Ibid.*, p. 72.

44. *Ibid.*, p. 77.

45. *Ibid.*

46. Kindleberger, *Economic Development.*

47. *Ibid.*, pp. 3, 14.

48. *Ibid.*, p. 14.

49. *Ibid.*

50. *Ibid.*, p. 15.

51. Simon Kuznets, "The Present Underdeveloped Countries and Past Growth Patterns," in T. Morgan and G. Betz, eds., *Economic Development* (Belmont, CA: Wadsworth Publishing Co., 1970), p. 16.

52. Ragnar Nurkse, *Problems of Capital Formation in Underdeveloped Countries* (New York: Oxford University Press, 1957), p. 11, 16-17.

53. *Ibid.*, pp. 127-128.

54. As opposed to the export of goods, which Nurkse seems to imply when he says: "advanced capitalist economies are under a compulsion to . . . dump their surplus *produce* abroad in order to keep the internal economy operating at a prosperous and profitable level of activity" (emphasis added). This is clearly a misreading of Lenin on the question of the export of capital, since Lenin points out that while under competitive capitalism the export of goods are decisive, under monopoly capital (or imperialism) it is the export of capital that plays a key role. See V. I. Lenin, *Imperialism, the Highest Stage of Capitalism,*

in *Selected Works*, vol. 1 (Moscow: Foreign Languages Publishing House, 1917, 1960).

55. Nurkse, *Problems of Capital Formation*, p. 128.

56. Irma Adelman and Cynthia Taft Morris, *Society Politics and Economic Development* (Baltimore, MD: The Johns Hopkins Press, 1967).

57. Irma Adelman and Cynthia Taft Morris, *Economic Growth and Social Equity in Developing Countries* (Stanford: Stanford University Press, 1973), p. 1.

58. *Ibid.*, p. 186.

59. *Ibid.*, p. viii.

60. *Ibid.*, p. 186.

61. *Ibid.*, pp. 186-189, 3.

62. *Ibid.*, p. 201.

63. *Ibid.*, p. 199.

64. *Ibid.*, pp. 201-202.

65. Dudley Seers, "The Birth, Life and Death of Development Economics," *Development and Change* 10 (1979), p. 712.

66. Deepak Lal, *The Poverty of "Development Economics"* (London: Institute of Economic Affairs, 1983), p. 109.

67. For a critical evaluation of these various, recent neoliberal responses in mainstream development theory, see Ankie M. M. Hoogvelt, *The Third World in Global Development* (London: The Macmillan Press, 1982), chap. 4. Also see P. W. Preston, *New Trends in Development Theory* (London: Routledge and Kegan Paul, 1985) and Andrew Webster, *Introduction to the Sociology of Development*, 2nd ed. (Atlantic Highlands, NJ: Humanities Press International, 1990).

CHAPTER 2

1. We refer here to the reformist structuralist "remedies" advocated by Raul Prebisch at the United Nations Economic Commission for Latin America (ECLA), who expressed concern with the deteriorating terms of trade and advocated the need for import-substitution industrialization in Latin America to promote growth. By the late 1960s and early 1970s it became apparent that this approach had failed because of its own particular contradictions, the main one being the fact that the approach remained within the framework of the capitalist mode and thus could not rise above the overwhelming forces of imperialism dominating the world economy. For a critical appraisal of the contribution of

Prebisch and the ECLA analysis, see Larrain, *Theories of Development*, pp. 102-110; Blomstrom and Hettne, *Development Theory in Transition*, pp. 38-44.

2. These social scientists, associated with the U.N. Latin American Social and Economic Planning Institute (ILPES), are Fernando H. Cardoso, Enzo Faletto, Anibal Quijano, Marcos Kaplan, Osvaldo Sunkel, and Celso Furtado. A more radical version of dependency theory, focusing on imperialism and the local ruling classes, was developed outside of establishment channels by Theotonio Dos Santos, Andre Gunder Frank, Susanne Bodenheimer, and Dale L. Johnson, primarily in an academic setting. For an overview of the basic dependency arguments as developed by proponents of the latter, radical version, see: Andre Gunder Frank, *Capitalism and Underdevelopment in Latin America* (New York: Monthly Review Press, 1967); Theotonio Dos Santos, "The Structure of Dependence," in K. T. Fann and Donald C. Hodges, eds., *Readings in U.S. Imperialism* (Boston: Porter Sargent Publisher, 1971); Susanne Bodenheimer, "Dependency and Imperialism: the Roots of Latin American Underdevelopment," *Politics and Society*, vol. 1, no. 3, (May 1971); Fernando H. Cardoso and Enzo Faletto, *Dependency and Development in Latin America*, (Berkeley: University of California Press, 1979); A. Murga, "Dependency: A Latin American View," *NACLA Newsletter*, vol. 4, no. 10, (February 1971); James D. Cockcroft, Andre Gunder Frank, and Dale L. Johnson, *Dependence and Underdevelopment: Latin America's Political Economy* (Garden City, NY: Anchor, 1972).

3. Andre Gunder Frank, "Economic Dependence, Class Structure, and Underdevelopment Policy," in Cockcroft et al. *Dependence and Underdevelopment*, p. 19.

4. Dos Santos, "The Structure of Dependence," p. 226.

5. A. Murga, "Dependency: A Latin American View," *NACLA Newsletter*, vol. 4, no. 10 (February 1971), p. 4.

6. *Ibid.*

7. Cockcroft et al., *Dependence and Underdevelopment*, p. xiii .

8. Murga, "Dependency," p. 5.

9. Osvaldo Sunkel, "Big Business and 'Dependencia'," *Foreign Affairs*, vol. 50, no. 3 (April 1972), p. 519. Also see an extensive discussion on this point in Andre Gunder Frank, *Capitalism and Underdevelopment in Latin America* (New York: Monthly Review Press, 1967), pp. 145-150.

10. Susanne Bodenheimer, "Dependency and Imperialism: The Roots of Latin American Underdevelopment," in Fann and Hodges, eds., *Readings in U.S. Imperialism*, p. 158 .

11. *Ibid.*, pp. 158-159.

12. *Ibid.*, p. 160.

13. The following outline is adopted from Bodenheimer, "Dependency and Imperialism"; Dos Santos, "The Structure of Dependence"; and Dale L. Johnson, " Dependence and the International System," in Cockcroft et al., *Dependence and Underdevelopment*, pp . 71-111.

14. Sunkel, "Big Business and 'Dependencia'," p. 521.

15. *Ibid.*

16. Theotonio Dos Santos, "The Changing Structure of Foreign Investment in Latin America," in James F. Petras and Maurice Zeitlin, eds., *Latin America: Reform or Revolution?* (New York: Fawcet, 1968), pp. 97-98.

17. Theotonio Dos Santos, "Foreign Investment and the Large Enterprise in Latin America: The Brazilian Case," in Petras and Zeitlin, eds., *Latin America: Reform or Revolution?*, p. 432.

18. *Ibid.*, pp. 444-445.

19. *Ibid.*, p. 445.

20. Bodenheimer, "Dependency and Imperialism," pp. 162-163.

21. Frank, "Economic Dependence," p. 20.

22. Cockcroft et al., *Dependence and Underdevelopment*, pp. xiv-xv.

23. Bodenheimer, "Dependency and Imperialism," p. 164.

24. James F. Petras and Thomas Cook, "Dependency and the Industrial Bourgeoisie" in James F. Petras, ed., *Latin America: From Dependence to Revolution* (New York: John Wiley & Sons, 1973), p. 144.

25. Dos Santos, "The Structure of Dependence," p. 225.

26. Murga, "Dependency," p. 5. An alternative conceptualization of dependence—that of "dependent development"—was developed by Fernando H. Cardoso to explain the simultaneous occurance of dependence *and* development, mainly in countries governed by "bureaucratic authoritarian" states. See Fernando H. Cardoso, "Associated-Dependent Development" in Alfred Stepan, ed., *Authoritarian Brazil* (New Haven: Yale University Press, 1973); Fernando H. Cardoso and Enzo Faletto, *Dependency and Development in Latin America* (Berkeley: University of California Press, 1979).

27. *Ibid.*

28. Frank, "Economic Dependence," p. 19.

29. Dos Santos, "The Structure of Dependence," p. 236.

30. See Ernesto Laclau, "Feudalism and Capitalism in Latin America," *New Left Review* 67 (May-June 1971), pp. 19-38. See also Raul A. Fernandez and

Jose F. Ocampo, "The Latin American Revolution: A Theory of Imperialism, Not Dependence," *Latin American Perspectives*, vol. 1, no. 1 (Spring 1974), pp. 30-61.

31. Regarding the discussion and debate on the transition from feudalism to capitalism in Western Europe, which originally took place in the pages of the journal *Science & Society* in the 1950s, see Rodney Hilton, ed., *The Transition from Feudalism to Capitalism* (London: New Left Books, 1976). For an assessment of the debate, see Berch Berberoglu, "The Transition from Feudalism to Capitalism: Another Look at the Sweezy-Dobb Debate," *Revista Mexicana de Sociologia*, vol. 39, no. 4 (1977). Also see Roger Gottlieb, "Feudalism and Historical Materialism: A Critique and a Synthesis," *Science & Society*, vol. 48, no. 1 (Spring 1984) and idem, "Historical Materialism, Historical Laws and Social Primacy: Further Discussion of the Transition Debate," *Science & Society*, vol. 51, no. 2 (Summer 1987).

32. Samir Amin, *Accumulation on a World Scale*, 2 vols. (New York: Monthly Review Press, 1974); Andre Gunder Frank, *Dependent Accumulation and Underdevelopment* (London: Macmillan, 1978) and idem, *World Accumulation, 1492-1789* (London: Macmillan, 1978).

33. For an alternative, liberal variant of the world system approach see Paul Kennedy, *The Rise and Fall of the Great Powers* (New York: Random House, 1987). Referring to the "history of the rise and later fall of the leading countries in the Great Power system since the advance of Western Europe in the sixteenth century," Kennedy argues that "there is detectable a causal relationship between the shifts which have occurred over time in the general economic and productive balances and the position occupied by individual Powers in the international system." Moreover, Kennedy goes on to argue that "there is a very clear connection *in the long run* between an individual Great Power's economic rise and fall and its growth and decline as an important military power (or world empire)." His main thesis is that there exists "a very significant correlation *over the longer term* between productive and revenue-raising capacities on the one hand and military strength on the other." In this context, the critical factor determining the rise and fall of the great powers is that the dominant powers/empires in the world system "steadily overextend themselves in the course of repeated conflicts and become militarily top-heavy for their weakening economic base." It is in this way, according to Kennedy, that shifts in global power centers occur and transformations in the world political economy take place. See Kennedy, *The Rise and Fall of the Great Powers*, pp. xv-xxv (emphases in the original).

34. Immanuel Wallerstein, *The Modern World System* (New York: Academic Press, 1974), p. 7.

35. *Ibid.*, p. xi.

36. Albert Bergesen, "The Class Structure of the World-System," in William R. Thompson, ed., *Contending Approaches to World-System Analysis* (Bev-

erly Hills, CA: Sage Publications, 1983), p. 53.

37. Wallerstein, *The Modern World System* and idem, "The Rise and Future Demise of the World Capitalist System," *Comparative Studies in Society and History* XVI (September 1974).

38. Terence K. Hopkins and Immanuel Wallerstein, "Structural Transformations of the World-Economy," in Richard Rubinson, ed., *Dynamics of World Development* (London: Sage Publications, 1981), p. 245.

39. *Ibid.*, pp. 245-146.

40. Amin, *Accumulation on a World Scale*, p. 24.

CHAPTER 3

1. The theoretical and empirical arguments developed around this thesis are to be found in the following accounts: Bill Warren, "Imperialism and Capitalist Industrialization, " *New Left Review* 81 (Sept.-Oct., 1973), pp. 3-45 and *Imperialism: Pioneer of Capitalism* (London: Verso, 1980); Albert Szymanski, "Marxist Theory and International Capital Flows," *Review of Radical Political Economics*, vol. 6, no. 3 (Fall 1974), pp. 20-40 (also see the debate on Szymanski's paper in vol. 8, no. 2 (Summer 1976) issue of the same journal); Patrick Clawson, "The Internationalization of Capital and Capital Accumulation in Iran and Iraq," *Insurgent Sociologist*, vol. 7, no. 2 (Spring 1977); and Albert Szymanski, *The Logic of Imperialism* (New York: Praeger Publishers, 1981). For a critique of this approach, in particular of Bill Warren's 1973 article, see Philip McMichael et al., "Imperialism and the Contradictions of Development," *New Left Review* 85 (May-June 1974).

2. Karl Marx, "The Future Results of the British Rule in India," *New York Daily Tribune*, July 11, 1953, reprinted in Berch Berberoglu, ed., *India: National Liberation and Class Struggles* (Meerut: Sarup & Sons, Publishers, 1986), p. 46.

3. *Ibid.*, pp. 47-49.

4. Marx to Engels, June 14, 1953, in *Ibid.*, p. 192.

5. V. I. Lenin, "Imperialism: The Highest Stage of Capitalism," in *Selected Works in Three Volumes*, vol. I, (Moscow: Progress Publishers, 1975), p. 681.

6. *Ibid.*, p. 707.

7. Marx, "The Future Results of the British Rule in India," p. 50.

8. *Ibid.*

9. V. I. Lenin, *Selected Works in Three Volumes*, vol. 1 (Moscow: Progress Publishers, 1975), p. 637.

10. *Ibid.*, pp. 712-713.

11. *Ibid.*, p. 640.

12. For a critique of circulationist arguments, see R. Brenner, "The Origins of Capitalist Development: A Critique of Neo-Smithian Marxism," *New Left Review* 104 (1977). Also see Ian Roxborough, *Theories of Underdevelopment* (Atlantic Highlands, NJ: Humanities Press, 1979), chap. 4; Gary Nigel Howe, "Dependency Theory, Imperialism, and the Production of Surplus Value on a World Scale," in Ronald H. Chilcote, ed., *Dependency and Marxism* (Boulder, CO: Westview Press, 1982), pp. 82-102; and Sheila Smith, "Class Analysis Versus World System: Critique of Samir Amin's Topology of Underdevelopment," in Peter Limqueco and Bruce McFarlane, eds., *Neo-Marxist Theories of Development* (London: Croom Helm; New York: St. Martin's Press, 1983), pp. 73-86.

13. See, for example, the works of Andre Gunder Frank, Samir Amin, and other dependency and world system theorists. For a recent elaboration on this point, see Amin, *Delinking: Towards a Polycentric World* (London: Zed Books, 1990) and idem, *Maldevelopment: Anatomy of a Global Failure* (London: Zed Books, 1990).

14. See Szymanski, *The Logic of Imperialism*; Howe, "Dependency Theory"; and Berch Berberoglu, *The Internationalization of Capital: Imperialism and Capitalist Development on a World Scale* (New York: Praeger Publishers, 1987).

15. See Ankie M. M. Hoogvelt, *The Third World in Global Development* (London: Macmillan, 1982), pp. 171-207. Also see Haldun Gulalp, "Frank and Wallerstein Revisited: A Contribution to Brenner's Critique," in Limqueco and McFarlane, *Neo-Marxist Theories of Development*, pp. 114-136; Magnus Blomstrom and Bjorn Hettne, *Development Theory in Transition: The Dependency Debate and Beyond* (London: Zed Books, 1984), chaps. 2-4, 8.

16. As an example of the latter approach, see Ernest Mandel, *Late Capitalism* (London: New Left Books, 1975).

17. See Jorge Larrain, *Theories of Development: Capitalism Colonialism, and Dependency* (Cambridge: Polity Press, 1989), pp. 188-211.

18. Andre Gunder Frank, *On Capitalist Underdevelopment* (Bombay: Oxford University Press, 1975), p. 94.

19. See James Petras, "Dependency and World System Theory: A Critique and New Directions," in Chilcote, *Dependency and Marxism*, pp. 148-155.

20. See Bill Warren, *Imperialism. Pioneer of Capitalism* (London: Verso, 1980); David Barkin, "Internationalization of Capital: An Alternative Approach," in Chilcote, *Dependency and Marxism*, pp. 156-161.

21. For these and other related criticisms of the dependency theory counterposed to Marxism, see Scott Werker, "Beyond the Dependency Paradigm,"

Journal of Contemporary Asia, vol. 15, no. 1 (1985); Chilcote, *Dependency and Marxism.*

22. *Ibid.* Also see Roxborough, *Theories of Underdevelopment,* pp. 55-69.

23. For a similar critique of underdevelopment theories, see Colin Leys, "Underdevelopment and Dependency: Critical Notes."

24. On this point, see Philip O'Brien, "Dependency: The New Nationalism?" in Colin Harding and Christopher Roper, eds., *Latin America Review of Books* (Palo Alto, CA: Ramparts Press, 1973).

25. See the various essays in Limqueco and McFarlane, eds., *Neo-Marxist Theories of Development* and Chilcote, ed., *Dependency and Marxism.* Also see Ivar Oxaal, Tony Barnett, and David Booth, eds., *Beyond the Sociology of Development* (London: Routledge & Kegan Paul, 1975); Ronaldo Munck, *Politics and Dependency in the Third World* (London: Zed Books, 1984); Cristobal Kay, *Latin American Theories of Development and Underdevelopment* (London: Routledge & Kegan Paul, 1989).

26. Samir Amin, *Delinking: Towards a Polycentric World* (London: Zed Books, 1990).

27. See, for example, Azzam Mahjoub, ed., *Adjustment or Delinking? The African Experience* (London: Zed Books, 1990).

28. See James F. Petras, *Critical Perspectives on Imperialism and Social Class in the Third World* (New York: Monthly Review Press, 1981). Also see Szymanski, *The Logic of Imperialism* and Berberoglu, *The Internationalization of Capital.*

29. Berberoglu, *The Internationalization of Capital.*

CHAPTER 4

1. Folker Frobel, Jurgen Heindrichs, and Otto Kreye, "Export-Oriented Industrialization of Underdeveloped Countries," *Monthly Review,* vol. 30, no. 6 (November 1978), p. 24.

2. See Martin Landsberg, "Export-Led Industrialization in the Third World: Manufacturing Imperialism," *Review of Radical Political Economics,* vol. 11, no. 4 (Winter 1979); Ernest Utrecht, ed., *Transnational Corporations and Export-Oriented Industrialization* (Sydney: University of Sydney, Transnational Corporations Research Project, 1986). For a broader discussion of this model, framed in mainstream economic parlance, see Gulten Kazgan, "Internal and External Constraints of Export Oriented Growth Strategy," *New Perspectives on Turkey,* vol. 3, no. 1 (Fall 1989).

3. The notion that a consistent increase in the share of industrial (relative

to agricultural) production in the GDP as an indicator of capitalist development in the noncommunist countries of the periphery is also advanced by Al Szymanski, *The Logic of Imperialism* (New York: Praeger, 1981), pp. 405-407.

4. See, for example, Clive Hamilton, "Capitalist Industrialization in East Asia's Four Little Tigers," *Journal of Contemporary Asia*, vol. 13, no. 1 (1983) and idem, *Capitalist Industrialization in Korea* (Boulder, CO: Westview Press, 1986); Sam Wynn, "The Taiwanese 'Economic Miracle'," *Monthly Review*, vol. 33, no. 11 (April 1982); Philippe Faucher, "Industrial Policy in a Dependent State: The Case of Brazil," *Latin American Perspectives*, vol. 7, no. 1 (Winter 1980); Leslie Sklair, *Assembling for Development: The Maquila Industry in Mexico and the United States* (Boston: Unwin Hyman, 1989).

5. See United Nations, *Yearbook of International Trade Statistics, 1987* (New York: United Nations, 1989), pp. 23, 103, 488; Republic of China, *Statistical Yearbook of the Republic of China, 1988* (Executive Yuan: Directorate General of Budget, 1988) p. 368; World Bank, *World Development Report, 1990* (New York: Oxford University Press, 1990).

6. Our focus on the proportionate shift in the structure of the labor force in favor of industrial employment should not be taken to mean the exclusive development of a wage labor force in the urban-industrial areas alone. Although the local and foreign-controlled industries in urban areas are clearly capitalist in nature, the presence or absence of wage-labor employment is determined neither by geographic location (urban/rural) nor by type of economic activity (agriculture/industry) per se, since industrial plants can also be found in rural areas and wage relations are widespread throughout the agricultural regions, where capitalist relations of production are well established in the agrarian sector of many countries. Thus it would be a serious error to characterize urban and rural areas as modern/capitalist and traditional/feudal respectively, as the dualistic theories of mainstream economics contend. However, regardless of the nature of production relations in the agrarian sector, we do know that wage-labor employment is the dominant form of exploitation on which industry (whether in manufacturing, mining, construction, or other branches) is based. Thus an increase in the proportion of industrial employment, together with other related factors, such as growth of manufacturing production and industrialization in general, would indicate further capitalist development. It is for this reason that focusing on the industrial sector as a definite indicator of capitalist development is so important.

7. In 1987 industrial workers accounted for 33 percent of all wage earners in the United States, and workers in the manufacturing sector accounted for 19 percent. U.S. Department of Commerce, *Statistical Abstract of the United States, 1989* (Washington, D.C.: Government Printing Office, 1989), p. 391.

8. We concentrate here on the growth in size of the industrial work force in the manufacturing sector (in line with the classical Marxist formulation) to

emphasize the central role of industrial workers in the revolutionary process. Marx's analysis of the development of workingclass consciousness was directly based on the objective, material conditions of production (large-scale socialized wage labor, which is best exemplified in factory-type production). According to the Marxist formulation, the politicization, hence class consciousness, of the working class is directly related to the very conditions of capitalist production which advance communication among workers of their common position in the productive process, and in society in general, leading to the formation of mass working-class organizations (unions, political parties, etc.). Our emphasis on industrial workers, then, is intended to signify the latter's central (but not exclusive) role in the revolutionary process.

9. It should be pointed out also that most of the workers employed in the electronics and other manufacturing industries in export production and processing zones in East and Southeast Asia, the U.S.-Mexican border, and elsewhere in the Third World—as well as, we might add, in California's Silicon Valley—are women workers employed at the lowest levels of the wage scale. Earning $3-5 a day, they stitch clothes in the sweatshops of Hong Kong, Taiwan, Malaysia, Brazil, and other cheap labor havens, assemble electronic appliances in South Korea, Taiwan, Singapore, and Mexico, and bond hair-thin wires to silicon chips in high-tech electronics factories in these and other countries of East Asia and Latin America. See the various essays in E. Utrecht, ed., *Transnational Corporations and Export-Oriented Industrialization*; and in Annette Fuentes and Barbara Ehrenreich, *Women in the Global Factory* (Boston: South End Press, 1983).

10. See Walden Bello and Stephanie Rosenfeld, *Dragons in Distress: Asia's Miracle Economies in Crisis* (San Francisco: Institute for Food and Development Policy, 1990).

11. One serious consequence of these policies has been a growing foreign debt. Both the principal and interest payments on this debt has grown beyond the ability of these states to pay them back. Brazil's foreign debt, for example, has grown from $4.4 billion in 1969 to over $130 billion in 1989—despite its annual payment to international creditors of $17 billion, as in 1988. Likewise, Mexico's foreign debt topped $100 billion in the late 1980s, reaching $107 billion in 1989. See Peter Korner et al., *The IMF and the Debt Crisis* (London: Zed Books, 1986) and Susan George, *A Fate Worse than Debt* (Harmondsworth: Penguin Books, 1988). Also see Sue Branford and Bernardo Kucinski, *The Debt Squads: The U.S., the Banks and Latin America* (London: Zed Books, 1986); Elmar Altvater, et al., eds., *The Poverty of Nations: A Guide to the Debt Crisis* (London: Zed Books, 1991); Cheryl Payer, *The Debt Trap: The IMF and the Third World* (New York: Monthly Review Press, 1975); and idem, *Lent and Lost: Foreign Credit and Third World Development* (London: Zed Books, 1991).

12. See Susan George, *A Fate Worse than Debt* and the author's earlier book, *How the Other Half Dies: The Real Reasons for World Hunger* (Montclair, NJ: Allanheld, Osmun, 1977). Also see references in the previous note.

13. See, for example, Martin Landsberg, "South Korea: The 'Miracle' Rejected," *Critical Sociology*, vol. 15, no. 3 (Fall 1988).

14. W. Olson, "Crisis and Social Change in Mexico's Political Economy," *Latin American Perspectives* 46 (1985), pp. 7-28; Frederick Deyo, Stephen Heggard, and Hagen Koo, "Labor in the Political Economy of East Asian Industrialization," *Bulletin of Concerned Asian Scholars*, vol. 19, no. 2 (April-June, 1987); Clive Hamilton, *Capitalist Industrialization in Korea* (Boulder, CO: Westview Press, 1986).

15. See I. Alexander, "Real Wages and Class Struggle in South Korea," *Journal of Contemporary Asia*, vol. 17, no. 4 (1987).

16. Data on strikes and demonstrations reported in this section are (unless otherwise cited) obtained from a variety of sources, including wire services, bulletins, reports, and newspapers.

17. International Labour Organization, *Yearbook of Labor Statistics, 1988* (Geneva: ILO, 1988), p. 1048.

18. R. Rew, "Brazil: Biggest Protest Ever," *The Guardian*, 8 Feb. 1984..

19. International Labour Organization, *Yearbook of Labour Statistics, 1982* (Geneva: ILO, 1982), p. 677; *1984*, p. 826; *1988*, p. 1049.

20. International Labour Organization, *Yearbook of Labour Statistics, 1988*, p. 1049.

21. International Labour Organization, *Yearbook of Labour Statistics, 1984*, p. 828; *1988*, p. 1051.

22. Lo Shiu Hing, "Political Participation in Hong Kong, South Korea, and Taiwan," *Journal of Contemporary Asia*, vol. 20, no. 2 (1990), p. 244.

CHAPTER 5

1. For a detailed discussion of the political implications of the internationalization of capital for the capitalist state and its role in the world economy, see Berch Berberoglu, *The Internationalization of Capital* (New York: Praeger, 1987), pp. 40-53, 157-195.

2. For a summary of the various major positions on the theory of the state, see Berch Berberoglu, *Political Sociology: A Comparative/Historical Approach* (New York: General Hall, Inc., 1990), chap. 2. Also see David Gold, Clarence Y. H. Lo, and Erik Olin Wright, "Recent Developments in Marxist Theories of the Capitalist State," *Monthly Review*, vol. 27, no. 5-6 (October/November 1985), and Albert Szymanski, *The Capitalist State and the Politics of Class* (Cambridge, MA: Winthrop, 1978), pp. 21-31 and chaps. 6-11, as well as the works of Ralph

Miliband, Nicos Poulantzas, Claus Offe, and the *Kapitalistate* collective.

3. For an analysis of positions contrary to this view, see Gosta Esping-Andersen, Roger Friedland, and Erik Olin Wright, "Modes of Class Struggle and the Capitalist State," *Kapitalistate*, no. 4-5 (Summer 1976); Fred Block, "The Ruling Class Does Not Rule: Notes on the Marxist Theory of the State," *Socialist Review* 33 (May-June, 1977), and idem, "Class Consciousness and Capitalist Rationalization: A Reply to Critics," *Socialist Review* 40-41 (July-October, 1978). These authors maintain that even today the capitalist state continues to be "relatively autonomous" of the capitalist class, despite the disproportionately favorable position of the monopolies within the economy and society. For a critique of such arguments, see Berberoglu, *Political Sociology*, pp. 32-45.

4. Albert Szymanski, *The Logic of Imperialism* (New York: Praeger, 1981); Mandel, *The Second Slump*.

5. Berberoglu, *The Internationalization of Capital*.

6. Barry Bluestone and Bennett Harrison, *The Deindustrialization of America* (New York: Basic Books, 1982) and idem, *The Great U-Turn: Corporate Restructuring and the Polarizing of America* (New York: Basic Books, 1988). Also see Howard Sherman, *Stagflation* (New York: Harper & Row, 1976); Jim Devine, "The Structural Crisis of U.S. Capitalism," *Southwest Economy and Society*, vol. 6, no. 1 (Fall 1982); and Victor Perlo, *Super Profits and Crises: Modern U.S. Capitalism* (New York: International Publishers, 1988), p. 512.

7. See Berch Berberoglu, *The Legacy of Empire: Economic Decline and Class Polarization in the United States* (New York: Praeger, 1992).

8. For corporatist interpretations of the Third World state, see Alfred Stepan, *The State and Society* (Princeton: Princeton University Press, 1978). On bureaucratic authoritarianism, see Guillermo O'Donnell, *Modernization and Bureaucratic Authoritarianism: Studies in South American Politics* (Berkeley: Institute of International Studies, University of California at Berkeley, 1973) and idem, "Tensions in the Bureaucratic Authoritarian State and the Question of Democracy," in David Collier, ed., *The New Authoritarianism in Latin America* (Princeton: Princeton University Press, 1979). On the neofascist character of the dependent states ruled by military dictatorships, see James Petras, *Class, State and Power in the Third World* (Montclair, NJ: Allanheld, Osmun, 1981), chaps. 7, 10. For a discussion of the nature of the bureaucratic authoritarian and other forms of the dependent state, see Berch Berberoglu, *The Internationalization of Capital*, chap. 7 and idem, *Political Sociology*, chap. 6. Also see Martin Carnoy, *The State and Political Theory* (Princeton: Princeton University Press, 1984), chap. 7.

9. James F. Petras, *Class, State and Power in the Third World* (Montclair, NJ: Allanheld, Osmun; London: Zed Press, 1981).

10. Berberoglu, *The Internationalization of Capital*, chap. 8.

CHAPTER 6

1. The definition of state capitalism used here is qualitatively different from both the notion of "state monopoly capitalism," as it is applied, for example, by James O'Connor for the case of the advanced capitalist countries, and "state interventionism" in a number of neocolonial Third World countries, such as Brazil in the 1970s and 1980s, Iran under the Shah, and the Philippines under Marcos. The definition that applies has certain specific requirements that need to be met in order for countries in the Third World to qualify for such a status.

The Brazilian-, pre-1979 Iranian-, and pre-1986 Philippine-type state intervention takes place within the framework of neocolonial arrangements, such that interventions of this type are fully harmonious with the interests of foreign capital and the local operations of transnational corporations in these countries. State-capitalist regimes, on the other hand, tend to challenge the neocolonial structure and move against foreign capital in order to facilitate national capitalist accumulation. This is so because class forces sympathetic to national capitalist development have captured state power and have replaced the rule of the old neocolonial power bloc. We will deal with these and other points in more detail throughout this chapter.

2. See Berch Berberoglu, *Turkey in Crisis: From State Capitalism to Neocolonialism* (London: Zed Press, 1982); Ellen Kay Trimberger, *Revolution from Above: Military Bureaucrats and Development in Japan, Turkey, Egypt and Peru* (New Brunswick, NJ: Transaction Books, 1977); Nora L. Hamilton, "Mexico: The Limits of State Autonomy," *Latin American Perspectives*, Vol. II, No. 2 (Summer 1975); Celso Furtado, *Economic Development of Latin America* (London: Cambridge University Press, 1970); Helio Jaguaribe, "The Dynamics of Brazilian Nationalism," in Claudio Veliz (ed.), *Obstacles to Change in Latin America* (New York: Oxford University Press, 1969).

3. See A. I. Levkovsky, *Capitalism in India* (Delhi: People's Publishing House, 1966); Mahmoud Hussein, *Class Conflict in Egypt: 1945-1970* (New York: Monthly Review Press, 1973); Karen Farsoun, "State Capitalism in Algeria," *MERIP Reports* 35 (1975); Hanna Batatu, *The Old Social Classes and the Revolutionary Movements of Iraq* (Princeton: Princeton University Press, 1978); Bob Fitch and M. Oppenheimer, *Ghana: End of an Illusion* (New York: Monthly Review Press, 1971); Issa G. Shivji, *Class Struggles in Tanzania* (New York: Monthly Review Press, 1976); Rene Antonio Mayorga, "National-Popular State, State Capitalism and Military Dictatorship," *Latin American Perspectives*, vol. 5, no. 2 (Spring 1978); E. V. K. Fitzgerald, *The Political Economy of Peru, 1956-78* (Cambridge: Cambridge University Press, 1979).

4. See Part III of this book.

5. "National bourgeoisie" here signifies that segment of the local capitalist class which owns and/or controls the means of industrial production. While the comprador bourgeoisie is mainly concentrated in import-export commerce

and is directly tied to the imperial centers, the national bourgeoisie has interests that are local and nationally-based and thus is "nationalistic." The "nationalism" of local industrial capitalists is the result of their interest to safeguard and protect property in the means of production located within the confines of "their own" national territory.

6. The national and petty bourgeoisies and the peasantry are not usually (and the working class almost never) included in this coalition; in instances when they are, they are always relegated to a peripheral position, where their presence would hardly be likely to alter the prevailing neocolonial arrangements.

7. Those regimes that have tried to challenge the existing neocolonial structure in favor of semi-independent national-capitalist development during "normal" periods have often been defeated by the imperial centers. Japan has been one of the few exceptions to this rule, but that is because it was never colonized.

8. The fact that the national industrialization process occurred in the relatively more developed countries and not in others is mainly related to differences in the economic and class structure of these countries previously generated by their relations with the colonial centers.

9. Furtado, *Economic Development of Latin America*, p. 106.

10. See chapter 7 of this book.

11. It must be pointed out, however, that petty-bourgeois, state-capitalist regimes have not been the sole beneficiaries of global wars, crises, and other disorders of transnational monopoly capitalism. During such periods since the First World War, socialism has made great advances worldwide: from the Russian Revolution to the Chinese, the Korean, the Cuban, and the Indochinese liberation struggles, as well as recent advances in Angola, Mozambique, Zimbabwe, Nicaragua, and elsewhere. What is crucial in this context is not so much the influence of external factors that would spark reaction against neocolonial forces in the Third World, *but the nature and intensity of the class struggle within each country*. The decisive factor in determining the nature of an anti-imperialist regime is the *balance of class forces* in the class struggle. Whether an imperialist crisis will produce a socialist or a state-capitalist regime in the Third World is thus dependent on whether the working class or the national and/or petty bourgeoisie is the dominant, leading force in the anti-imperialist liberation struggle.

12. See, for example, Raul Fernandez and Jose F. Ocampo, "The Andean Pact and State Capitalism in Colombia," *Latin American Perspectives*, vol. II, no. 3 (Fall 1975).

13. Shivji, *Class Struggles in Tanzania*. Also see Issa Shivji, ed., *The State and the Working People in Tanzania* (Dakar: CODESRIA, 1986).

14. V. Solodovnikov and V. Bogoslovsky, *Non-Capitalist Development* (Moscow: Progress Publishers, 1975).

15. *Ibid.*, pp. 25-26.

16. *Ibid.*, p. 29.

17. R. A. Ulyanovsky, *On Some Questions of the Non-Capitalist Development of the Countries of Asia and Africa* (Moscow: Progress Publishers, 1969).

18. Ulyanovsky, *On Some Questions*, p. 119, cited in Solodovnikov and Bogoslovsky, *Non-Capitalist Development*, p. 20.

19. See, for example, the works of Frank, Furtado, Sunkel, Cardoso, and Faletto.

20. In instances when the class nature of these regimes are discussed and the petty bourgeoisie is identified as the leading force in control of the state, too much hope and emphasis is placed on the progressive nature of this class in seeing it as an instrument of social transformation in a socialist direction—a conception that is fundamentally at odds with Marxist theory. See, for example, R. Ulyanovsky, *Socialism and the Newly Independent Nations* (Moscow: Progress Publishers, 1974), p. 83.

21. These are basically similar to criticisms directed at dependency and world system theories which we have discussed in earlier chapters.

22. R. B. Sutcliffe, *Industry and Underdevelopment* (London: Addison-Wesley, 1971), p. 285.

23. In the early phase of the state-capitalist regime, therefore, there is no necessary contradiction between state and national private capital, as the state's task is to promote—not to go against—the interests of national capitalists. State-controlled investment at this stage is minimal and national private capital is given every opportunity to expand industrial production and with it the accumulation of capital.

24. We use this concept in a fashion similar to that in the works of Hussein and Shivji, who identify the bureaucratic stratum as a ("neo-") "capitalist class"—one which loses its previously petty-bourgeois character once it comes to power and begins to take on the role of capitalist, temporarily substituting for, or replacing, the national industrial bourgeoisie. In this sense, the concepts "bureaucratic bourgeoisie" and "state bourgeoisie" are viewed by these authors as synonymous. See Hussein, *Class Conflict in Egypt* and Shivji, *Class Struggles in Tanzania*. While we generally agree with this formulation on the subsequent class position of the bureaucratic stratum, we shall here refer to this stratum as "petty-bourgeois," to highlight its intermediate class origin and current status vis-à-vis the dominant and exploited classes.

25. James F. Petras, "State Capitalism and the Third World," *Journal of*

Contemporary Asia, vol. 6, no. 4 (1976), p. 433.

26. Tamas Szentes, *The Political Economy of Underdevelopment* (Budapest: Akademiai Kiado, 1976), pp. 314-315.

27. This is also done through the issuance of government bonds—in the form of shares of ownership in industrial enterprises—by which landlords are compensated for land transferred to the state in a forced attempt to transform landlords into industrial capitalists, as was attempted in Peru under the Velasco regime during the years 1968-75 (see chapter 10 of this book). It is usually after the failure of such an initial attempt that the state moves in and expropriates large tracts of land without compensation.

28. See A. Mafeje, "Neo-Colonialism, State Capitalism, or Revolution?" in P. C. Gutkind and P. Waterman, eds., *African Social Studies* (London: Heinemann, 1977).

29. Of course they would not want to articulate their program in these terms, and instead attempt to give the regime a "socialist" facade, in order to maintain a mass base among the people and not to lose aid from (and the protection of) the socialist states after expelling the imperialists. But their real, projected interest is to lay the foundations of an independent, national capitalist state.

CHAPTER 7

1. This was the allocation of parcels of conquered lands to *sipahis* (rural cavalry with military and administrative functions in the provinces) and to the civilian sector of the *devsirmes* (top officials of the central bureaucracy) in the form of fiefs *(timar)*. The *sipahis* and the civilian *devsirmes* were given these lands for the purpose of administering them in the name of the state. This system of land allocation was put into effect during the reign of Suleyman I and continued for quite some time.

2. As the central state began gradually to lose its authority in the countryside, however, the *sipahis* and other fief holders increasingly evaded their obligations to the state and attempted to take over the ownership of state lands. In reaction to these developments, and the fact that the old rural military-administrative system had outlived its usefulness, the state moved against the *sipahis* and displaced them. This was done, above all, by the introduction of tax farming *(iltizam)*.

3. Although private property in land and feudal relations of production began to develop in the Ottoman formation in the seventeenth century and rapidly expanded and surpassed that owned by the state in many parts of the empire by the eighteenth century, the feudal lords were never able to overthrow the central state and exert political domination over the empire's affairs. Never-

theless, in one instance at least, a rebellion in the late nineteenth century by the landlords, led by Mehmet Ali Pasa, the governor of Egypt, nearly succeeded, but the rebellion was put down with the aid of the French and British armies. The *ayans* nevertheless continued to exercise economic control over vast areas of the empire.

4. See the collection of essays in Rodney Hilton, ed., *The Transition from Feudalism to Capitalism* (London: New Left Books, 1976). Also see Maurice Dobb, *Studies in the Development of Capitalism* (London: Routledge & Kegan Paul, 1963).

5. E. M. Earle, *Turkey, The Great Powers, and the Bagdad Railway: A Study in Imperialism* (New York: Russell & Russell, 1966), p. 13; T. Chavdar, "Cumhuriyet Devri Başlarken Türkiye Ekonomisi," (The Turkish economy at the beginning of the republican era), in *Türkiye Ekonomisinin 50 Yili Semineri* (Bursa: I. ve T. I. Akademisi, 1973), p. 62.

6. Thus, for example, while the value of exports of cotton fabrics from England to Turkey was only £10,834 in 1828, it rose to £39,920 in 1829, to £95,355 in 1830, and to £105,615 in 1831—a tenfold increase in just four years. O. C. Sarc, "Ottoman Industrial Policy, 1840-1914," in Charles Issawi, ed., *The Economic History of the Middle East, 1800-1914* (Chicago: University of Chicago Press, 1966), p. 49.

7. *Ibid.*, pp. 52-55.

8. However, this did not mean a complete blockage of capitalist development in Turkey, but a temporary halt in the development of a Turkish industrial bourgeoisie. The limited capitalism that did develop in the Empire from the nineteenth to the beginning of the twentieth centuries was effected through the intermediary of the Ottoman comprador bourgeoisie.

9. Bernard Lewis, *The Emergence of Modern Turkey*, 2nd ed. (New York: Oxford University Press, 1969).

10. Niyazi Berkes, *The Development of Secularism in Turkey* (Montreal: McGill University Press, 1964), p. 329.

11. H. Derin, *Türkiye'de Devletcilik* (Statism in Turkey) (Istanbul, 1940), p. 83.

12. S. Aksoy, *Türkiye'de Toprak Meselesi* (The land question in Turkey) (Istanbul: Gerçek Yayinevi, 1971), pp. 52-67. Thousands of acres of land were transferred to peasants; by 1934 a total of 7,114,315 *dönüm* (or 17,785,787 acres) had been distributed to those without land. See Aksoy, *Türkiye'de Toprak Meselesi*, p. 58. Among those receiving land were newly arrived immigrants from the old Ottoman provinces in the Balkans. However, all this land was state-owned public land, as the state was as yet reluctant to confront the powerful landlords by expropriating "their" land.

13. Doğu Ergil, *From Empire to Dependence: The Evolution of Turkish Under-development* (Ph.D. dissertation, State University of New York at Binghamton, 1975), p. 364.

14. *Ibid.*, pp. 355-356.

15. Özlem Özgür, *Sanayileşme ve Türkiye* (Industrialization and Turkey) (Istanbul: Gerçek Yayinevi, 1976), p. 170.

16. To all these we should add that 1929 was also the year when the repayment of Ottoman debts was to begin, according to the terms of the Lausanne Treaty. Thus, the immense burden of these debts (the annual repayments of which accounted for between 13 and 18 percent of the state's budget) also hindered the industrialization process.

17. For an analysis of the nature and extent of foreign investment in Turkey during this period, see Berch Berberoglu, *Turkey in Crisis: From State Capitalism to Neocolonialism* (London: Zed Press, 1982), pp. 35-37, 49.

18. For example, the distribution between 1923 and 1938 of about 25.3 million acres of unused, state-owned land.

19. Lewis, *The Emergence of Modern Turkey*, p. 475.

20. In early 1941, Prime Minister Refik Saydam threatened the comprador bourgeoisie with nationalization of import-export trade, and said: "I am deeply dissatisfied with the import merchants. . . . I will try to explain to them that their task must not be limited solely to the maximization of their own interests, but, above all, must serve the higher (public) interest. . . . If my efforts prove to be futile, I will work to bring import-export commerce under state monopoly." Quoted in Doğan Avcioğlu, *Türkiye'nin Düzeni* (Turkey's social order) (Istanbul: Tekin Yayinevi, 1975), p. 475.

21. While up until World War II the army had been kept relatively small and defense expenditure had been reduced to 28 percent of the budget, with the onset of war it was rapidly expanded and defense expenditures rose to between 50 and 60 percent of the budget for the duration.

22. Çağlar Keyder points out that: "Seventy percent of the tax was collected in Istanbul, and 65 percent from non-Moslems and foreigners. Non-Moslems were assessed at ten times the Moslem rate, and Dönmes [Moslem converts] at twice. Christian and Jewish businessmen not readily able to obtain the sums needed were forced to sell their businesses and real estate to Moslem profiteers. Most of these businessmen left Turkey immediately after the war." See Çağlar Keyder, *State and Class in Turkey* (London: Verso, 1987), p. 113. Also see, E. C. Clark, "The Turkish Varlik Vergisi Reconsidered," *Middle Eastern Studies* (May 1972), p. 205; Faik Ökte, *Varlik Vergisi Faciasi* (The tragedy of the capital tax) (Istanbul, 1951). Ökte was the head of the tax office in Istanbul.

23. Avcioğlu, *Türkiye'nin Düzeni*, p. 481. Suat Aksoy, in reporting the findings of a study conducted by the Ministry of Village Affairs in the mid-1960s, notes the persistence of feudal land tenure practices throughout Eastern and Southeastern Turkey, where it was still not surprising to find individual *ağas* who owned literally dozens of villages and, in league with other landlords, ruled over entire provinces. "Here in Urfa," reads a recent news story on the land question in Turkey, "51 villages are owned by one *ağa* and 72 by a single family or clan. Whole villages are sometimes given as a bride's dowry." (*The New York Times*, 6 Apr. 1977). Areas where precapitalist relations of production are still predominant today include the provinces of Urfa, Gaziantep, Diyarbakir, Mardin, Tunceli, Siirt, Erzurum, Hatay, Ağri, and Elaziğ. See Aksoy, *Türkiye'de Toprak Meselesi*, pp. 107-108.

24. State Institute of Statistics, *Türkiye'de Toplumsal ve Ekonomik Gelişmenin 50 Yili* (Fifty years of social and economic development in Turkey) (Ankara: Devlet Istatistik Enstitüsü Matbaasi, 1973), p. 241.

25. Quoted in Aksoy, *Türkiye'de Toprak Meselesi*, pp. 108-109.

26. Ergil, *From Empire to Dependence*, pp. 485-486.

27. State Institute of Statistics, *Türkiye'de Toplumsal ve Ekonomik Gelişmenin 50 Yili*, table 19, p. 38.

28. Y. N. Rozaliev, *Türkiye Sanayi Proletaryasi* (The industrial proletariat of Turkey) (Istanbul: Yar Yayinlari, 1974), p. 63. While workers in manufacturing industry numbered less than half a million, the size of the industrial proletariat as a whole was substantially larger, numbering 643,000. *Ibid.*, p. 57.

29. H. Kivilcimli, *Türkiye'de İşçi Sinifinin Sosyal Varliği* (The social condition of the working class in Turkey) (Istanbul, 1935).

30. Based on Aydemir's unofficial figures on the total number of workers in Turkey in 1935 and 1938, Fişek puts the average annual wages of workers in all industries at 196.7 and 249.3 T.L. respectively (the former indicating a further decline compared to 1934 levels, while the latter reflected a slight increase over the 1932 average). See K. Fişek, *Türkiye'de Kapitalizmin Gelişmesi ve Işçi Sinifi* (The development of capitalism and the working class in Turkey) (Ankara: Doğan Yayinevi, 1969), p. 75.

31. *Ibid.*, p. 80.

32. Özlem Özgür, *Türkiye'de Kapitalizmin Gelişmesi* (The development of capitalism in Turkey) (Istanbul: Gerçek Yayinevi, 1972), p. 96. As a result, industrial accidents almost tripled during this period—from 4,691 in 1937 to 11,958 in 1943. Rozaliev, *Türkiye Sanayi Proletaryasi*, p. 118.

33. According to Article 14 of the Labor Law, 48- and 56-hour work weeks "are taken as the base"; in line with Article 37, the work week could be

further extended if employers so wished, provided they obtained permission from the Regional Directorate of Employment. M. Gorkey, *İş Kânunu İle İlgili Kararname*, no. 63, p. 159. Moreover, as Article 6 clarifies, in certain branches of industry the work day would be designated as 11 hours, with no days off. Thus, the document continues, "in general, a work week could be extended to 77 hours, whenever the need arises." *Ibid.* This was put into effect in all major state-run industries soon after the outbreak of the Second World War.

34. State Institute of Statistics, *Türkiye'de Toplumsal ve Ekonomik Gelişmenin 50 Yili*, p. 155.

35. *Ibid.*, p. 367.

36. Rozaliev, *Türkiye Sanayi Proletaryasi*, pp. 122-124.

37. Özgür, *Sanayileşme ve Türkiye*, p. 179.

38. For the influence of Germany on Turkey (and of fascist ideology on Turkey's nationalist leadership) during this period, see Keyder, *State and Class in Turkey*, pp. 107-112.

39. Ergil, *From Empire to Dependence*, pp. 523-524.

40. General Directorate of Press, *Ayin Tarihi* (History of the month) (May 1952), p. 103.

41. *Ibid.*

42. Doğu Ergil, "Class Conflict and Turkish Transformation," *Studia Islamica*, 41 (1975), pp. 141-42.

43. *Ibid.*, p. 141.

44. The oil, electrical, processing, and assembly industries are notable examples.

45. State Planning Organization, *A Survey on Foreign Capital Investment in Turkey* (Ankara: Devlet Planlama Teskilati, 1964), p. 17.

46. Avcioğlu, *Türkiyenin Düzeni*, pp. 712-17; N. Behramoğlu, *Türkiye-Amerikan İlişkileri: Demokrat Parti Dönemi* (Turkish-American relations: The demokrat party period) (Istanbul: Yar Yayinlari, 1973), pp. 120-21; Ismail Cem, *Türkiye'de Geri Kalmişliğin Tarihi* (The history of underdevelopment in Turkey) (Istanbul: Cem Yayinevi, 1970), pp. 463-68.

47. Feroz Ahmad, *The Turkish Experiment in Democracy, 1950-1975* (Boulder, CO: Westview Press, 1977), pp. 279 and 286, f. 35.

48. Demir, "Turkey in the Grip of Reaction," p. 21.

49. See Keyder, *State and Class in Turkey*, pp. 117-140.

50. There is no reliable data on the extent of capitalist relations in Turkish agriculture during this period. Nevertheless, if Moiseyef's estimates are correct, in nearly two-fifths of the large farms (i.e., on 3 to 3.5 million hectares of land, out of 8.5 million hectares) production was carried out on a capitalist basis. Given that there were 17 million hectares of cultivated land in Turkey as a whole in 1957, this means that 18 to 20 percent of all cultivated land was operated by large capitalist farmers. And if we add to this figure the area cultivated by rich peasants utilizing wage labor, we would see a further increase in the percentage of cultivated land operated on a capitalist basis. See Y. Sertel, *Türkiye'de Ilerici Akimlar* (Progressive movements in Turkey) (Istanbul: Ant Yayinlari, 1969), p. 80.

51. See Berberoglu, *Turkey in Crisis*, pp. 67-86.

52. Sertel, *Türkiye'de Ilerici Akimlar*, pp. 76-114.

53. See Irvin C. Schick and Ertugrul Ahmet Tonak, eds., *Turkey in Transition: New Perspectives* (New York: Oxford University Press, 1987).

54. Cem, *Türkiye'de Geri Kalmişliğin Tarihi*, p. 410.

55. For a detailed discussion and documentation of the size of the trade deficit, foreign debt, and debt servicing during the 1960s and 1970s, see Berberoglu, *Turkey in Crisis*, pp. 93-97, 109-113.

56. See Alpaslan Işikli, "Wage Labor and Unionization," in Irvin C. Schick and Ertugrul Ahmet Tonak, eds., *Turkey in Transition* (New York: Oxford University Press, 1987), pp. 317-21.

57. *Ibid.*, p. 316.

58. R. Yürükoğlu, *Turkey—Weak Link of Imperialism* (London: Işçinin Sesi Publications, 1979), p. 87.

59. *Ibid.* Also see T. Arinir and S. Öztürk, *Işçi Sinifi, Sendikalar, ve 15/16 Haziran* (The working class, trade unions, and June 15/16) (Istanbul: Sorun Yayinlari, 1976).

60. The statement to the press of Istanbul's martial law commander General Faik Turun is indicative of the military's conception of developments during 1970-71, when he said: "We were on the verge of a civil war; this war had even begun. They called it 'People's War' . . . Martial law was declared under these conditions." Quoted in Ahmad, *The Turkish Experiment*, p. 321, f. 18.

61. The Turkish press reported "rumors" of a meeting on March 11 between the commanders, Ambassador Handley, and Richard Helms, Director of the CIA, at the U.S. Embassy in Ankara—thus directly implicating the CIA in the March 12 coup. See Ahmad, *The Turkish Experiment*, p. 265, f. 56.

62. On real wages, see Işikli, "Wage Labor and Unionization, " p. 324.

OECD and Turkish government data on unemployment are both cited in *Turkey Today* 44 (March 1979), p. 17.

63. Işikli, "Wage Labor and Unionization," p. 325.

64. *Turkey Today* 33-34 (May-June 1978), pp. 4-6.

65. *İşçinin Sesi* (The Worker's Voice) (December 17, 1979), p. 1.

66. See Feroz Ahmad, "Military Intervention and the Crisis in Turkey," in Huseyin Ramazanoglu, ed., *Turkey in the World Capitalist System* (Aldershot: Gower Publishing Co., 1985), pp. 191-221.

CHAPTER 8

1. See Anupam Sen, *The State, Industrialization, and Class Formations in India* (London: Routledge & Kegan Paul, 1982).

2. Irfan Habib, *The Agrarian System of Mughal India* (London: Asia Publishing House, 1963), p. 115.

3. Sen, *The State, Industrialization, and Class Formations in India*, p. 28.

4. The war between Prussia and Austria and the Seven Years' War, in both of which France and Britain were on opposite sides, led to an Anglo-French struggle in India. Faced with a superior British naval force, France's hold on India was weakened following a series of military defeats: the failure of French general Thomas Arthur Lally's attempt to recapture Madras in 1758-59 was compounded by British commander Robert Clive's victory over the French garrison of the Northern Sarkars, while Sir Eyre Coote succeeded in defeating the French decisively at Wandiwash in 1760. Following this, Marquis de Bussy-Castelnau, who had been recalled from Hyderabad, was captured; and Lally retreated to Pondichery, where, after an eight-month siege, he surrendered in 1761. The French threat to British power in India had thus ended.

5. Berch Berberoglu, ed., *India: National Liberation and Class Struggles* (Meerut: Sarup & Sons, 1986).

6. Sen, *The State, Industrialization, and Class Formations in India*.

7. Hamza Alavi, "India and the Colonial Mode of Production," *Economic and Political Weekly*, August 1975.

8. Bipan Chandra, "The Indian Capitalist Class and Imperialism Before 1947," *Journal of Contemporary Asia*, vol. 5, no. 3 (1975).

9. A. I. Levkovsky, *Capitalism in India* (Delhi: People's Publishing House, 1966).

10. Paresh Chattopadhyay, "India's Capitalist Industrialization," in Berch

Berberoglu, ed., *Class, State and Development in India* (New Delhi and London: Sage Publications, 1991).

11. *Ibid.*

12. Levkovsky, *Capitalism in India*, p. 409.

13. Sen, *The State Industrialization and Class Formations in India*, p. 92.

14. A. R. Desai, *India's Path of Development* (Bombay: Popular Prakashan, 1984), p. 46.

15. Chattopadhyay, "India's Capitalist Industrialization."

16. M. R. Bhagavan, "Indian Industrialization and the Key Role of the Capital Goods Sector," *Journal of Contemporary Asia*, vol. 15, no. 3 (1985), p. 310.

17. Chattopadhyay, "India's Capitalist Industrialization."

18. Levkovsky, *Capitalism in India*, p. 467.

19. Ranjit Sau, *India's Economic Development* (New Delhi: Orient Longman, 1981), p. 44-45.

20. *Ibid.*

21. Chattopadhyay, "India's Capitalist Industrialization."

22. 1 crore=10 million Rs (rupees).

23. Government of India, Ministry of Law, Justice, and Company Affairs, *Report of the High-Powered Expert Committee on Companies and MRTP Acts* (New Delhi: GOI, 1978), p. 251.

24. Chattopadhyay, "India's Capitalist Industrialization."

25. Levkovsky, *Capitalism in India*, pp. 448-449, 472.

26. This debate, with additional commentary by other authors, has been published in *Studies in the Development of Capitalism in India* (Lahore: Vanguard Books, Ltd., 1978).

27. See Gail Omvedt, "Capitalist Agriculture and Rural Classes in India," *Bulletin of Concerned Asian Scholars*, vol. 15, no. 3 (1983).

28. Levkovsky, *Capitalism in India*, p. 410.

29. *Ibid.*, pp. 410-11.

30. *Ibid.*, p. 414.

31. *Ibid.*, pp. 414-15.

32. Chattopadhyay, "India's Capitalist Industrialization."

33. Sen, *The State, Industrialization, and Class Formations in India*, p. 180.

34. *Ibid.*, p. 181.

35. *Ibid.*

36. *Ibid.*

37. Cited in *Ibid.*

38. *Ibid.*

39. Prabhat Patnaik, "A Perspective on the Recent Phase of India's Economic Development," in Berberoglu, ed., *Class, State and Development in India.*

40. *Ibid.*

41. International Labour Office, *Yearbook of Labour Statistics* (Geneva: ILO, various years).

42. In the early 1980s workers in the manufacturing industry accounted for 23.4 percent of all workers in the United States, 20.3 percent of all workers in Canada, and 23.8 percent of all workers in Sweden. See International Labour Office, *Yearbook of Labour Statistics, 1981, 1983* (Geneva: ILO). In 1988, while industrial workers as a whole accounted for 33 percent of all wage earners in the United States, workers in the manufacturing sector accounted for less than 19 percent of all wage earners. See U.S. Department of Commerce, *Statistical Abstract of the United States, 1990* (Washington, DC: Government Printing Office, 1990), p. 394.

43. Levkovsky, *Capitalism in India*, p. 484.

44. *Ibid.*, p. 488.

45. See Chattopadhyay, "India's Capitalist Industrialization."

46. Kathleen Gough, "Socio-Economic Change in Southeast India, 1950s to 1980s," *Journal of Contemporary Asia*, vol. 17, no. 3 (1987), p. 285.

47. Sau, *India's Economic Development*, p. 49.

CHAPTER 9

1. See John Sender and Sheila Smith, *The Development of Capitalism in Africa* (London: Methuen & Co., 1986).

2. Colin Leys, *Underdevelopment in Kenya* (Berkeley: University of California Press, 1975); Mahmood Mamdani, *Politics and Class Formation in Uganda* (New York: Monthly Review Press, 1976).

3. See D. M. P. McCarthy, *Colonial Bureaucracy and Creating Underdevelop-*

ment (Ames, Iowa: The Iowa State University Press, 1982).

4. *Ujamaa* refers to the system of collective agriculture organized around cooperatives in villages throughout Tanzania. For an extended discussion on this, see Julius Nyerere, "Ujamaa—the Basis of African Socialism," in his *Freedom and Unity* (Nairobi: Oxford University Press, 1966), pp. 162-71. Also see Bismarck U. Mwansasu and Cranford Pratt, eds., *Towards Socialism in Tanzania* (Toronto: University of Toronto Press, 1979), part III; Andrew Coulson, *Tanzania: A Political Economy* (Oxford: Clarendon Press, 1982), chap. 22.

5. See Ahmed Mohiddin, *African Socialism in Two Countries* (London: Croom Helm, 1981). For a critical assessment of this concept and its practical content, see A. R. M. Babu, *African Socialism or Socialist Africa?* (London: Zed Press, 1981).

6. Julius Nyerere, *Freedom and Socialism* (Nairobi: Oxford University Press, 1968), p. 231.

7. *Ibid.*, pp. 231-32.

8. Idrian N. Resnick, *The Long Transition: Building Socialism in Tanzania* (New York: Monthly Review Press, 1981), pp. 17, 24.

9. *Ibid.*, p. 26.

10. *Ibid.*, p. 16.

11. Babu, *African Socialism or Socialist Africa?* p. xv.

12. Issa G. Shivji, *The State and the Working People in Tanzania* (Dakar: CODESRIA, 1986), p. 3.

13. *Ibid.* Also see Dan Nabudere, *Imperialism in East Africa* (London: Zed Press, 1981), pp. 97-110.

14. David J. Vale, "Ujamaa as a Social Philosophy and Economic Development," in his *Technology for Ujamaa Village Development in Tanzania* (Syracuse, NY: Eastern African Studies Center, Syracuse University, 1975), p. 2.

15. *Ibid.*

16. Julius Nyerere, "Socialism and Rural Development," in his *Freedom and Socialism.*

17. Vale, "Ujamaa as a Social Philosophy," p. 16.

18. *Ibid.*

19. *Ibid.*, pp. 11-12.

20. Andrew Coulson, *Tanzania: A Political Economy* (New York: Oxford University Press, 1982), p. 178.

21. *Ibid.*, p. 179.

22. *Ibid.*, pp. 179-80.

23. Issa G. Shivji, *Class Struggles in Tanzania* (New York: Monthly Review Press, 1976).

24. Dan Nabudere, *Imperialism in East Africa*, vol. 1 (London: Zed Press, 1981), p. 106.

25. M. R. Bhagavan, "Problems of Socialist Development in Tanzania," *Monthly Review*, vol. 24, no. 1 (May 1972), p. 32.

26. *Ibid.*

27. Quoted in *Ibid.*, p. 32.

28. NDC and STC refer to the National Development Corporation and the State Trading Corporation, both of which are state organizations in charge of national economic development. Quoted in *Ibid.*, pp. 34-35.

29. From an interview quoted in *Ibid.*, p. 35.

30. See Shivji, *The State and the Working People in Tanzania.*

31. See Nabudere, *Imperialism in East Africa*, vol. 1, pp. 97-110.

CHAPTER 10

1. Celso Furtado, *Economic Development of Latin America* (Cambridge: Cambridge University Press, 1970), pp. 35-42.

2. H. Olden, *U.S. Over Latin America* (New York: International Publishers, 1955), p. 33.

3. See Berch Berberoglu, *The Internationalization of Capital* (New York: Praeger, 1987), pp. 64-72.

4. *Ibid.* Analysis of the evolution of U.S. direct investment in Latin American manufacturing industries reveals that capital held by parent companies rose from $780 million in 1950 to $4.2 billion in 1970 to $17.9 billion in 1988. U.S. Department of Commerce, *Survey of Current Business* (August 1989), p. 62.

5. For a detailed discussion on the social and class background of the members of the ruling junta that came to power in 1968, see James F. Petras and Nelson Rimensnyder, "The Military and the Modernization of Peru," in James F. Petras, *Politics and Social Structure in Latin America* (New York: Modern Reader, 1971), pp. 132-133 and pp. 152-153.

6. "What Is the Peruvian Revolution?" in *Petroleum in Peru* (Lima: General Bureau of Information, 1969), p. 56.

7. *Ibid.*, p. 59.

8. Petras and Rimensnyder, "The Military and the Modernization of Peru," p. 138.

9. *Ibid.*, p. 156.

10. "What Is the Peruvian Revolution?" p. 55.

11. See *The New York Times*, 30 Jan. and 28 Sept. 1969.

12. Quoted in Anibal Quijano, *Nationalism and Capitalism in Peru* (New York: Monthly Review Press, 1971), p. 37.

13. "Peru and Foreign Investments," in *Petroleum in Peru*, pp. 46-47.

14. See Michael Locker, "Perspective on the Peruvian Military," NACLA *Newsletter*, vol. 3, no. 6 (October 1969); Petras and Rimensnyder, "The Military and the Modernization of Peru"; Quijano, *Nationalism and Capitalism in Peru*; Hugo Blanco, "The Government, the Oligarchy, and the Exploited," in his *Land or Death: The Peasant Struggle in Peru* (New York: Pathfinder Press, 1972), pp. 145-155; James D. Cockcroft, "Last Rites for the Reformist Model in Latin America," in Cockcroft et al., *Dependence and Underdevelopment* (Garden City, NY: Anchor Books, 1972), esp. pp. 141-145; and Elizabeth Dore and John Weeks, "The Intensification of the Assault Against the Working Class in 'Revolutionary' Peru," *Latin American Perspectives*, vol. 3, no. 2, (Spring 1976), pp. 55-83.

15. Julio Cotler, "The New Mode of Political Domination in Peru," in Abraham F. Lowenthal, ed., *The Peruvian Experiment: Continuity and Change under Military Rule* (Princeton: Princeton University Press, 1975), p. 44.

16. *Ibid.*, p. 51.

17. *Ibid.*, p. 45.

18. Quijano, *Nationalism and Capitalism in Peru*, pp. 85-86.

19. Dore and Weeks, "The Intensification of the Assault Against the Working Class," pp. 59-63.

20. *Ibid.* Also see John Weeks, "Backwardness, Foreign Capital, and Accumulation in the Manufacturing Sector of Peru, 1954-1975," *Latin American Perspectives*, vol. 4, no. 3 (Summer 1977), pp. 124-45.

21. Dore and Weeks, "The Intensification of the Assault Against the Working Class," p. 66.

22. *Ibid.*

23. Elizabeth Dore and John Weeks, "Class Alliances and Class Struggle in Peru," *Latin American Perspectives*, vol. 4, no. 3 (Summer 1977), p. 16.

24. William Bollinger, "The Bourgeois Revolution in Peru, " *Latin American Perspectives*, vol. 4, no. 3 (Summer 1977), pp. 18-56.

25. *Ibid.*, p. 20.

26. *Ibid.*, p. 51. Obviously, such positions have serious political implications for class alliances and the support for (or struggle against) a given regime, which we have discussed in previous chapters in different settings. This will also become clear in the context of the Peruvian case in the remainder of this chapter.

27. E. V. K. Fitzgerald, *The Political Economy of Peru, 1956-78* (Cambridge: Cambridge University Press, 1979), p. 62.

28. *Ibid.*

29. *Ibid.*, p. 191.

30. *Ibid.*, p. 59.

31. *Ibid.*

32. *Ibid.*

33. David Slater, *Territory and State Power in Latin America: The Peruvian Case* (New York: St. Martin's Press, 1989), p. 144.

34. *Ibid.*, p. 147.

35. *Ibid.*, p. 164.

36. *Ibid.*, pp. 164-65. Slater points out that "initially, the military government did make the agricultural owners an offer which entailed the reinvestment of a part of their expatriated capital into industrial activities, an amount which was to be equalled by the state in the form of bonds, but the offer was not taken up, thus marking the political eclipse of a once hegemonic social class." *Ibid.*, p. 187.

37. Quijano, *Nationalism and Capitalism in Peru*, p. 111.

38. Slater, *Territory and State Power in Latin America*, p. 165.

39. Abraham Lowenthal points out that protesting miners and peasants have been gunned down; the press has been muzzled; expressing opposition to the agrarian reform is prohibited; and dissident union leaders have been jailed and deported. See Abraham F. Lowenthal, "Peru's Ambiguous Revolution," in Lowenthal, ed., *The Peruvian Experiment*, p. 11.

40. *Ibid.*, p. 158.

41. Fitzgerald, *The Political Economy of Peru*, p. 60.

42. *Ibid.*

43. Petras and Rimensnyder, "The Military and the Modernization of Peru," pp. 144-151; Dore and Weeks, "The Intensification of the Assault Against the Working Class," pp. 55-83, esp. pp. 59-70; Cockcroft, "Last Rites for the Reformist Model in Latin America," pp. 141-145; Quijano, *Nationalism and Capitalism in Peru*, pp. 41-46, 101-108.

44. Richard E. Ward, "Peru: Regime Moves to the Right," *The Guardian*, 11 and 25 Aug. 1976, p. 10.

45. *Ibid.*

46. *Ibid.*

47. *Ibid.*

48. *Ibid.*

CONCLUSION

1. A similar argument, which sees the emergence and development of these theories as an outgrowth of (or corresponding to) the material conditions in the global political economy, and which explains paradigmatic shifts in development theory in terms of changes in the nature of the development process and its impact on theory, is also made by a number of other authors. See, for example, Magnus Blomstrom and Bjorn Hettne, *Development Theory in Transition* (London: Zed Books, 1984); Jorge Larrain, *Theories of Development* (Cambridge: Polity Press, 1989).

2. See Chapter 2, note 1 above.

3. Susanne Bodenheimer correctly identifies modernization theory, and developmentalism in general, not as a theory but as an ideology—a sophisticated intellectual tool of imperialism. See Bodenheimer, "The Ideology of Developmentalism," *Sage Professional Papers in Comparative Politics* (New York: Sage Publishers, 1971).

4. That is, questions such as which class would be leading the anti-imperialist national liberation struggle and, therefore, which class would hold state power in the postrevolutionary society, and what would be the class nature of that society and state, were never seriously addressed or discussed.

5. See, for example, the large number of articles published in the *Journal of Contemporary Asia* and *Latin American Perspectives* during the late 1970s and throughout the 1980s. Also see the series of recent volumes on development from a variety of Marxist perspectives, published by Zed Books (London).

6. See the essays in Ronald H. Chilcote, ed., *Dependency and Marxism: Toward a Resolution of the Debate* (Boulder, CO: Westview Press, 1982); Peter Limqueco and Bruce McFarlane, eds., *Neo-Marxist Theories of Development* (London: Croom Helm, and New York: St. Martin's Press, 1983); Scott Werker, "Beyond the Dependency Paradigm," *Journal of Contemporary Asia*, vol. 15, no. 1 (1985); and Jorge Larrain, *Theories of Development* (Cambridge: Polity Press, 1989), pp. 188-211.

7. See Albert Szymanski, *The Logic of Imperialism* (New York: Praeger, 1981), chaps. 12 and 13; Berch Berberoglu, *The Internationalization of Capital*, chap. 8.

8. For example, Walden Bello points out that in South Korea export-oriented industrialization policies "produced a 58-hour work-week—the longest of any country surveyed by the International Labor Organization; the world's highest industrial accident rate; and a working class that remains relatively impoverished. In 1985, 60% of South Korean workers earned less than $110 per month, far below the government's estimated minimum monthly income of $335 needed to support a family of five." Walden Bello, "Asia's Miracle Economies: The First and Last of a Dying Breed," *Dollars & Sense* 143 (January-February 1989), p. 14. The same can easily be said about other countries that are pursuing export-oriented industrialization, such as Brazil, Mexico, Taiwan, Hong Kong, Singapore, and the Philippines.

9. *Ibid.* Also see Walden Bello and Stephanie Rosenfeld, *Dragons in Distress: Asia's Miracle Economies in Crisis* (San Francisco: Institute for Food and Development Policy, 1990).

10. In fact, this is exactly what is happening in South Korea, Taiwan, Hong Kong, and other export-oriented countries that are part of the original group of countries that embarked on this path nearly three decades ago. Thus: "An estimated $1.5 billion of capital from Taiwan and Hong Kong has moved to China, where labor is *ten times cheaper* than in those countries. Even as the Kuomintang government continues to emit anti-communist propaganda, Taiwanese capitalists now view the workers of a socialist society as the key to their continued profitability. Currently, South Korean capital is considering moving to China and following Taiwanese and Hong Kong capital to other cheap labor havens like the Caribbean and Southeast Asia." Bello, "Asia's Miracle Economies," p. 15 (emphasis added).

11. This is especially the case when such regimes are under attack by imperialism and/or confront a serious challenge from the labor movement. Iraq, Syria, and Libya are good examples of such regimes in the world today.

12. See Berch Berberoglu, *Turkey in Crisis: From State Capitalism to Neocolonialism* (London: Zed Press, 1982); Mahmoud Hussain, *Class Conflict in Egypt 1945-1970* (New York: Monthly Review Press, 1973).

13. The potential exists for such an eventuality in Algeria, Syria, Iraq, and other state-capitalist regimes still in power today.

14. See Albert Szymanski, *Is the Red Flag Flying? The Political Economy of the USSR Today* (London: Zed Press, 1979). Also see Zaki Laidi, ed., *The Third World and the Soviet Union* (London: Zed Books, 1988).

15. *Ibid.*

16. It is in this context that U.S. direct intervention in Central America (Nicaragua, El Salvador, Honduras); the invasion of Grenada and of Panama; and the intervention in the Persian Gulf by some 500,000 U.S. troops and the war against Iraq, that one must assess the significance of changes in the global political-economic situation. They are in essence a manifestation of changes in the balance of forces at the global level based on rivalry for empire status between the major imperialist powers in their battle for control of world resources (such as oil), hence the world economy and polity.

BIBLIOGRAPHY

Abrahamian, Ervand. 1982. *Iran: Between Two Revolutions*. Princeton, NJ: Princeton University Press.

Adelman, Irma, and Cynthia Taft Morris. 1967. *Society, Politics, and Economic Development*. Baltimore, MD: The Johns Hopkins Press.

————. 1973. *Economic Growth and Social Equity in Developing Countries*. Stanford: Stanford University Press.

Alavi, Hamza. 1975. "India and the Colonial Mode of Production." *Economic and Political Weekly* (August).

————. 1982. "State and Class under Peripheral Capitalism." In *An Introduction to the Sociology of "Developing Societies"*, ed. H. Alavi and T. Shanin. London: Macmillan.

Alexander, I. 1987. "Real Wages and Class Struggle in South Korea." *Journal of Contemporary Asia*. Vol. 17, no. 4.

Altvater, Elmar, et al., eds. 1991. *The Poverty of Nations: A Guide to the Debt Crisis*. London: Zed Books.

Amin, Samir. 1974. *Accumulation on a World Scale*. New York: Monthly Review Press.

————. 1976. *Unequal Development: An Essay on the Social Formations of Peripheral Capitalism*. New York: Monthly Review Press.

———. 1978. *The Arab Nation: Nationalism and Class Struggles.* London: Zed Books.

———. 1990. *Maldevelopment: Anatomy of a Global Failure.* London: Zed Books.

———. 1990. *Delinking: Towards a Polycentric World.* London: Zed Books.

Avcioğlu, D. 1975. *Türkiye'nin Düzeni* (Turkey's social order). Istanbul: Ant Yayinevi.

Babu, Abdul Rahman Mohamed. 1981. *African Socialism or Socialist Africa?* London: Zed Books.

Baran, Paul. 1957. *The Political Economy of Growth.* New York: Monthly Review Press.

Baran, Paul, and Paul M. Sweezy. 1966. *Monopoly Capital.* New York: Monthly Review Press.

Batatu, Hanna. 1978. *The Old Social Classes and the Revolutionary Movements of Iraq.* Princeton, NJ: Princeton University Press.

Beinin, Joel. 1982. "Egypt's Transition Under Nasser." *MERIP Reports* 107 (July-August).

Bello, Walden, and Stephanie Rosenfeld. 1990. *Dragons in Distress: Asia's Miracle Economies in Crisis.* San Francisco: Institute for Food and Development Policy.

Berberoglu, Berch. 1982. *Turkey in Crisis: From State Capitalism to Neocolonialism.* London: Zed Books.

———. 1986. *India: National Liberation and Class Struggles.* Meerut: Sarup & Sons.

———. 1987. *The Internationalization of Capital: Imperialism and Capitalist Development on a World Scale.* New York: Praeger.

———. 1989. *Power and Stability in the Middle East.* London: Zed Books.

———. 1990. *Political Sociology: A Comparative/Historical Approach.* New York: General Hall, Inc.

———. 1991. *Class, State, and Development in India.* London and New Delhi: Sage Publications.

———. 1992. *The Legacy of Empire: Economic Decline and Class Polarization in the United States.* New York: Praeger.

Bernstein, Henry. 1971. "Modernization Theory and the Sociological Study of Development," *Journal of Development Studies.* Vol. 7, no. 2.

Bhagavan, M. R. 1972. "Problems of Socialist Development in Tanzania."

Monthly Review. Vol. 24, no. 1 (May).

——— . 1990. *Technological Advance in the Third World.* London: Zed Books.

Blanco, Hugo. 1972. *Land or Death: The Peasant Struggle in Peru.* New York: Pathfinder Press.

Block, Fred. 1977. "The Ruling Class Does Not Rule: Notes on the Marxist Theory of the State." *Socialist Review* 33 (May-June).

——— . 1978. "Class Consciousness and Capitalist Rationalization: A Reply to Critics." *Socialist Review* 40-41 (July-October).

Blomstrom, Magnus, and Bjorn Hettne. 1984. *Development Theory in Transition: Dependency Theory and Beyond.* London: Zed Books.

Bluestone, Barry, and Bennett Harrison. 1982. *The Deindustrialization of America.* New York: Basic Books.

Bodenheimer, Susanne. 1971. "Dependency and Imperialism: The Roots of Latin American Underdevelopment." In *Readings in U.S. Imperialism,* ed. K. T. Fann and Donald C. Hodges. Boston: Porter Sargent Publisher.

——— . 1971. "The Ideology of Developmentalism." *Sage Professional Papers in Comparative Politics.* New York: Sage Publishers.

Bollinger, William. 1977. "The Bourgeois Revolution in Peru." *Latin American Perspectives.* Vol. 4, no. 3 (Summer).

Branford, Sue and Bernardo Kucinski. 1986. *The Debt Squads: The U.S., the Banks and Latin America.* London: Zed Books.

Brenner, R. 1977. "The Origins of Capitalist Development: A Critique of Neo-Smithian Marxism." *New Left Review* 104 (July/August).

Cameron, Kenneth Neill. 1977. *Humanity and Society: A World History.* New York: Monthly Review Press.

Cardoso, Fernando H., and Enzo Faletto. 1979. *Dependency and Development in Latin America.* Berkeley: University of California Press.

Carnoy, Martin. 1984. *The State and Political Theory.* Princeton: Princeton University Press.

Ceyhun, Fikret. 1988. "The Politics of Industrialization in Turkey." *Journal of Contemporary Asia.* Vol. 18, no. 3.

Chaliand, Gerard, ed. 1980. *People Without a Country: The Kurds and Kurdistan.* London: Zed Books.

Chaliand, Gerard, and Yves Ternon. 1983. *The Armenians: From Genocide to Resistance.* London: Zed Books.

Chattopadhyay, Paresh. 1991. "Some Trends in India's Capitalist Industrialization." In *Class, State, and Development in India*, ed. Berch Berberoglu. London and New Delhi: Sage Publications.

Cheru, Fantu. 1989. *The Silent Revolution in Africa: Debt, Development and Democracy*. London: Zed Books.

Chilcote, Ronald H., ed. 1982. *Dependency and Marxism: Toward a Resolution of the Debate*. Boulder, CO: Westview Press.

Clawson, Patrick. 1977. "The Internationalization of Capital and Capital Accumulation in Iran and Iraq." *Insurgent Sociologist*. Vol. 7, no. 2 (Spring).

Cockcroft, James D., et al. 1972. *Dependence and Underdevelopment: Latin America's Political Economy*. New York: Anchor.

Cooper, Mark. 1983. "Egyptian State Capitalism in Crisis." In *The Middle East*, ed. Talal Asad and Roger Owen. New York: Monthly Review Press.

Cotler, Julio. 1975. "The New Mode of Political Domination in Peru." In *The Peruvian Experiment: Continuity and Change under Military Rule*, ed. Abraham F. Lowenthal. Princeton: Princeton University Press.

Coulson, Andrew. 1982. *Tanzania: A Political Economy*. Oxford: Clarendon Press.

Desai, A. R. 1984. *India's Path of Development*. Bombay: Popular Prakashan.

Devine, Jim. 1982. "The Structural Crisis of U.S. Capitalism." *Southwest Economy and Society*. Vol. 6, no. 1 (Fall).

Deyo, Frederick, Stephen Heggard, and Hagen Koo. 1987. "Labor in the Political Economy of Asian Industrialization." *Bulletin of Concerned Asian Scholars*. Vol. 19, no. 2.

Dore, Elizabeth, and John Weeks. 1976. "The Intensification of the Assault Against the Working Class in 'Revolutionary' Peru." *Latin American Perspectives*. Vol. 3, no. 2 (Spring).

———. 1977. "Class Alliances and Class Struggle in Peru." *Latin American Perspectives*. Vol. 4, no. 3 (Summer).

Dos Santos, Theotonio. 1970. *Dependencia economica y cambio revolucionario en America Latina*. Caracas: Editorial Nueva Izquierda.

———. 1971. "The Structure of Dependence." In *Readings in U.S. Imperialism*, ed. K. T. Fann and Donald C. Hodges. Boston: Porter Sargent Publisher.

Dube, S. C. 1988. *Modernization and Development: The Search for Alternative Paradigms*. London: Zed Books.

Emmanuel, Arghiri. 1972. *Unequal Exchange: A Study of the Imperialism of Trade*. New York: Monthly Review Press.

Ergil, Dogu. 1975. *From Empire to Dependence: The Evolution of Turkish Underdevelopment* (PhD Dissertation). Binghamton, NY: State University of New York.

Esping-Andersen, Gosta, Roger Friedland, and Erik Olin Wright. 1976. "Modes of Class Struggle and the Capitalist State." *Kapitalistate* 4-5 (Summer).

Fann, K. T., and Donald C. Hodges, eds. 1971. *Readings in U.S. Imperialism.* Boston: Porter Sargent Publisher.

Farsoun, Karen. 1975. "State Capitalism in Algeria." *MERIP Reports* 35.

Farsoun, Samih. 1973. "Student Protests and the Coming Crisis in Lebanon." *MERIP Reports* 19 (August).

Faucher, Philippe. 1980. "Industrial Policy in a Dependent State: The Case of Brazil." *Latin American Perspectives.* Vol. 7, no. 1 (Winter).

Fernandez, Raul, and Jose F. Ocampo. 1974. "The Latin American Revolution: A Theory of Imperialism, Not Dependence." *Latin American Perspectives.* Vol. 1, no. 1 (Spring).

———. 1975. "The Andean Pact and State Capitalism in Colombia." *Latin American Perspectives.* Vol. 2, no. 3 (Fall).

Fişek, K. 1969. *Türkiye'de Kapitalizmin Gelişmesi ve İşçi Sinifi* (The development of capitalism and the working class in Turkey). Ankara: Doğan Yayinevi.

Fitch, Bob, and Marty Oppenheimer. 1971. *Ghana: End of an Illusion.* New York: Monthly Review Press.

Fitzgerald, E. V. K. 1979. *The Political Economy of Peru. 1956-78.* Cambridge: Cambridge University Press.

———. 1979. *The New International Division of Labor.* New York: Cambridge University Press.

Foster-Carter, A. 1973. "Neo-Marxist Approaches to Development and Underdevelopment." *Journal of Contemporary Asia.* Vol. 3, no. 1.

Frank, Andre Gunder. 1967. *Capitalism and Underdevelopment in Latin America.* New York: Monthly Review Press.

———. 1972. "Sociology of Development and the Underdevelopment of Sociology." In *Dependence and Underdevelopment,* ed. James Cockcroft, et al. Garden City, NY: Anchor.

———. 1975. *On Capitalist Underdevelopment.* Bombay: Oxford University Press.

Frobel, Folker, Jurgen Heindrichs, and Otto Kreye. 1978. "Export-Oriented Industrialization of Underdeveloped Countries." *Monthly Review.* Vol. 30, no. 6 (November).

Fuentes, Annette, and Barbara Ehrenreich. 1983. *Women in the Global Factory.* Boston: South End Press.

Furtado, Celso. 1970. *Economic Development of Latin America.* London: Cambridge University Press.

Gallaher Jr., Art, ed. 1968. *Perspectives in Developmental Change.* Lexington, KY: University of Kentucky Press.

George, Susan. 1977. *How the Other Half Dies: The Real Reasons for World Hunger.* Montclair, NJ: Allanheld, Osmun.

————. 1988. *A Fate Worse than Debt.* Harmondsworth: Penguin Books.

Gerstein, Ira. 1977. "Theories of the World Economy and Imperialism." *Insurgent Sociologist.* Vol. 7, no. 2 (Spring).

Ghai, Dharam, ed. 1991. *The IMF and the South.* London: Zed Books.

Glavanis, Kathy, and Pandeli Glavanis, eds. 1990. *The Rural Middle East.* London: Zed Books.

Gold, David, Clarence Y. H. Lo, and Erik Olin Wright. 1985. "Recent Developments in Marxist Theories of the Capitalist State." *Monthly Review.* Vol. 27, nos. 5-6 (October, November).

Griffin, Keith. 1973. "Underdevelopment in History." In *The Political Economy of Development* and *Underdevelopment,* ed. Charles K. Wilber. New York: Random House.

Gulalp, Haldun. 1981. "Frank and Wallerstein Revisited: A Contribution to Brenner's Critique." *Journal of Contemporary Asia.* Vol. 11, no. 2.

————. 1987. "Dependency and World System Theories: Varying Political Implications." *Journal of Contemporary Asia.* Vol. 17, no. 2.

Gunnarsson, Christer. 1985. "Development Theory and Third World Industrialization." *Journal of Contemporary Asia.* Vol. 15, no. 2.

Halliday, Fred. 1979. *Iran: Dictatorship and Development.* New York: Penguin.

Hamilton, Clive. 1983. "Capitalist Industrialization in East Asia's Four Little Tigers." *Journal of Contemporary Asia.* Vol. 13, no. 1.

————. 1986. *Capitalist Industrialization in Korea.* Boulder, CO: Westview Press.

Hamilton, Nora L. 1975. "Mexico: The Limits of State Autonomy." *Latin American Perspectives.* Vol. 2, no. 2 (Summer).

Harris, Richard, ed. 1975. *The Political Economy of Africa.* Cambridge, MA.: Schenkman.

Harrison, Bennett, and Barry Bluestone. 1988. *The Great U-Turn: Corporate Restructuring and the Polarizing of America.* New York: Basic Books.

Hing, Lo Shiu. 1990. "Political Participation in Hong Kong, South Korea, and Taiwan." *Journal of Contemporary Asia.* Vol. 20, no. 2.

Hobson, John A. 1965. *Imperialism: A Study.* Ann Arbor: University of Michigan Press.

Hooglund, Eric. 1982. *Land and Revolution in Iran, 1960-1980.* Austin: University of Texas Press.

Hoogvelt, Ankie M. M. 1982. *The Third World in Global Development.* London: Macmillan.

Hoselitz, Bert F. 1960. *Sociological Factors in Economic Development.* New York: The Free Press.

Howe, Gary Nigel. 1982. "Dependency Theory, Imperialism, and the Production of Surplus Value on a World Scale." In *Dependency and Marxism*, ed. Ronald H. Chilcote. Boulder, CO: Westview Press.

Hussein, Mahmoud. 1973. *Class Conflict in Egypt. 1945-1970.* New York: Monthly Review Press.

International Labour Organization. 1978. *Yearbook of Labour Statistics, 1978.* Geneva: ILO.

——— . 1982. *Yearbook of Labour Statistics, 1982.* Geneva: ILO.

——— . 1988. *Yearbook of Labour Statistics, 1988.* Geneva: ILO.

Isikli, Alpaslan. 1987. "Wage Labor and Unionization." In *Turkey in Transition: New Perspectives*, ed. Irvin C. Schick and Ertugrul Ahmet Tonak. New York: Oxford University Press.

Issawi, Charles, ed. 1966. *The Economic History of the Middle East.* Chicago: University of Chicago Press.

——— . 1980. *The Economic History of Turkey, 1800-1914.* Chicago: University of Chicago Press.

Jalee, Pierre. 1968. *The Pillage of the Third World.* New York: Monthly Review Press.

Jayawardena, Kumari. 1986. *Feminism and Nationalism in the Third World.* London: Zed Books.

Jelin, Elizabeth, ed. 1990. *Women and Social Change in Latin America.* London: Zed Books.

Johnson, Dale L. 1972. "Dependence and the International System." In *Depen-*

dence and Underdevelopment, ed. James D. Cockcroft et al. Garden City, NY: Anchor.

————. 1973. *The Sociology of Change and Reaction in Latin America*. New York: The Bobbs-Merrill Co.

Kay, Cristobal. 1989. *Latin American Theories of Development and Underdevelopment*. London: Routledge & Kegan Paul.

Kay, Geoffrey. 1975. *Development and Underdevelopment: A Marxist Analysis*. New York: St. Martin's Press.

Kazgan, Gulten. 1989. "Internal and External Constraints of Export Oriented Growth Strategy." *New Perspectives on Turkey*. Vol. 3, no. 1 (Fall).

Kennedy, Paul. 1987. *The Rise and Fall of the Great Powers*. New York: Random House.

Keyder, Caglar. 1987. *State and Class in Turkey*. London: Verso.

Kidron, Michael. 1970. *Western Capitalism Since the War*. Harmondsworth, England: Penguin.

Kindleberger, Charles P. 1965. *Economic Development*. New York: McGraw-Hill Book Co.

Kolko, Joyce. 1988. *Restructuring the World Economy*. New York: Pantheon Books.

Korner, Peter, et al. 1986. *The IMF and the Debt Crisis*. London: Zed Books.

Kruijer, Gerald J. 1987. *Development Through Liberation: Third World Problems and Solutions*. Atlantic Highlands, NJ: Humanities Press.

Kuznets, Simon. 1970. "The Present Underdeveloped Countries and Past Growth Patterns." In *Economic Development*, ed. T. Morgan and G. Betz. Belmont, CA: Wadsworth.

Laclau, Ernesto. 1971. "Feudalism and Capitalism in Latin America." *New Left Review* 67 (May-June).

Laidi, Zaki, ed. 1988. *The Third World and the Soviet Union*. London: Zed Books.

Landsberg, Martin. 1979. "Export-Led Industrialization in the Third World: Manufacturing Imperialism." *Review of Radical Political Economics*. Vol. 11, no. 4 (Winter).

————. 1988. "South Korea: The 'Miracle' Rejected." *Critical Sociology*. Vol. 15, no. 3 (Fall).

Larrain, Jorge. 1989. *Theories of Development: Capitalism, Colonialism, and Dependency*. Cambridge: Polity Press.

Lenin, V. I. 1917. *Imperialism: The Highest Stage of Capitalism.* In *Selected Works,* Vol. 1. Moscow: Foreign Languages Publishing House, 1960.

————. 1975. *Selected Works in Three Volumes.* Moscow: Progress Publishers.

Levkovsky, A. I. 1966. *Capitalism in India.* Delhi: People's Publishing House.

Lewis, Arthur W. 1955. *The Theory of Economic Growth.* Homewood, IL: Richard D. Irwin, Inc.

Lewis, Bernard. 1969. *The Emergence of Modern Turkey,* 2nd ed. New York: Oxford University Press.

Leys, Colin. 1975. *Underdevelopment in Kenya.* Berkeley: University of California Press.

————. 1976. "The 'Overdeveloped' Post-Colonial State: A Re-evaluation." *Review of African Political Economy* 5.

————. 1977. "Underdevelopment and Dependency: Critical Notes." *Journal of Contemporary Asia.* Vol. 7, no. 1.

Limqueco, Peter, and Bruce McFarlane, eds. 1983. *Neo-Marxist Theories of Development.* London: Croom Helm; New York: St. Martin's Press.

Locker, Michael. 1969. "Perspective on the Peruvian Military." *NACLA Newsletter.* Vol. 3, no. 6 (October).

Longuenesse, Elizabeth. 1979. "The Class Nature of the State in Syria." *MERIP Reports.* Vol. 9, no. 4 (May).

Lowenthal, Abraham F., ed. 1975. *The Peruvian Experiment: Continuity and Change under Military Rule.* Princeton: Princeton University Press.

Luxemburg, Rosa. 1913. *The Accumulation of Capital.* Reprint. New Haven: Yale University Press, 1951.

Mafeje, A. 1977. "Neo-colonialism, State Capitalism, or Revolution?" In *African Social Studies,* ed. P. C. W. Gutkind and P. Waterman. London: Heinemann.

Magdoff, Harry. 1969. *The Age of Imperialism.* New York: Monthly Review Press.

————. 1978. *Imperialism: From the Colonial Age to the Present.* New York: Monthly Review Press.

Mahjoub, Azzam, ed. 1991. *Adjustment or Delinking? The African Experience.* London: Zed Books.

Mamdani, Mahmood. 1976. *Politics and Class Formation in Uganda.* New York: Monthly Review Press.

Mandel, Ernest. 1975. *Late Capitalism*. London: New Left Books.

———. 1980. *The Second Slump*. London: Verso.

Marcus, Tessa. 1990. *Modernizing Super-Exploitation*. London: Zed Books.

Markakis, John. 1990. *National and Class Conflict in the Horn of Africa*. London: Zed Books.

Marx, Karl. 1967. *Capital*. 3 vols. New York: International Publishers.

———. 1986. "The Future Results of the British Rule in India." *New York Daily Tribune*, 11 July 1953. Reprinted in *India: National Liberation and Class Struggles*, ed. Berch Berberoglu. Meerut: Sarup & Sons, Publishers.

Mayorga, Rene Antonio. 1978. "National-Popular State, State Capitalism, and Military Dictatorship." *Latin American Perspectives*. Vol. 5, no. 2 (Spring).

McClelland, David. 1963. "The Achievement Motive in Economic Growth." In *Industrialization and Society*, ed. Bert F. Hoselitz and Wilbert E. Moore. Paris: UNESCO.

McMichael, Philip, James Petras, and Robert Rhodes. 1974. "Imperialism and the Contradictions of Development." *New Left Review* 85 (May/June).

Mies, Maria. 1986. *Patriarchy and Accumulation on a World Scale: Women in the International Division of Labor*. London: Zed Books.

Mohiddin, Ahmed. 1981. *African Socialism in Two Countries*. London: Croom Helm.

Munck, Ronaldo. 1984. *Politics and Dependency in the Third World*. London: Zed Books.

———. 1990. *Latin America: The Transition to Democracy*. London: Zed Books.

Murga, A. 1971. "Dependency: A Latin American View." *NACLA Newsletter*. Vol. 4, no. 10 (February).

Murray, Martin. 1976. "International Capital Flows and the Meaning of Capitalist Expansion." *Review of Radical Political Economics*. Vol. 8, no. 2 (Summer).

Mwansasu, B. U., and C. Pratt, eds. 1979. *Towards Socialism in Tanzania*. Toronto: University of Toronto Press.

Nabudere, Dan. 1977. *The Political Economy of Imperialism*. London: Zed Books.

———. 1981. *Imperialism in East Africa*. Vol. 1. London: Zed Books.

Nash, Manning. 1963. "Approaches to the Study of Economic Growth." *Journal of Social Issues*. Vol. 19, no. 1.

Nolan, Peter. 1990. "Assessing Economic Growth in the Asian NICs." *Journal of Contemporary Asia.* Vol. 20, no. 1.

Nurkse, Ragnar. 1957. *Problems of Capital Formation in Underdeveloped Countries.* New York: Oxford University Press.

Nyerere, Julius. 1968. *Freedom and Socialism.* Nairobi: Oxford University Press.

O'Connor, James. 1973. *The Fiscal Crisis of the State.* New York: St. Martin's Press.

O'Donnell, Guillermo. 1973. *Modernization and Bureaucratic Authoritarianism: Studies in South American Politics.* Berkeley: Institute of International Studies, University of California at Berkeley.

———. 1979. "Tensions in the Bureaucratic Authoritarian State and the Question of Democracy." In *The New Authoritarianism in Latin America,* ed. David Collier. Princeton: Princeton University Press.

Olden, H. 1955. *U.S. Over Latin America.* New York: International Publishers.

Olson, W. 1985. "Crisis and Social Change in Mexico's Political Economy," *Latin American Perspectives 46.*

Onimode, Bade. 1985. *An Introduction to Marxist Political Economy.* London: Zed Books.

———. 1989. *A Political Economy of the African Crisis.* London: Zed Books.

———. 1989. *The IMF, the World Bank, and the African Debt.* 2 vols. London: Zed Books.

Oxaal, Ivar, Tony Barnett, and David Booth, eds. 1975. *Beyond the Sociology of Development.* London: Routledge & Kegan Paul.

Ozgur, Ozlem. 1972. *Turkiye'de Kapitalizmin Gelismesi* (The development of capitalism in Turkey). Istanbul: Gercek Yayinevi.

Payer, Cheryl. 1975. *The Debt Trap: The IMF and the Third World.* New York: Monthly Review Press.

———. 1982. *The World Bank: A Critical Analysis.* New York: Monthly Review Press.

———. 1991. *Lent and Lost: Foreign Credit and Third World Development.* London: Zed Books.

Peet, Richard, ed. 1987. *International Capitalism and Industrial Restructuring.* Boston: Allen & Unwin.

Perlo, Victor. 1988. *Super Profits and Crises: Modern U.S. Capitalism.* New York: International Publishers.

Petras, James F., ed. 1973. *Latin America: From Dependence to Revolution*. New York: John Wiley & Sons.

———. 1978. *Critical Perspectives on Imperialism and Social Class in the Third World*. New York: Monthly Review Press.

———. 1981. *Class, State and Power in the Third World*. Montclair, NJ: Allanheld, Osmun.

———. 1982. "Dependency and World System Theory: A Critique and New Directions," In *Dependency and Marxism*, ed. Ronald H. Chilcote. Boulder, CO: Westview Press.

———. 1983. *Capitalist and Socialist Crises in the Late Twentieth Century*. Totowa, NJ: Rowman & Allanheld.

Petras, James F., and Maurice Zeitlin, eds. 1968. *Latin America: Reform or Revolution?* New York: Fawcett.

Petras, James F., and Nelson Rimensnyder. 1971. "The Military and the Modernization of Peru." In *Politics and Social Structure in Latin America*, ed. James F. Petras. New York: Modern Reader.

Poulantzas, Nicos. 1979. "The Political Crisis and the Crisis of the State." In *Critical Sociology: European Perspectives*, ed. Jay Freiberg. New York: Irvington Publishers.

Preston, P. W. 1985. *New Trends in Development Theory*. London: Routledge and Kegan Paul.

Quijano, Anibal. 1971. *Nationalism and Capitalism in Peru*. New York: Monthly Review Press.

Rahman, Atiur. 1987. *Peasants and Classes*. London: Zed Books.

Ramazanoglu, Huseyin, ed. 1985. *Turkey in the World Capitalist System*. Aldershot: Gower Publishing Co.

Resnick, Idrian, N. 1981. *The Long Transition: Building Socialism in Tanzania*. New York: Monthly Review Press.

Rhodes, Robert I. 1970. *Imperialism and Underdevelopment*. New York: Monthly Review Press.

Rodney, Walter. 1972. *How Europe Underdeveloped Africa*. London and Dar es Salaam: Tanzania Publishing House and Bogle L'Ouverture Publications.

Rostow, W. W. 1960. *Stages of Economic Growth: A Non-Communist Manifesto*. New York: Cambridge University Press.

Roxborough, Ian. 1979. *Theories of Underdevelopment*. Atlantic Highlands, NJ: Humanities Press.

Rozaliev, Y. N. 1974. *Türkiye Sanayi Proletaryasi* (The industrial proletariat of Turkey). Istanbul: Yar Yayinlari.

Sau, Ranjit. 1978. *Unequal Exchange, Imperialism, and Underdevelopment*. Delhi: Oxford University Press.

———. 1981. *India's Economic Development*. New Delhi: Orient Longman Ltd.

Sayigh, Rosemary. 1979. *Palestinians: From Peasants to Revolutionaries*. London: Zed Books.

Schick, Irvin C., and Ertugrul Ahmet Tonak, eds. 1987. *Turkey in Transition: New Perspectives*. New York: Oxford University Press.

Sen, Anupam. 1982. *The State, Industrialization, and Class Formations in India*. London: Routledge & Kegan Paul.

Sender, John, and Sheila Smith. 1986. *The Development of Capitalism in Africa*. London: Methuen & Co.

Sharma, Hari, and Kathleen Gough, eds. 1973. *Imperialism and Revolution in South Asia*. New York: Monthly Review Press.

Sherman, Howard. 1976. *Stagflation*. New York: Harper & Row.

Shiva, Vandana. 1990. *The Violence of the Green Revolution: Ecological Degredation and Political Conflict*. London: Zed Books.

Shivji, Issa G. 1976. *Class Struggles in Tanzania*. New York: Monthly Review Press.

———. 1986. *The State and the Working People in Tanzania*. Dakar: CODESRIA.

Sinha, Arun. 1990. *Against the Few: Struggles of India's Rural Poor*. London: Zed Books.

Sklair, Leslie. 1989. *Assembling for Development: The Maquila Industry in Mexico and the United States*. Boston: Unwin Hyman.

Slater, David. 1989. *Territory and State Power in Latin America*. New York: St. Martin's Press.

Smith, Sheila. 1982. "Class Analysis Versus World System: Critique of Samir Amin's Typology of Underdevelopment." *Journal of Contemporary Asia*. Vol. 12, no. 1.

Solodovnikov, V. and V. Bogoslovsky. 1975. *Non-Capitalist Development*. Moscow: Progress Publishers.

Stepan, Alfred. 1978. *The State and Society: Peru in Comparative Perspective*. Princeton: Princeton University Press.

Stork, Joe. 1989. "Class, State, and Politics in Iraq." In *Power and Stability in the Middle East,* ed. Berch Berberoglu. London: Zed Books.

Sunkel, Osvaldo. 1972. "Big Business and 'Dependencia'." *Foreign Affairs.* Vol. 50, no. 3 (April).

Sutcliffe, R. B. 1971. *Industry and Underdevelopment.* London: Addison-Wesley.

————. 1972. "Imperialism and Industrialization in the Third World." In *Studies in the Theory of Imperialism,* ed. Roger Owen and Bob Sutcliffe. London: Longman.

Sweezy, Paul M. 1942. *The Theory of Capitalist Development.* New York: Monthly Review Press.

Szentes, Tamas. 1976. *The Political Economy of Underdevelopment.* Budapest: Akademiai Kiado.

————. 1989. *The Transformation of the World Economy.* London: Zed Books.

Szymanski, Albert. 1974. "Marxist Theory and International Capital Flows." *Review of Radical Political Economics.* Vol. 6, no. 3 (Fall).

————. 1977. "Capital Accumulation on a World Scale and the Necessity of Imperialism." *Insurgent Sociologist.* Vol. 7, no. 2 (Spring).

————. 1978. *The Capitalist State and the Politics of Class.* Cambridge, Mass.: Winthrop.

————. 1979. *Is the Red Flag Flying? The Political Economy of the Soviet Union Today.* London: Zed Books.

————. 1981. *The Logic of Imperialism.* New York: Praeger.

Taylor, J. 1974. "Neo-Marxism and Underdevelopment—A Sociological Phantasy." *Journal of Contemporary Asia.* Vol. 4, no. 1.

————. 1979. *From Modernization to Modes of Production.* London: Macmillan.

Trimberger, E. K. 1977. *Revolution from Above: Military Bureaucrats and Development in Japan, Turkey, Egypt and Peru.* New Brunswick, NJ: Transaction Books.

Ulyanovsky, R. A. 1969. *On Some Questions of the Non-Capitalist Development of the Countries of Asia and Africa.* Moscow: Progress Publishers.

United Nations. 1989. *Yearbook of International Trade Statistics, 1987.* New York: United Nations.

United States Bureau of the Census. 1990. *Statistical Abstract of the United States, 1990.* Washington, DC: Government Printing Office.

United States Department of Commerce. 1990. *Survey of Current Business* (August).

Utrecht, Ernest, ed. 1986. *Transnational Corporations and Export-Oriented Industrialization.* Sydney: University of Sydney, Transnational Corporations Research Project.

Vale, David J. 1975. *Technology for Ujamaa Village Development in Tanzania.* Syracuse, NY: Eastern African Studies Center, Syracuse University.

Veliz, Claudio, ed. 1969. *Obstacles to Change in Latin America.* New York: Oxford University Press.

Vickers, Jeanne. 1991. *Women and the World Economic Crisis.* London: Zed Books.

Wallerstein, Immanuel. 1974. *The Modern World System.* New York: Academic Press.

——— . 1979. *The Capitalist World Economy.* Cambridge: Cambridge University Press.

——— . 1984. *The Politics of the World Economy. The States, The Movements and the Civilizations.* Cambridge: Cambridge University Press.

Warren, Bill. 1973. "Imperialism and Capitalist Industrialization." *New Left Review* 81 (Sept./Oct.).

——— . 1980. *Imperialism, Pioneer of Capitalism.* London: Verso.

Webster, Andrew. 1990. *Introduction to the Sociology of Development,* 2nd ed. Atlantic Highlands, NJ: Humanities Press International.

Weeks, John. 1977. "Backwardness, Foreign Capital, and Accumulation in the Manufacturing Sector of Peru, 1954-1975." *Latin American Perspectives.* Vol. 4, no. 3 (Summer).

Werker, Scott. 1985. "Beyond the Dependency Paradigm." *Journal of Contemporary Asia.* Vol. 15, no. 1.

Wilber, Charles K., ed. 1973. *The Political Economy of Development and Underdevelopment.* New York: Random House.

Wynn, Sam. 1982. "The Taiwanese 'Economic Miracle'." *Monthly Review.* Vol. 33, no. 11 (April).

Zaalouk, Malak. 1989. *Power, Class and Foreign Capital in Egypt.* London: Zed Books.

INDEX